Boiling Energy

To the Zhutwasi

Contents

Illustrations

Foreword by Richard Lee

THE KUNG, a former gathering and hunting society living in the Kalahari Desert of southern Africa, have been intensively filmed, studied, and interviewed by anthropologists for over thirty years. What is the special appeal of these people? For one, they are among the few remaining representatives of a way of life – foraging – which was, until 12,000 years ago, the universal mode of human existence. For another, observers are attracted by their extraordinary culture, their narrative skills, their dry wit and earthy humor, and the rich social life they have created out of the unpromising raw materials of their simple technology and semidesert surroundings.

Despite the many reports written about the Kung, certain areas of their life remain little understood. The ritual of the healing dance is one such area. This dance has been the main focus of religious life among the Kung. At weekly dances, while the women clap and sing, men and women dancers enter a trance-like state and go among the assembled Kung, laying on hands and casting a shield of spiritual energy over the group.

The main contours of this dance and its associated beliefs had been described, but no study in depth from a psychological perspective had ever been attempted. Much remained to be learned of the altered state of consciousness in the dance, of the long and painful training process, of the folk theory of illness and healing that lies behind the ritual, and of the esoteric knowledge held by the masters of healing, the handful of charismatic "gurus" who personify the most sacred of Kung traditions.

Richard Katz has now given us such a study. A community psychologist long interested in human potential, Katz is well qualified to bridge the chasm between humanistic disciplines and field anthropology. He is comfortable in both fields and skillful at rendering intelligible the arcane mysteries of other cultures without reductionism and without condescension to either the reader or the subjects.

Responding to the Kung request to "tell our story," Katz sets himself five tasks. He describes the fascinating healing rituals themselves in graphic detail, and he shows how they are perceived at the experiential level in the words of the healers and other Kung. He attempts to trace the role that healing plays in the lives of the healers and for the community at large, and he offers a compelling sociological analysis of how the form and function of healing are molded by the specific character of the Kung social order, based as it is on political egalitarianism, food sharing, and collective ownership of resources. Finally, he tells how this social order is being challenged by the economic changes sweeping Africa.

We learn, for example, that traditionally the healing power, though in the hands of individuals, is not hoarded, to be doled out for a fee; it is freely given to the community as the need arises. An important point, this, but not the whole story. We also learn that not all healers adhere to this ideal. In fact, during Katz's study, the question of fee for services was a major controversy which sharply divided the healers. Several who had received goods or cash for treating members of other ethnic groups argued that if others placed a cash value on their services, they could not continue to provide the same service to the community for less. Against this view were the majority of healers who continued to heal other Kung as they always had, for free. This issue fascinated me. We know that the Kung are changing and are being rapidly drawn into the cash economy. This debate among healers graphically illustrates how individuals attempt to grapple at the level of consciousness with the wrenching changes that accompany the shift from a communally based economy to an economy based on the impersonal forces of the marketplace.

It is hard not to be captivated by the Kung; many have fallen under their spell. Yet a danger lies here, the real danger of romanticizing them and portraying them in utopian terms as all-sharing, all-loving, and selfless primitives. Such a portrayal, however tempting, would not only be inaccurate but ultimately do a disservice to the Kung. The Kung are part of the contemporary world and not of the mythological past; like the rest of us, they share all of contemporary humanity's frailties. To his credit, Katz is aware of the danger and he struggles largely successfully to avoid its pitfalls. Further, throughout the book he keeps us constructively aware of Katz the observer. Instead of hiding behind a mask of objectivity, he uses his likes and dislikes creatively, as an instrument of discovery.

There are treasures here to be savored. The spiritual strengths of the healers are drawn from the community, and the community in turn benefits from the lonely battles healers carry on with the malevolent ghosts of ancestors and with their own inner fears. The net effect is of a body of protective spiritual energy endlessly recycled from healer to community and back in a process that extends deep into the past. What do the Kung have to teach us? Plenty! With Richard Katz as your guide, read on!

Acknowledgments

THIS BOOK developed out of a request, almost a charge. The Kung said, "Tell our story of healing to your people." To whatever extent the book tells that story, it is the Kung who are speaking. To whatever extent the book obscures that story, I am responsible.

My love and gratitude go to the Kung people with whom I lived and spoke and danced. They opened their lives to me, willingly but with care. They helped me feel at home, naturally but with understanding. They showed me how to laugh when things seemed most solemn, and how to speak my mind when I was trying to be "nice." They simply were being themselves, and I still look to that for inspiration.

Four Kung healers extensively shared their understanding of healing. Their talks are the heart of this book. Out of respect for their knowledge, I use their names. Two of them, Kinachau and Toma Zho, are still alive, and they eagerly agreed. Two others, Kau Dwa and Wa Na, are now dead, and it is as a memorial to their lives that I name them. Pseudonyms are used for all other Kung.

I am greatly indebted to Richard Lee, who played a significant part in creating this book. He invited me to join the Harvard Kalahari Research Group, initiating a collaborative process that still continues. In the field, he was my guide, my co-worker, and my interpreter. His was a selfless expenditure of energy, for he interrupted his own research to assist mine. Only through his ongoing relationship with the Kung could I in fact do my research and gain entry to so much in so little time. After we returned from the field, he continued to work with me, discussing the data, sharing his own field notes, and criticizing my writings. The book has been shaped by his perceptiveness and sensitivity.

Megan Biesele also has a special relationship to this book. Before she left for her field work with the Kung, she talked to me about my research. After her return, I went to hear of her research. Since then, we have had many talks, helping each other develop an understanding of the Kung approach to healing. She too freely shared her field notes and was a source of perceptive criticism.

The work of the Harvard Kalahari Research Group (Lee and DeVore, 1976) is the context for my own research. Members of the group who contributed to my field work are Irven DeVore, whose intellectual and administrative leadership was truly enabling, balancing creativity on a sound empirical base; Pat Draper; Henry Harpending; John Yellen; and especially Nancy Howell, who made important methodological suggestions and helped turn our field site into a home. With appropriate humor, Gakekgoshe Isak provided a variety of on-site help. The research was supported by the National Institute of Mental Health, Grant #MH 13611. The government of the Republic of Botswana graciously allowed us to work in their country. In cooperation with the Botswana government, we established the Kalahari People's Fund, a nonprofit foundation, to make resources available to the Kung and other San in their struggle to secure their land and develop their communities. This fund is part of our continuing responsibilities to people who have given us so much.

The Marshall Research Expeditions served an important role in providing a wealth of data. In particular I thank Lorna Marshall, for her critical studies on Kung religion and healing, her gentle inspiration, and her enduring support, and John Marshall, for his rich storehouse of film and his giving nature.

I am also grateful to Maxwell Katz, who offered perceptive views about both the book's conception and some unrecognized implications of my language, and freed me from writing blocks; Marjorie Shostak, for her generous and helpful response to my frequent queries, providing valuable comments and making orthographic recommendations; Nancy DeVore, for her creative assistance with photographic materials; Mel Konner, whose help, though more implicit, was strongly felt; and Virginia LaPlante, who gave generously of skillful and sensitive editorial assistance.

Others who offered stimulating comments were Daniel

Brown, Mel Bucholtz, Marie Cantlin, Jane Maslow Cohen, Harvey Cox, Daniel Goleman, Jane Isay, John Pfeiffer, Florence Trefethen, Judy Salzman, Cynde Shambaugh, and Polly Wiessner. Michael Bodkin, Robert Kaufman, and Dennis Shulman performed data analyses with enthusiasm. Jean Blair worked with commitment and care in final preparation of the manuscript. The suggestions of Gary Bisbee, Donna Gold, Gabrielle Kasper, Bonnie Nelson, and Mary Norman, typists at various stages, were another important ingredient.

Portions of the book have appeared in my works *Preludes to Growth* (Free Press, 1973); "Education for Transcendence: Trance-Curing with the Kalahari !Kung," *Journal of Transpersonal Psychology* 5, no. 2 (1973); and "Education as Transformation: Becoming a Healer Among the !Kung and Fijians," *Harvard Educational Review* 51, no. 1 (1981), copyright (c) 1981 by the President and Fellows of Harvard University. Chapter 9 and the part of Chapter 15 dealing with the Trees dance derive from the paper "Male and Female Approaches to Healing Among the !Kung," co-authored with Megan Biesele. I thank her for permission to use both that material and the folktale in Chapter 2. My thanks also to Richard Lee for allowing use of his interview with Wa Na in Chapter 13. The photographs are courtesy of Richard Katz/Anthro Photo.

I am deeply grateful to my family – Mary Maxwell Katz, Laurel Katz, Alex Katz, and Ruth Katz – for their patience, endurance, and encouragement during the long writing process.

Then there were the many persons with whom I shared my experiences and understanding of the Kung. They told me – with their words, their expressions, their hearts – that some of the Kung story was coming through. As Laurel, my then seven-year-old daughter, once said, "Dick is up in his study now working with the Kung people."

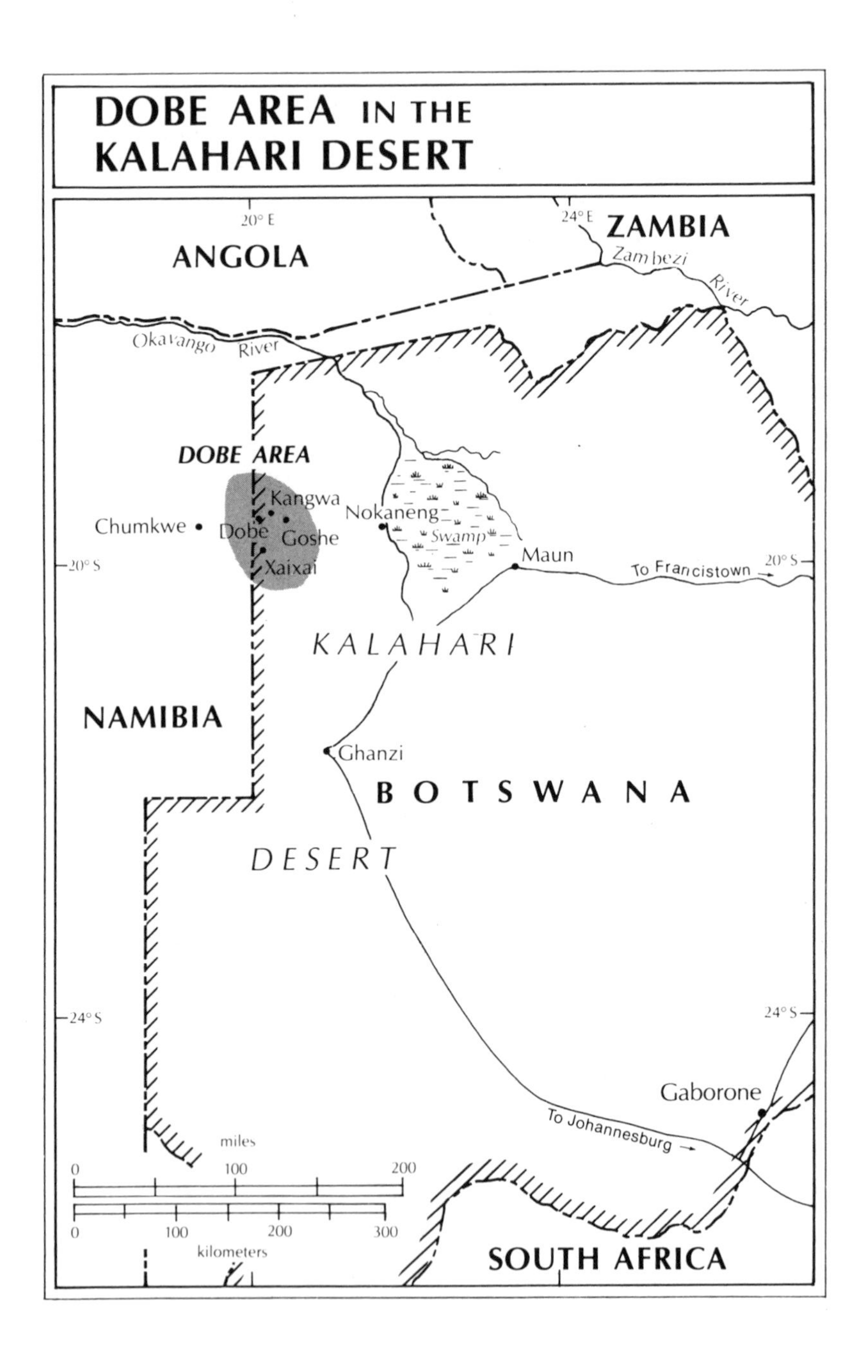
DOBE AREA IN THE KALAHARI DESERT
20° E
24° E
ZAMBIA
ANGOLA
Zambezi River
Okavango River
DOBE AREA
Kangwa
Chumkwe
Dobe
Goshe
Xaixai
Nokaneng
Swamp
Maun
To Francistown
20° S
20° S
KALAHARI
NAMIBIA
Ghanzi
BOTSWANA
DESERT
24° S
24° S
Gaborone
To Johannesburg
miles
0
100
200
0
100
200
300
kilometers
SOUTH AFRICA

Kung Who Speak in This Book

Bau claims to have long experience with healing and strong healing power, facts acknowledged by those who live with her at the Xaixai water-hole. Already past sixty, she remains physically active and alert.

Bo, a young man just over twenty, is dedicated in his search for healing power and is already past the first phase in the process of learning to heal. Everyone says he will become "a strong healer." He is Gau's nephew and lives in the same camp at Xaixai.

Chuko, a strong, experienced healer, lives with her family at Xaixai in a close economic relationship with a Herero family. Approaching sixty, she is an important figure at the water-hole; her moody behavior is accepted, a sharp wit piercing through periods of pensive detachment.

Dau, Chuko's son who lives with her at Xaixai, is a soft-spoken person in his early thirties. An enthusiastic dancer, he is considered inexperienced as a healer.

Debe, one of Toma Zho's sons, is a serious person in his mid-twenties. He seeks to learn about healing but often holds back in fear. He has yet to experience the first phase in the process of learning to heal.

Gau, proud and politically astute though not yet forty, is already emerging as a leader at Xaixai. Though somewhat inexperienced as a healer, his efforts are respected.

Kaha, a quiet though striking man in his early fifties, is a strong and experienced healer. He lives at the Kangwa water-hole.

Kana, one of Toma Zho's sons, is easy-going and quiet. Nearly forty, he is still unmarried. He is an active though inexperienced healer at Xaixai.

Kashay, a well-liked and respected man in his late fifties, is something of an enigma at Xaixai, especially in regard to his healing activities. Though he says he no longer heals, others suggest he still can.

Kau Dwa, in his mid-fifties, lives at Kangwa. Along with Wa Na, he is considered one of the most powerful healers in the entire Dobe area. He heals both within the traditional camp context and as a professional.

Kinachau, an active and experienced healer in his late sixties, lives at Xaixai. Though his healing efforts are focused primarily within his own camp, his power is respected throughout the four Kung camps at Xaixai.

Koto, the dignified man who adopted me into his family as his grandson, is already approaching eighty and is one of the oldest persons at Xaixai. He is the acknowledged expert on kinship, his wife having descended from those who originally settled around the water-hole. Each of these facts establishes his importance at Xaixai; together, they make him a greatly valued resident. Koto has never healed. His nephew Kinachau, who lives in the same camp, often treats him for his numerous ailments.

Kumsa, Nau's husband, now lives at Ghanzi, an area a good distance from Xaixai that is dominated by the large farms of white Afrikaners. Though only in his early forties, Kumsa has already developed a strong reputation, based as much on his dancing ability as on his healing power. He has become very much a professional performer.

Nau, a vigorous and outgoing woman, is approaching forty. Originally from outside of Xaixai, she has become an important member of the community. She is a strong singer at the healing dances, though she herself does not heal.

Tikay has created his own healing dance, an unusual occurrence, and he is trying to learn to heal in that dance. Almost thirty, he is one of the more intriguing and enigmatic figures at Xaixai. He is Gau's brother-in-law and lives in the same camp.

Toma Zho is a complex and controversial figure at Xaixai. An experienced and respected healer in his late fifties, he is in transition. He is trying to move toward a more professional status, which takes him away from the traditional approach to healing practiced within the camp. He is Kinachau's nephew.

Tsaa, who is past seventy, his mood mellowed and his physical condition weakened by age, has retired from active healing. He is Kumsa's father and lives in the same Xaixai camp as his daughter-in-law, Nau. It is said that, on occasion, he will heal members of his immediate family.

Tsama, in his mid-teens, is one of Toma Zho's sons. He dances but does not yet seriously seek healing power.

Wa Na, who lives at the Goshe water-hole, is an awesome person in her early eighties. Despite her age, she is considered the most powerful healer in the entire Dobe area. She heals both within the traditional approach practiced in the camp and as a professional. She maintains a central social and political position at Goshe, her family having been one of the first residents.

Wi, nearly seventy, is another experienced healer at Xaixai, but he is no longer active, dancing and healing infrequently. He says that physical ailments have "taken his strength," but his humor and strong opinions remain unaffected.

1 Starting Points

XAIXAI is our destination. It sits isolated in the Kalahari Desert, on the far northwestern edge of Botswana. It is there that I will begin my study of Kung healing. As we drive toward Xaixai, the sun comes down brightly, the heat increases its influence. Sitting on top of our four-wheel-drive truck, I am first amazed, then secretly proud that I am not sweating like my companions. "Must be that I'm in pretty good shape," I muse.

A short time later, it hits me, a direct and terrifying realization. I am in an enormous oven, baking beyond what I have learned to experience, with no release into cool. Nowhere in this open, arid land, with its tall walk-through grasses, scrubby bushes, and scattered trees covering the flat, sandy ground, nowhere is the cool I knew. Shade yes, shade enough. But the sun-heat lingers on, drifting only slightly diminished under shade branches. I am in the oven of that land, and there is no way out. Terror is of no breathing space. Terror is of dying.

In an instant – sooner even than the "next" instant – I accept the oven I am in. I have no choice. I do not want a choice. Before I can decide, I have decided. I am there, and I accept the fact of where I am. From that point on, the summer temperatures remain high, sometimes reaching 110° fahrenheit during the mid-day. But from that point on I live and work in the Kalahari. The terror of heat-death is no more. And my body shows its wisdom. Soon I am sweating along with all the other proper inhabitants of that climate.

As so often happens, my body leads my emotions and mind in learning to live in a new situation. It takes somewhat longer for me to put my expectations aside so that I can begin to understand what is actually happening with the Kung.

What has brought me to the Kung, a remote group of hunter-gatherers living in the Kalahari Desert? I received my

Page 1: Family at the morning meal

doctorate in clinical psychology from the interdisciplinary Department of Social Relations at Harvard University, which gave me the opportunity to pursue studies in personality and social psychology as well as sociology and cultural anthropology. My personal interests in health and healing, altered states of consciousness, and human potential fueled my professional research. I view healing as a process of transition toward meaning, balance, wholeness, and connectedness, both within individuals and between individuals and their environments. States of consciousness are patterns of human experience which include ways of acting, thinking, perceiving, and feeling. An altered state of consciousness is radically different from the usual everyday patterns (Bateson, 1972; Tart, 1969, 1975). One example is the experience of transcendence. A particularly powerful form of healing occurs when the process of transition is accomplished through an altered state, as in conversion experience (James, 1958). I saw the possibility that the study of healing and consciousness might provide important insights into human nature and potential (Bourguignon, 1973, 1979; Durkheim, 1915; Levi-Strauss, 1963; LeVine, 1973; Van Gennep, 1960). Individuals and communities which seek healing may be in the midst of crises, confusion, or a search for fulfillment. In their vulnerability and openness to change, they reveal fundamental aspects of behavior, such as fears and hopes. As they participate in a healing process that is accomplished through an altered state, these fears and hopes are acknowledged as the context for the healing transition, their resolution or fulfillment as the aim of that transition. In this way the study of healing and consciousness deals with the intensification and enhancement of human potential.

Then I learned that more than one-third of the adult Kung routinely and without drugs alter their state of consciousness, thereby releasing healing energy to the entire community. I knew that was an important combination of factors, especially in view of the enduring nature of the Kung approach. Their model of community healing seemed to speak with particular eloquence and relevance to what is missing in the healing approaches of the industrialized West. Also, the process of culture change was accelerating among the Kung. The disappearance of the hunting-gathering way of life seemed imminent. And so working with the Kung became a special opportunity for me to study these dual themes of healing and consciousness. Both my professional research and my personal search motivated me in the same direction – toward the Kalahari.

It was an opportunity with other special characteristics. There were no comprehensive studies of healing in its ecological and cultural context among hunter-gatherers. That was to be my aim. Nor did the existing references have a psychological perspective or employ a theory of altered states of consciousness. That was to be my orientation.

Finally, working with the Kung offered a special opportunity because of their mode of adaptation. The Kung are hunter-gatherers, a rare way of living today, which is representative of what until 10,000 years ago was the universal pattern of human existence. It is generally agreed that the basic dimensions of human nature were forged during that huge span of history when people lived as foragers (Lee and DeVore, 1968). Any statement about the particular evolutionary significance of the Kung has to take into account their own history, including instances of contact with other cultures, which may have differentiated them from their earliest ancestors, as well as the fact that the Kung are only one of several living hunter-gathering groups. Yet there remains an enormous potential in studying the Kung to learn about the nature of hunting-gathering life. According to Lee (1979), by "understanding the adaptions of the past, we can better understand the present and the basic human material that produced them both" (p. 433). A study of Kung community healing could generate crucial insights into the understanding of healing and consciousness.

My fieldwork in the Kalahari occurred over three months in 1968, from September through November, a period dominated by hot, dry weather. In reporting that work in this book, I will use the present tense, what is called in anthropology the "ethnographic present." But the time frame of the fieldwork must be stressed. The book focuses on healing among hunting and gathering Kung in the late 1960s. Although I call this the "traditional" Kung approach to healing, it is traditional only in a relative sense, because of the fast-changing circumstances of those Kung who have since become more sedentary and less reliant on their hunting-gathering pattern of subsistence. The significance of the fieldwork has in fact increased because this hunting-gathering way of life is rapidly vanishing.

Most of my time in the field is spent at Xaixai, a permanent water-hole surrounded by four Kung camps. To say that there are no electricity or roads or stores at Xaixai is both accurate and an understatement. What we in the industrialized West take for granted as the bare essentials of living, such as clothing and shelter which keep out the cold or heat or rain, are conspicuously absent with the Kung. Even the minimal creature-comforts of the simplest sedentary life-style are generally absent among the nomadic Kung of Xaixai.

I live in a little compound made up of my small tent, a larger tent for my two co-workers, the anthropologist Richard Lee and the sociologist Nancy Howell, and a tiny mud kitchen with a canvas roof. Our little compound is about one-half mile from the water-hole and 300 yards from the nearest Kung camp.

The tent architecture of our compound affords more privacy than the open, thatched huts of the Kung camp, but the Kung easily and naturally enter into our space. Their laughter and joking, their animated conversations, fill our compound throughout the day. Their informal coming and going, visiting and staying, keep our boundaries permeable. On their side, the Kung are friendly and open to receiving us into their homes and lives.

My research program focuses on the all-night healing dances, in which the entire community participates. This dance is the central event in the Kung approach to healing. The men, joined at times by some women, dance around a group of women who sit around a fire singing. The dancing and singing activate a healing power, and through the efforts of individual healers, both men and women, that healing is released to the entire community. I attend these dances whenever possible and manage to participate in eighteen of them. I take field-notes at all of the dances, make detailed behavior observations, including a running time account, at a selection of dances, interview participants afterward about the meaning of their various behaviors, and administer psychological tests.

More than twenty Kung, both healers and others, participate in the interviews, which sometimes last for several hours. I offer compensation to the Kung for these interviews, in a form of their choosing, such as the provision of a meal, a desired item of clothing, the ever-valued tobacco, or the exchange of some of my belongings for some of theirs. Their conversation is characterized by the use of repetition for emphasis and by a certain discomfort with the Western form of direct questioning, which requires an immediate and precise response; the Kung prefer at times to develop an idea rather than answer a question. Moreover, as there are more male than female healers among the Kung, the men's descriptions of healing predominate. The similarities in the male and female experience of healing are such that these descriptions generally remain valid for both sexes, although my understanding, and that of my research colleagues, of the particularly female perspective on healing is less well developed.

What ties together all this research, and in itself provides important insights, is my participant-observation. During the first healing dance I attend, I struggle to stay awake as the singing continues into the early morning hours. By the second dance, it is clear that I will have to do something more than watching if I am to remain awake and see the complete dance – which usually lasts from dusk to dawn. And the most natural thing for me to do is to start dancing. Without really planning it, I have begun trying to learn about healing by participating in the dance.

As my participation increases and intensifies, more penetrating and informative observations emerge. The healers I interview take me more seriously and share more of their knowledge. Toma Zho, one of the more powerful Xaixai healers, takes me aside one day. "Dick," he says, "I noticed you are dancing more seriously. Your eyes are straight ahead, you don't look around, and you dance hard. Why is this so?"

"I'm very interested in healing," I reply, "and I want to learn all I can about it."

"Well," Toma Zho exclaims in mock surprise, "why didn't you say so. Let me tell you." Of course, I have spoken many times of my interest in healing – I am known as the "European who wants to know *about* healing" – but my interest in learning *to* heal opens new doors.

Participant-observation as a methodology is just one expression of my increasing involvement in Kung life. I find that, as I expand my focus and stop trying always to "turn the conversation" to healing, I begin to understand more about healing. I spend more time just being with the Kung in their daily lives. I see new aspects of their culture, the context for healing. The Kung begin to share more with me. One experience stands out as an initiation into the culture. After a three-hour walk back to Xaixai through the bush in the mid-day desert sun with two Kung – at *their* pace, since I want to do it their way and could not otherwise have communicated very easily – the Kung say of me, "Ah, he walks just like a Kung." Of course, I spend a good part of the next day totally exhausted, but thankful I have avoided heat prostration.

Coupled with the brevity of my stay, my minimal understanding of Kung presents a problem. It is solved by Lee, who serves as my interpreter. That function unfolds most intensively and creatively in our collaboration during the in-depth interviews.

Another helpful factor is that my particular study of healing is part of a larger, ten-year research project with the Kung which focuses on a variety of topics, including archeology, ecology, population biology, child-rearing, and folklore (Lee and DeVore, 1976). Being part of that team opens up for me new perspectives on the phenomenon of healing. For example, Lee's ecological studies provide a balance to my psychological orientation. As I come to understand the Kung's daily patterns of adaptation, I increase my understanding of their healing dance. These ecological data also remind me that the Western categories of "material" and "immaterial" are neither important nor distinctly separate in Kung experience. The demographic work of Lee and Howell is the basis of my sample selection and provides a necessary context for all the data I collect.

Still another factor that helps my work is the strong emphasis in Kung culture, especially in the healing dance, on nonverbal communication and experience. Professionally, I am well-trained in nonverbal methodologies; and personally I am more comfortable with nonverbal approaches. I develop an intimate relationship with the old Kung man who adopts me as his grandson, even though we never exchange more than one or two words of greeting. Whenever the old man and I see each other, we embrace and rub heads, or rub heads on each other's chests. Though this is not typical behavior for either him or me, it communicates for us both. My inability to speak Kung may actually make intimacy with him easier in some respects. There is another example of this nonverbal communication. One hot, lazy, afternoon a group of Kung women, mostly in their fifties and sixties, are sitting, talking. Their mood is jovial, their conversation full of laughter. Suddenly about five of them come toward me and Richard and, with a variety of raucous, blatant, and joyous sex-play, jump over us, hold us, and pull us down. A mass of bodies form briefly in the sand, joined together by playful sexualized contacts. The raucous attitude toward sex allowed older Kung women has been expressed. No words are spoken, yet everybody understands what is happening.

The Kung healing dance is a uniquely nonverbal phenomenon. Words are not a dominant feature of the dance. Sounds are much more frequent. And the experience of *kia*, that altered state of the consciousness which is the key to healing, is essentially nonverbal, or even beyond words.

Over and over the Kung tell me, "We want to teach you about our healing, and then we wish you will tell that story to your people." Eventually, I realize that their wish is simple; they mean exactly what they say. But to fulfill their wish, I have to go beyond my preconceptions, to listen carefully and see clearly.

In telling their story, I try to let the Kung speak for themselves. This demands an honesty which makes writing difficult but very educational. I cannot be invisible, a transparent vehicle through which the Kung material passes. Nor can my desires to explain and interpret remain neutral; they often serve my own self-interests. Keeping track of these desires is a full-time job, possible only when leavened with a sense of humor.

That job is not made easier by the dominant trend in the social sciences toward explanation and interpretation of data. The necessary first step in research, and one that I seek to emphasize – the full and accurate description of the phenomenon – is often overlooked. Premature explanation and overinterpretation occur at the expense of accurate description. This imbalance characterizes much of the research on traditional or spiritual healing systems.

I also try to avoid presumptions of similarity and a reductionistic approach. The fact that the Kung experience of healing is being described in English introduces a fundamental problem. The act of reading and interpreting the translation presumes similarities in Kung and American experiences, not all of them valid. I intentionally do not rely on an explicit comparative framework. I do not, for example, compare at length the Kung spiritual energy, called *num*, with spiritual energy in other cultures, nor do I consistently place the Kung approach to healing in the context of other studies of healing and consciousness. The influences of reductionism are also pervasive in the social sciences. Again, I try to check these influences, not judging, for example, whether certain data are "real" or not, or more "real" than others.

It has been more than ten years since I came back from the Kalahari. I began writing this book soon after my return. It has taken a long time. I have felt a need for the Kung material to simmer a while before it could be assimilated sufficiently. I made this kind of effort primarily out of respect for the Kung way of healing. I wanted to present a phenomenon of incredible excitement and subtlety without first having to dessicate it. I also wanted to find a way to tell their story of spiritual knowledge so that it is less vulnerable to misunderstanding or misapplication.

My attitude about the Kung story is very much a product of my own socialization. As a twentieth-century Westerner, I am led to treat spiritual knowledge as "secret" and for the "few." This applies not only to describing such knowledge, but especially to teaching such knowledge. For the Kung, however, the situation is different. They stress that spiritual knowledge can be described to all. And so in describing the enhanced state of consciousness in kia to others, including myself, they see few dangers. Dangers arise only when they try to teach others actually to experience kia. To hear about kia is one thing; to risk, as the Kung say, "dying during kia," is another matter entirely.

A question was once put to me after a lecture I had given in America on Kung healing: "I would like to learn to do Kung healing. Are there any Kung healers or schools where they teach that here in America?" In America, the hunger is often great and yet the judgment is faulty, so that spiritual material is easily distorted and diluted, especially when it is marketed within a commercial format. "Overeating" of that knowledge can occur; indigestion rather than understanding results. The thought of one of the Kung healers being catapulted to late twentieth-century America is incongruous to the point of absurdity; yet the possibility of such an event is there. The unlimited potential for misapplication of the Kung's story is compounded by the use of a mass-market medium such as the printed book.

Several things have eased my concern about potential misunderstandings and helped bring this book to fruition. I have become more realistic. Writing a book about healing is one of the ways I can help to tell the Kung's story. With all its limitations, it is something I can do. Moreover, it is only *a* story, not *the* story. As further research is done, and as Kung healers continue to speak out, a more complete and accurate picture will emerge. Even then, it is not the Kung way to have one, universally-agreed-upon story. Finally, this book is only a study of Kung healing, not a primer on it. It can point toward healing, describe the general outlines of its nature and structure, perhaps even suggest something of the atmosphere in which it exists. But learning to heal requires direct personal contact with the Kung community which activates num, the healing energy. The preservation of Kung healing must therefore lie with those who become healers and their future students. In some small way, I hope, this book may encourage such transmissions.

One other thing has proved decisive in bringing this book to fruition. It is remembering my Kung friends, and keeping their presence alive in me. When I was in the field, writing furiously in my notebook, trying to catch every word, my friends were sometimes both perplexed and amused. They did not want to hurt my feelings, but they found it hard to understand why I worked so hard putting down on paper what was in fact taking place around me. Back from the field, during periods of intense concentration at my desk when I was searching for a way to unravel a mysterious jumble of material, or simply typing and retyping material, I called to mind certain images. They were of my Kung friends, and I could hear what they might say. "Why do you struggle so with those words and thought?" they asked, their curiosity spilling over into laughter. "Write your book, if that is what you want to do. Just simply write your book. And don't forget, there is a long day each day, and much time for joking and good talk."

2 Kung Hunter-Gatherers

THE KUNG APPROACH to healing and consciousness is rooted in their environment and culture. As a central event in Kung life, the healing dance both defines and expresses their culture and its adaptation to the environment (see Lee, 1968a, 1979; Marshall, 1969, 1976).

The Kung live primarily as hunter-gatherers. In a trial formulation of that life-style as offered by Lee and DeVore (1968), its economic system is based on several features: a home base or camp, a division of labor in which men hunt and women gather, and most important, a pattern of sharing the collected food resources. Since in the hunter-gatherer social organization individuals and groups must move around to get food, personal property is kept to a minimum. The nature of the food supply keeps the living groups small. Food-gathering units must be maintained at an effective level, usually about fifty persons. Also, local groups do not usually maintain exclusive rights to food resources; a "reciprocal access" prevails. Furthermore, food surpluses are not prominent in hunter-gatherer societies. The environment itself acts as the "storehouse"; food is not gathered until needed. Frequent visiting among the areas where different bands gather and hunt mitigates the effect of localized shortages. Allied bands cooperate; territories are not defended. With so little personal or collective property, there is substantial freedom of movement. The resolution of conflict by fission or parting company rather than by confrontation is common.

This hunting-gathering life-style has enormous significance for understanding patterns of human adaptation. As Lee and DeVore (1968) note: "Cultural Man has been on earth for some 2,000,000 years; for over 99 per cent of this period he has lived as a hunter-gatherer. Only in the last 10,000 years has man begun to domesticate plants and animals, to use metals, and to harness energy sources other than the human body . . . To date, the hun-

Page 12: Women enjoying each other's company

ting way of life has been the most successful and persistent adaptation man has ever achieved" (p. 3). Basic patterns of human adaptation were forged largely in and from that hunting-gathering situation. Thus, learning about the Kung affords a rare opportunity to learn about healing and consciousness in what might be a variant of one of its earliest and most basic forms.

There are about 50,000 San people, living in Botswana, Namibia, and southern Angola. The word *San* applies to people who speak click languages, one of which is Kung, and who share physical characteristics that set them apart from the neighboring black-skinned people. In the anthropological literature, these people have been referred to as "Bushmen," which is a pejorative term that implies those "savages" who live in the bush. Recent researchers have substituted the word *San*, a more respectful term from the Cape Hottentot dialect which means "aborigines" or "settlers proper" (Lee and DeVore, 1976). When speaking of themselves, the Kung San use the word *"Zhutwasi,"* which means "true" or "real people," "we people," or just "people." Throughout this book they are called simply "Kung."

The San are short, averaging about 155 centimeters, with a bronze-yellow skin and high cheekbones. Most San have undergone intensive acculturation and have become attached to black Africans as serfs or to Europeans as servants and laborers. About 3000 San still live primarily as hunter-gatherers and reside mainly in the Kalahari Desert. Among these groups of hunter-gatherers are the Kung of the Dobe area in Botswana, an area that embraces nine permanent water-holes, including Dobe and Xaixai.

Of the nearly 500 Dobe-area Kung, about 400 cluster together in more than a dozen independent, economically self-sufficient camps or become attached in a more dependent status to black cattle posts. The groups associated with the cattle people usually consist of one or two Kung families whose men work on the cattle (Lee, 1979). About 350 black pastoralists, primarily from the Herero and Tswana tribes, live at the cattle posts around the permanent water-holes throughout the year. Nearly 100 San from outside the Dobe area visit at different times of the year for extended periods. During the long dry season, all the Kung in the area locate around one or other of the nine permanent water-holes, some of the larger holes, like the one at Xaixai, supporting as many as five independent camps. Each camp usually serves as a home base for about 15 to 20 Kung, most of them closely related. But the number of camps at each water-hole and the size of each camp change often during the year. As Lee (1972a) puts it, the camp is "an open aggregate of cooperating persons which changes in size from day to day" (p. 344).

Hunting and gathering are not the only sources of food for the Dobe area Kung. Particularly during the long dry season, when the Kung stay close to the permanent water and have more access to the black cattle posts, milk may enter their diet. Groups attached to their pastoral neighbors usually depend on the blacks' milk, meat, and grain for their subsistence, though if the group is large, much food comes from hunting-gathering. Most of these groups are temporary aggregations, the exception being those who remain associated with a single black patron for years. The Kung have not "stood still" since Pleistocene times, when hunting-gathering was apparently the universal mode. But hunting and gathering remain the dominant pattern of adaptation among the Dobe area Kung.

The Dobe area is in the northwestern part of the Kalahari Desert. It is a semi-arid environment, sparse and harsh. The Kalahari sands support an array of plant foods, but gathering them is arduous. Hunting is difficult. Game herds are nowhere nearly as numerous as in the better-watered sectors of Africa.

The Kung year begins with the coming of the rains in October and November, a season called the spring rains. The vegetation of trees, small bushes, and grasses can become quite lush in the following months of the main summer rains – December, January, February, and March. Exceptionally heavy rains in 1974 turned a small stream near the Kangwa water-hole into a river, and to celebrate that fact, a hippopotamus appeared one day and remained submerged in the newly created river basin. But the land quickly takes on a bare, brown complexion through the long, dry season, which begins with the brief autumn of April or May, goes into the cool winter of June, July, and August, and extends into the spring dry season, which ends in October or early November when the spring rains break the surface of a parched, sandy ground. Water resources are scarce and variable, especially during the long, dry season. Temperatures are extreme, sometimes reaching 115° F during summer days and below freezing during the nights of winter.

The Kung dress simply. The men wear a small piece of leather tied around the waist which covers their genitals. The women wear a large leather hide, called a *kaross,* draped over one shoulder and wrapped around the waist. Smaller skin aprons, usually decorated with beadwork, cover their genitals and rear. The kaross hangs loosely over the shoulder, turning into an excellent carrying device for a child or for that bulging mound of roots or nuts or melons which can accumulate from a gathering expedition. In colder weather, a blanket may be wrapped around the head and shoulders. Contact with blacks and Europeans has brought about marked changes in dress. Men sometimes wear shorts, or a shirt, and the women, dresses. None of these imported styles recognize the facts of the Kalahari environment, and they quickly become rags as the Kung move about their daily affairs.

Half a dozen or so huts, usually forming a half- or quarter-circle, face into an open area and physically define each camp. The huts are domelike, made of sticks and grasses woven over a flimsy structure of larger branches. They are quickly constructed and insubstantial. They provide a focus for the families; next to each hut is a cooking and sitting fire, around which food and conversation are exchanged throughout the day and into the night. In the winter nights, people sleep outside around the fires. During the summer months, they may sleep inside the hut, especially seeking its shade for daytime resting and napping. The hut is also a storage space for the Kung's few possessions – some skins to sit on, a blanket or two, hunting bow and arrows, digging sticks, musical instruments, ostrich eggshell water containers, pipes, cosmetics, children's toys, beads, and the ubiquitous imported iron cooking pot. But the hut is not an effective shelter. The heavy rains fall through the porous thatch, and the cold winds of winter easily sift through the many large cracks.

During the spring dry season, as the sun picks away at once-cool places, the Kung diligently seek new areas of shade. For several hours around mid-day, the sun filters through the denser foliage, giving all shady areas a mottled effect. Then the Kung try to be quiet, sleeping or talking softly. They present a low profile to the merciless heat.

In the warm weather, Kung families sleep in close physical proximity, but with a spacing that allows the air to circulate around their bodies. During the cold winter nights, the family stays closer to each other and to the fire, which burns low through the night. They wrap themselves more tightly in their blankets. Yet always some skin surface appears, because the blankets are inevitably too small, and a tug of the covering toward one's stomach exposes a part of one's back to the winds. Periodically someone feeds the fire, the flames providing a temporary burst of warmth. The Kung remain very much under the influence of the weather. Their clothing and shelter offer only minimal protection.

The Kung of the Dobe area move their camps as often as five or six times a year, but never very far. In moving out from a permanent water-hole into the bush during the rainy season to settle around the temporary shallow summer pools, they may locate no more than ten miles away. During the dry season, when they return to the permanent water-hole, the new campsite may be only a few hundred yards from the previous one, since the Kung must stay near their permanent water supply. Camps are informal, easily dismantled.

There is little investment in what could be called a "capital sector" of the economy. Needs of the material culture are easily met, and there is ample leisure time to meet them. All adults make and maintain the utensils they need for daily activities. A hut for the rainy season is built in a day; a shelter for the dry season, in a morning. Fixed facilities, like storage places and fenced enclosures, are not needed. The digging stick, used to dig up roots, can be whittled in an hour and lasts several months. The bow and arrow may take three or four days to make and last several years. In short, there is no incentive for accumulating, or buying and selling, items that all Kung can make for themselves easily, partly because the Kung must at some time carry all that they own. The total weight of an individual's personal property is usually less than twenty-five pounds (Lee, 1972b).

The Kung's emphasis on sharing and the frequency of their moves keep food accumulation to a minimum. Since they know what to expect from their environment, they see no reason to bring food into the village before it is actually needed. The food that is collected is distributed and consumed without delay; surpluses are not built up. To meet their food needs, the Kung must therefore work throughout the year, collecting food every third or fourth day. Agriculturalists, in contrast, have seasonal bursts of work activity and seasonal unemployment. Industrial work patterns are still less related to daily physical hunger; their work and vacation schedules are determined by calendar calculations based on other considerations. But the fact that the Kung must work throughout the year to survive does not mean that survival is constantly at issue. Their diet is composed largely of nutritious foodstuffs, constantly available and readily procured by those who know how.

Although the term *hunter-gatherer* is used to describe the Kung, it can be misleading. About 60 to 80 percent of the Kung diet by weight consists of wild vegetable foods (Lee, 1979). The highly nutritious, protein-rich mongongo nut, the major staple food in the Dobe area, is easily gathered throughout most of the year. Various roots and melons, available on a more seasonal basis, complete the vegetable diet. These foods are gathered primarily by the women. The men's major contribution to the diet is in the hunting of small and large game. But hunting is a less reliable source of food than gathering. Women provide about 50 percent more food than men by weight and calories. In the Kung pattern of food procurement, "hunting is a *high-risk, low-return* subsistence activity, while gathering is a *low-risk, high-return* subsistence activity" (Lee, 1968b, p. 40).

Adults spend approximately two and one-half days, or twelve to nineteen hours, a week securing food (Lee, 1969). In one day a woman can gather enough food for her family for three days. When women are at home, their daily routine includes cooking, collecting firewood, and fetching water, which may take one to three hours. Men's hunting schedules are uneven. A man may hunt actively for a week and then cease hunting for several weeks or more. Hunting is unpredictable and "subject to magical control" (Lee, 1968b). Much time is therefore available among the Kung for other things, such as resting, talking, visiting, entertaining, craftwork, and the all-night healing dances.

Adults between the ages of twenty and sixty provide most of the food. Boys and girls are not expected to provide food until they marry – girls typically between fifteen and twenty years of age, boys about five years later. Other adult responsibilities are also assumed at a relatively late age. When age prevents the Kung from continuing to hunt or gather, they are cared for by their children and grandchildren. The aged occupy a respected position in Kung society. Their knowledge of ritual is revered, and they are effective camp elders. The Kung have a "relatively carefree childhood and adolescence and a relatively unstrenuous old-age" (Lee, 1968b, p. 36).

Although general statements about the health of any group are always subject to qualification, the Kung enjoy good health. Their nutrition seems good, their caloric intake adequate. According to a conservative viewpoint, the Kung are adequately nourished, though during the difficult dry season their caloric intake may at times be less than desirable (Truswell and Hansen, 1976). Emphysema and chronic bronchitis, probably due to the Kung's inveterate smoking, are common, as are tuberculosis and malaria. Venereal diseases, imported from the Johannesburg mines, affect many young adults. Yet there is no high blood pressure or evidence of coronary heart disease among the Kung. The rate of infant mortality is high, the chance of death about 20 percent within the first year of life, about 50 percent by age fifteen. Birth spacing is relatively long, the modal length about four years. Life expectancy at birth is approximately thirty-two years; at age fifteen it is approximately fifty-five years (Howell, 1976). The percentage of persons over sixty is about 10 percent, which compares favorably with the proportion of elderly in Third World societies (Lee, 1979).

Life among the Kung is obviously not trouble-free. Friction and conflict, arguments and fights occur. Extremes of mood are seen, as in the young man who experiences a temporary lethargy attributed to "tired blood," or in the woman who others in the camp say "laughs too loudly and at the wrong times." The Kung exhibit behavior that they themselves consider "crazy" (*di*). An example they give of such behavior is a woman who rolls on her back and spreads her legs: "Nobody who was not crazy would do that!" Another example is a man who lives alone in the bush with his wife and his sister and is said to have sexual relations with both. Still another example is a boy who breaks a food taboo and subsequently loses his wits and can only repeat the word *kwara*, which means "absent" or "none." The Kung consider all three cases to represent unacceptable behavior, whose cause they link with craziness. But avenues for working out tensions and dealing with deviations in behavior are constantly available to the Kung and are quite effective.

One of the features of Kung life that contributes to both their sensed and actual security is their emphasis on sharing. Resources of all kinds circulate among members of a village and between villages, so that any one person can draw upon resources far beyond his or her own capacities to obtain.

One of the most pervasive examples of sharing is the Kung's mutual and flexible use of land, made possible by their group structure. The Kalahari's highly variable rainfall and its sparse distribution of standing water apparently affect the group's structure (Lee, 1976). Flexible group structure becomes an asset, perhaps even an adaptive requirement. Groups may form and reform, splitting apart to follow the vagaries of rainfall and the different ripening times of plant foods, coalescing again to take advantage of a large game migration. Allied bands come together when resources permit in a given area, or live apart when times are bad and food or water sources are widely scattered.

Although the Kung have a secure economic base, they suffer; their environment does not treat them gently. Their subsistence activities are strenuous, and some days people go to sleep hungry. The scarcity of water is a fact never forgotten, and during a drought that scarcity is a constant preoccupation. But a joke always pierces the air, a loud laugh always breaks through the talk, and the Kung retain a sense of perspective. The Kung continually complain about their lot, sometimes with a basis in fact, sometimes just as a habit. But their sense of humor and ability to laugh remain. Sitting next to her full pot of boiling meat, a Kung woman says: "Just look at us! We get nothing to eat in this place." Then glancing at the pot, without a change in expression, she continues, "And you call this meat food?"

At the core of the camp are several siblings or cousins who are considered to be the owners (*kausi*) of the water-hole, around which the camp orients itself. Surrounding each water-hole is an area of land, the *nore*, which contains the basic subsistence resources for the group, including food and other sources of water. But a local group's area does not imply exclusivity. Anyone who has a relative in the camp can enjoy the resources of the area round the camp; that standing invitation is simply good manners. And within the camp, food is distributed so that all, residents and visitors alike, receive an equitable share. As the Kung go about meeting their subsistence needs, there is very little friction with neighboring Kung groups. Intergroup visiting is frequent, keeping group composition in flux, opening up boundaries among different groups. Consequently, each group's subsistence space is bounded, "but these boundaries are vague and not defended" (Lee, 1976, p. 79). The Kung make no sharp distinction between the resources of the natural environment and social wealth. The unimproved land is itself "the means of production, and since it is owned by no one exclusively, it is available to everyone to make use of" (Lee, 1972b, p. 361).

The Kung method of meat distribution is another instance of the sharing ethos (Lee, 1972b; Marshall, 1961). While relieving the fear of hunger and minimizing the stress and hostility aroused on the appearance of meat, the distribution system also reinforces the Kung networks of mutual obligation. A distribution "draws the good feelings of one's neighbors, a feeling that later on will make one a favored guest at the neighbor's distributions" (Lee, 1972b, p. 349).

Depending on the size of the kill, the custom of meat sharing is more or less formally organized. The owner of the meat, often but not always the hunter who killed the animal, is responsible for butchering and distributing it. With the smallest game – hares, birds, young duikers – the animal is butchered, cooked, and eaten by the hunter's immediate family and whoever else might join them at their family fire. With medium-size game of about 20 to 40 pounds, such as adult duiker, the animal is butchered and cooked by the hunter's immediate family and portions are distributed throughout the village.

It is with big game, which is deliberately hunted by organized hunting parties, that meat sharing is most formally organized. When animals such as kudu, gemsbok, wildebeest, warthog, and the occasional eland and buffalo are killed, they are butchered and divided into three portions: about one-fifth remains with the meat owner's immediate family; about one-fifth is cut into strips for drying into biltong, and about three-fifths is distributed to the closely related households in the village. This last and largest portion then undergoes a secondary distribution to more distantly related households in the camp and to visitors. Each family cooks the meat at its own family fire. On subsequent days, when word gets around about the kill, visitors from neighboring camps may come by to eat some of the fresh meat and take home several strips of dried biltong.

Given the enormous size of these large animals, a mass distribution of the fresh meat is essential. Meat spoils quickly in the Kalahari heat; even dried biltong turns after about three days if it is rained upon. As a result, "Nothing is wasted; all is distributed" (Marshall, 1961, p. 237). The conditions of the Kalahari present the Kung with an opportunity to share, and they use that opportunity, intentionally and carefully.

The positive social meaning of meat distribution is clearly understood and underlies all decisions about distribution. But how this positive social act is translated into specific interactions with specific persons is another matter. It is then that the Kung put their own particular emphasis on sharing, favoring some more than others, setting up certain obligations that they value. The primary division of the meat is done with great care. Many decisions must be made about who gets what, and in the process many factors must be weighed. For example, what are the taboo relationships between the owner of the meat and the potential recipients? What is the size of the recipient's family, and to how many persons must he in turn distribute his portion? What are the possible tensions between owner and recipient?

Although the meat from every kill is shared, the owner is not required to give everyone that portion he or she presumably "deserves." Disagreements are often expressed by giving out smaller or less desirable portions of meat, and in rare cases by withholding meat entirely from an appropriate recipient. But these specific and perhaps biased criteria do not disrupt the general sharing ethic. The fact that the Kung convey their attitudes and wishes about each other through the meat distribution confirms their intense investment in that process. The goal of each ritual of meat sharing remains unchallenged: to establish and reconfirm social cohesion and solidarity in the group.

Although the distribution of meat is more formal, vegetable foods are also distributed throughout the camp. The Kung use of the land makes a sufficient quantity of food available. Their patterns of distribution bring sufficient food to each person.

A final example of sharing among the Kung is their custom of *hxaro* or "gift-giving" (Marshall, 1961; Wiessner, 1977). The Kung use this term for their distinctive process of exchanging material goods. The particular objects involved are not rigidly exchanged one for the other. When something is given, it carries no specific implication as to what in particular should be given in return, nor when in particular it should be given. And when something is received, no specific calculation is made as to whether the object received is as valuable as the object given. The objects exchanged generally should be of comparable value. If an obvious imbalance exists, complaints ensue. If the imbalance is repeated, the hxaro partnership sometimes is terminated. When someone wants to express an especially deep affection or recognize an especially strong obligation, the object given may be especially lovely or well crafted. Again, however, this is not usually the case, for the hxaro is primarily concerned with maintaining everyday relationships. The Kung's primary purpose in giving to others, is to reduce jealousies and ensure a reciprocal generosity.

In these everyday exchanges, two rules prevail: a person must not refuse a proffered gift, and then must give something in return. The time between giving and receiving varies, often lasting months. One person may give another person the gift of a spear while both are camped together around a permanent water-hole. As the summer rains begin, they part; their separate camps seek different summer water. The next winter, they may meet again at the permanent water-hole, at which time the recipient of the spear may give a stringed musical instrument in return. A person may have dozens of hxaro partners, many of whom are seen less than once a year.

The exchange does not begin with a particular giving nor end with a particular receiving. Hxaro is a continuous, open-ended process of giving and receiving in no logical order. Hxaro establishes an organic network among persons. The flow of material objects facilitates and objectifies a series of reciprocating obligations. Hxaro is not used to celebrate specific holidays nor to acknowledge important events, such as a birth or death. It is not like trade or barter. In hxaro, a person does not give back the object received. What is more subtle, the person does not give something too soon after receiving something. Hxaro is a medium of material exchange which conveys a significant cultural message, expressing the fluid quality of social relationships and confirming a commitment to maintaining harmony.

The objects exchanged are the ordinary materials and artifacts of everyday life, such as ostrich eggshell beads, dance rattles, knife sheaths, snares, and walking sticks. Such objects are immediately put to everyday use. They are usually made of durable material and are well cared for. As objects move through the varied exchange routes between hxaro partners, they appear and reappear at different times in different places. In fact, "everything a person has may have been given to him and may be passed on to others in time" (Marshall, 1961, p. 241). But since every Kung can make what he or she needs because the resources are available from the land and the skills have been taught, no Kung is dependent upon acquiring objects in hxaro. The very fact that the objects exchanged are so ordinary and available does not diminish the importance of hxaro. Instead, it allows the materials themselves to become somewhat transparent, letting the social message shine through. One Kung describes hxaro this way: "The worst thing is not giving presents. If people do not like each other but one gives a gift and the other must accept, this brings a peace between them. We give to one another always. We give what we have. This is the way we live together" (Marshall, 1961, p. 245).

The Kung's emphasis on sharing has obvious survival value. Their flexible access to the land, their mutual exploitation of the resources of the land, and their reciprocal distribution of those resources ensure an adequate and nourishing diet for all. These mechanisms of sharing also produce their own jealousies and conflicts, either through imperfect operation or intentional slights. Yet the Kung support these mechanisms because their primary intention is to establish social and psychological harmony among persons who live in close quarters and who must relate continually in intimate, face-to-face contact. They help keep the balance in a situation that is extremely sensitive to social injustices or even social slights.

The Kung are an intensely egalitarian people (Lee, 1979). There is a marked absence of disparities in wealth among them. Any surplus is quickly equalized by social pressure, because accumulation has distinct disadvantages. But equality is not merely material; it affects all aspects of Kung life. Hierarchical and evaluative differentiations not expressed in the material culture also are not expressed in the social and emotional culture. Individual differences of course exist, such as that some Kung are better hunters than others or some healers are considered more powerful than others. Their special hunting skill or healing power is highly valued. But as these individual differences do not stimulate the differential accumulation of property, they also do not imply differential social and political privileges. No individuals have authority over any others. Each man's and each woman's voice counts in decision-making. There is a definite prohibition against one person's "standing out" from the rest of the group. No one is supposed to be "special" in the eyes of others, and certainly not by one's own proclamation. A Kung does not make much of personal achievements or exploits. If someone were to come back from a successful hunt manifesting excessive pride, he would be put firmly back into his place even if the kill were a large animal. With the freshly killed meat still over his shoulder, such an improperly proud hunter would hear the pointed teasing of his village: "What is that you have there? What a scrawny little thing! You didn't kill that. It looks so sick and scrawny that it must have fallen dead into your arms!"

Sexual egalitarianism, or at least a nonsexist attitude, characterizes the relationship between men and women among the Kung (Draper, 1974; Lee, 1979; Shostak, 1981). This is not to say that men and women do the same thing or have the same attitudes toward issues, though their roles often overlap. Generally, however, they have relatively equal access to power, prestige, and satisfaction.

Women have much autonomy and influence in Kung culture. The relationship between men and women is relaxed and filled with balanced exchanges, with neither male nor female subordinate to the other. In the area of political and economic power, both men and women can be central figures: with no official leaders, informal leadership is based upon personality, and women have strong personalities as often as men. Women participate actively in decision-making. Perhaps the basis among the Kung of this shared power is the fact that the women contribute two-thirds of the food supply. Their food gathering gives the women a large degree of economic independence; they retain control over the distribution of gathered foods. Gathering in the Kalahari also ensures that women have a mobility similar to men's. Then, too, there is a low degree of task specialization by sex in Kung culture, probably related to the small group size, and this flexibility is echoed in patterns of child socialization. Men often do women's tasks, such as gathering and water-collecting, with no trace of shame. A few women have hunted, and this is accepted by the men.

Physical layout and structure in the Kung camp support and express the easy relationships between sexes (Draper, 1975). There are no rules limiting access because of sex. Nor are there architectural features like walls and fences, or separate eating and sleeping arrangements, which some societies use to manage sexual interactions. The Kung camp is open and intimate, and persons of both sexes move about it freely. In a typical camp during leisure hours one sees "small clusters of people in conversation. Men and women (children too) sit together – talking, joking, cracking and eating nuts, passing around tobacco. Individuals pass among these groups without causing a rift in the ambience, without attracting attention. In general, the sexes mix freely and unself-consciously" (Draper, 1975, p. 93).

Everything is visible in the camp. Persons can converse from opposite ends of the camp without raising their voices. With such extensive contact and lack of privacy, it becomes essential that the sexes interact casually and matter-of-factly.

Few experiences of the growing child set one sex apart from the other. Since the Kung live in such small groups, children must seek playmates of both sexes and different ages. Playing in these heterogeneous groups helps minimize sexual differences.

The relationship between Kung fathers and their children provides yet another view of the prevailing sexual egalitarianism (Draper, 1975). In cultures where men occupy a dominant, superordinate status, women and children are expected to show deference to the male head of the family by generally staying out of his way and by observing certain formalities. Kung fathers, however, have a relaxed, easy relationship with their children. They spend time with their children, playing with them physically when they are young, talking with them and showing them things when they are somewhat older. There is an intimate and ongoing involvement between father and children. Furthermore, Kung women deal directly with their children when discipline is required. They do not resort to the threat, "If you don't do that, I'll tell your father!" (Draper, 1975).

Authoritarian behavior toward children is in fact avoided by parents of both sexes, as are physical aggression or abuse. When a child misbehaves, a parent physically intervenes, removing the child from the situation where the trouble lies, and then tries to interest the child in some other activity. The general rules for Kung infant life are "indulgence, stimulation and non-restriction" (Konner, 1976, p. 245).

The life of the spirit is an inextricable aspect of everyday life among the Kung. To say that what in the West are called the "profane" and "sacred," or the "ordinary" and "extraordinary," are merged in Kung life would obscure the fact that the Kung do not even categorize their experience in such a dualistic fashion in the first place. Such things as the sacred and profane are constantly and playfully mingled in Kung life. "Religion" as a separate enterprise does not exist for the Kung; it is simply their way of living. The

Kung speak of the gods directly, not of their beliefs about the gods. The nature of these gods and their relationships to the Kung are an animating force in Kung life. The gods are the source of both sickness and the healing power to combat sickness.

Information on the Kung gods is neither codified nor consistent. The gods and one's relationship to them remain very individual matters. This creates a predicament for Westerners when interviewing the Kung about their gods, as Marshall (1962) found: "I could discover no formulated myth of [the great god's] creation which . . . [all the Kung] knew or anything which told how he created himself. People simply said they did not know . . . [One Kung woman] turned on me and asked me if I knew. When I said I did not, she snapped, 'How then did I expect her to know?' " (p. 234).

There is an ordinary, open quality to the Kung gods. Most Kung believe that there are two gods, a great god, Gao Na, and a lesser god, Kauha (Marshall, 1962). Each god has a wife and children, and both are attended by the spirits of the dead, the *gauwasi*. All these beings live in the sky. The great god sends both good and bad fortune to the people through the spirits and the lesser god. But the Kung consider the spirits primarily as bearers of sickness and misfortune, and fear them accordingly.

The lesser god is named after the great god, which according to Kung custom places the two gods in a "joking" relationship with each other. The namesake relationship is in fact the most open, informal, and free relationship available in the society. This relationship between the lesser and greater gods allows for a full and varied set of interactions between them, including trickery and laughter as well as deference and obedience.

There are two dominant characterizations of the great god Gao Na (Marshall, 1962). In the older image, the great god is human in appearance but has supernatural powers. Like humans, he is subject to passion, stupidity, and frustration. He can be tricked and humiliated. Like the Kung today, his dominant interests are eating and sex. Without shame, he commits what are the worst sins for a Kung—

cannibalism and incest. He is a great magician but is not much concerned with humanity or morality. For example, though he gave fire to mankind, it was only as an afterthought to the satisfaction of his own desire for cooked food. The Kung laugh raucously at tales of the great god cast in this mold.

The more contemporary characterization of Gao Na stresses his power. It presents the great god as the creator and controller of all things. He has so much power that he is dangerous; he might destroy a whole camp if he came into it. The Kung speak of him in a whisper, avoiding his name. Reportedly the great god named himself in order to praise himself, saying: "I am unknown, a stranger. No one can command me . . . I am a bad thing. I take my own way" (Marshall, 1962, p. 223). Yet in contrast to the older image, the great god as creator is also "deeply involved with humanity, constantly aware of what people do." He reacts with pleasure or displeasure to human behavior and "favors, punishes, or ill-treats man accordingly" (p. 244).

The great god is anything but abstract. The fullness of his flavor comes out in Kung stories about him:

> Even people were different in the beginning. We were definitely not like people. We were like animals; we were made the same way animals were made. Animals were created just like people were.
>
> When . . . [God] was on the earth, when . . . [God] first came to the earth, he wanted to sleep with his wife but didn't know how. He tried sticking his penis up her nose, he tried putting it into her ears. He did it this way for awhile until people told him, "Don't you know you're supposed to do it this way?"
>
> One day . . . [God] was sitting with his wife and he caught a glimpse of her crotch. He stared and stared at it and wondered, "What's that? What can that be?"
>
> The others told him, "That's something for you to eat." So . . . [God] listened to their advice and he took his wife the right way.
>
> She gave birth, and . . . [God] had children. They slept together and slept together and had a lot of children. Then they all came out of the hole in the ground in which they lived. "Yes," people said to him, "This is how you take a woman."

> From there he went on to create things. He began to go about making things and giving them names. He named his two sons Kana and Xoma. Then he made all the other people. At first we were not people but were something else. (Biesele, 1975, I, 46).

It is to such gods that the Kung pray. They pray as individuals, each speaking directly to the gods, silently or aloud, as though thinking aloud, without special postures, and at any time they feel it is necessary. The prayers are often "in the form of questions which imply accusation," but the Kung "mean to plead mildly, without displaying anger" (Marshall, 1962, p. 246). A typical prayer is: "You have created me and given me power to walk about and hunt. Why do you guide us so that we do not get animals?" Another prayer says: "Give us your water [rain]. Give us a chance to rest. Give us food. We have nothing else if you do not give us food. Let food grow" (p. 246). The Kung voice anxieties and hopes to the gods, seeking from their great reservoir of power benefits to balance out the difficulties of existence in the Kalahari.

The gods are at once human in their follies and pleasures and godlike in their powers, at once apart from and part of everyday Kung life. The Kung both fear and expect some good from the gods, both revere them and make matter-of-fact demands of them. Symbols are not merely symbolic; they are also real. The same fire that is god's gift is also what keeps someone warm and cooks the food. The fire means both things to the Kung. Their spiritual life is profound precisely because they approach it directly, simply, and with a primal humor.

In the Kung camp, that cluster of huts facing an open center and crowded together in the great empty spaces of the Kalahari, permeable from without, boundaryless within, the reciprocal networks of community seek to resolve the tensions of small group living. The Kung exist in an intimate setting with continuous face-to-face contact. This colors the whole of Kung life and is the unchanging context for their activities. Whether in a hunting party or on a gathering expedition, whether cracking nuts in the camp or collecting water from the water-hole, whether eating at a fire or singing at a healing dance, whether trekking through the bush to a new camp site or putting the last few branches on a new hut, the Kung are probably with persons they know well and have known their whole life. Certainly, most of the Kung's activities, especially those geared toward basic survival, require a group effort involving people who know each other's weaknesses and strengths.

Although the community is pragmatically strong and provides enduring support for its members, it is not idyllic. Tensions or disagreements emerge, and sometimes hostilities flare into the open. A premium is placed on keeping such divisive tendencies in check, for the community must remain intact if each person is to survive. Persons are encouraged to express their criticism and grievances in public and to direct them to the source of the problem. People are always complaining about some injustice or other. One who feels that he did not get the portion of food he deserved grumbles: "That is a stingy way to give out meat. It is me you are treating that way." Another airs a family problem: "That husband of mine! He can't get it up anymore!" (Lee, personal communication). Most often these complaints have an element of humor in them that softens their sting.

But if the grievance cannot be resolved through argument and talk, if the hostility smolders or bursts into open conflict, more drastic solutions are necessary. The Kung wish to avoid actual fighting at all costs. They have seen fighters resort to the poisoned hunting arrows, and they know the results can be fatal (Lee, 1979). Before disagreements turn into fights, a camp often decides to break up. The disputing parties take their immediate families with them and set up separate camps. This fission is the preferred last resort for conflict.

Community is expressed in many ways for the Kung, from the method of food distribution to the shared belief in the healing power of the dance. People are encouraged to act and believe in ways to increase the common good, though there is respect for individual differences. And as parents "teach" their children simply by living together, day after day, the fact of community continues.

3 The Kung Approach to Healing

FOR THE KUNG, healing is more than curing, more than the application of medicine. Healing seeks to establish health and growth on physical, psychological, social, and spiritual levels; it involves work on the individual, the group, and the surrounding environment and cosmos. Healing pervades Kung culture, as a fundamental integrating and enhancing force. The culture's emphasis on sharing and egalitarianism, its vital life of the spirit and strong community, are expressed in and supported by the healing tradition. The central event in this tradition is the all-night healing dance.

Four times a month on the average, night signals the start of a healing dance. The women sit around the fire, singing and rhythmically clapping. The men, sometimes joined by women, dance around the singers. As the dance intensifies, *num* or spiritual energy is activated in the healers, both men and women, but mostly among the dancing men. As num is activated in them, they begin to *kia* or experience an enhancement of their consciousness. While experiencing kia, they heal all those at the dance. Before the sun rises fully the next morning, the dance usually ends. Those at the dance find it exciting, joyful, powerful. "Being at a dance makes our hearts happy," the Kung say.

The dance is a community event in which the entire camp participates. The people's belief in the healing power of num brings substance to the dance. All who come are given healing. In the dance, the people confront the uncertainties and contradictions of their experience, attempting to resolve issues dividing the group, reaffirming the group's spiritual cohesion. And they do so in a way which is harmonious with their own and their culture's maintenance and growth.

The Kung do not look upon their healing dances as separate from the other activities of daily life. Like hunting, gathering, and socializing, dancing is another thing they do.

Page 33: Healing dance at dawn

The dance is a point of marked intensity and significance in their daily lives.

As if to underscore the unity of the dance with their ongoing lives, the Kung make some of their spiciest jokes in the dance. A healer works himself into a state of kia, dancing energetically and sweating profusely, when someone outside the dance circle yells to him: "Hey, your large black penis is dragging around the circle." The dance lightens up for a moment. But the joke does not disrupt the dance or the healer. If there is a sudden crisis at the dance, such as an inexperienced healer losing control, the humor immediately subsides, not because it is inappropriate, but because other activities, such as physically restraining the frightened healer, require the participants' complete attention. The earthiness of the Kung's jokes is very much a part of their contact with the supernatural.

The healing dance is open and public, a routine cultural event to which all Kung have access. To become a healer is to follow a normal pattern of socialization. Healing is not reserved for a few persons with unique characteristics or extraordinary powers. Nor is there a special class or caste or guild of healers, enjoying special privileges in the culture. By the time they reach adulthood, more than half the men and 10 percent of the women have become healers.

These characteristics of the dance establish its importance in the study of healing and consciousness. Moreover, the dance seems to be an old part of Kung hunting-gathering life. The rock paintings of South Africa include depictions of a healing dance much like the *dwa*, or Giraffe, the dominant healing dance of today (Lewis-Williams, 1980; Vinnicombe, 1975). The healing dance must therefore be at least several hundred years old, and perhaps older.

A broad range of fundamental activities are focused in the dance. Healing in the most generic sense is provided. It may take the form of curing an ill body or mind, as the healer pulls out the sickness; or of mending the social fabric, as the dance provides for a manageable release of hostility and an increased sense of social solidarity; or of protecting the village from misfortune, as the healer pleads with the gods for relief from the Kalahari's harshness. And the healing takes the form of enhancing consciousness, as the dance brings its participants into contact with the spirits and gods.

The dance provides the training ground for aspiring healers. It also provides the healers with opportunities for fulfillment and growth, where all can experience a sense of well-being, and where some may experience what Westerners would call a spiritual development. In the dance, the Kung find a vehicle for artistic expression. And from the dance, they receive profound knowledge, as the healer reports on those extended encounters with the gods which can occur during especially difficult healing efforts.

These activities are integrated with and reinforce each other, forming a continuous source of curing, counsel, protection, and enhancement. The healing is stimulated by the atmosphere generated at the dance. As individual healers go into kia, other Kung participating in the dance in various ways and to various degrees themselves experience an alteration of their state of consciousness, even if they do not go into kia. An atmosphere develops in which one person's experience of kia has a contagious effect on others.

The dance provides the focal point for what anthropologists consider to be the central features of a culture. The dance is the Kung's primary expression of "religion," "medicine," and "cosmology." It is their primary "ritual." For the Kung, the dance is, quite simply, an orienting and integrating event of unique importance.

Certain events or happenings make a dance more likely to occur, such as a severe illness, especially if it is sudden; the killing of a big game animal; the return of absent family members; and visits from close relatives or "important" persons, like the anthropologists. Most often dances are held because people want to sing and dance together, as part of their continuing effort to prevent incipient sickness, which they believe resides in everyone, from becoming severe and manifest; as part of their desire to contact the gods and seek their protection; as part of their wish to have an evening of enjoyment and companionship.

The actual frequency of dances is influenced by ecological and sociological factors, a most important one being whether the Kung are camped at a permanent water-hole or out in the bush. When they are camped around the permanent water-holes, though their hunting and gathering remain demanding, camps move infrequently and then only for short distances. This leaves more time and energy available for dances, which can occur once, perhaps twice a week. When the Kung are out in the bush, especially as the dry season approaches, they are constantly on the move, and their hunting, gathering, and water collection can require greater effort. Less time and energy are available for dancing. Dances occur perhaps two or three times a month, and then usually to treat a specific illness.

The number of persons in the camp who can support a dance is another important factor in the number of dances. While the Kung are located at a permanent water-hole, there are usually enough strong singers and dancers to begin and maintain a dance, though sometimes persons from several camps are needed. In the bush, where the Kung move about in much smaller groups, there is a personnel shortage. A typical group may have only four adult males, and they must often be out hunting. The number needed for a dance is often missing.

The composition of a camp is also a factor in the frequency of dances. At the permanent water-hole of Xaixai, the different Kung camps have different amounts of dancing. One camp, for example, has many young and middle-aged people but few children and old persons as compared to the other camps. Because the children need supervision at a dance, they subtract from the resources available to maintain the dance. The very old are usually not active participants. So this camp has more dances than other Xaixai villages.

Finally, the prevailing social climate affects the number of dances. For a period of time at Xaixai when there is much tension between the two main camps, no healing dances take place. Persons simply do not want to spend the long intimate hours of the dance in each other's company.

Yet a large dance finally brings the camps together to resolve their conflicts. As the small Kung groups move about in the bush, they may not see other groups for weeks, even months. When the groups do meet, a dance is in their hearts and quickly comes to fruition. As they sing and dance together, their sense of isolation vanishes. The dance is an organic event, its occurrence remaining sensitive to the moods and hopes of the people at the time. When a camp is in good spirits, there may be a period of frequent and intense dancing. At other times when a mood of lethargy prevails in the camp, the dancing seems to shrivel up the same as the green bushes in the blistering heat of the desert dry season. A compelling reason for a dance may then exist, yet no dance occurs.

The size of dances varies. A large dance, in which several camps participate, includes about fifty to eighty persons. There are infants and little ones, frisky adolescents and slow-moving old people. In such a large dance, fifteen to thirty women may be singing at different times. The singers are usually adults, joined by some of the more enthusiastic adolescents. Their ages vary across the full range of adulthood, though rarely including the very old. About seven to fifteen men may be dancing at any one time, most of them young or middle-aged.

Smaller dances, usually started and maintained by a single camp, have about fifteen to twenty persons at the dance, with seven to ten women singing and four or five men dancing. At these, younger boys and girls may participate to bring the complement of singers and dancers up to a sufficient level. Perhaps one-quarter of the singers and two-thirds of the dancers may be healers at any one dance regardless of its size. The potential for healing is thus everpresent and pervasive.

Occasionally there are very large dances, usually to celebrate special events. These may go on continuously for several days, sustained through the long, hot days by a few hardy singers and dancers, accelerating during the cooler hours of the night when the crowds build. There can be up to two hundred persons at such a dance, with perhaps thirty to forty singers at any one time sitting two or three deep in a circle around the fire, and perhaps fifteen to twenty-five dancers. Sometimes it becomes impossible for so many dancers to form one circle. Two dance fires are built, with the singers divided up around each one, and the dancers circling both fires in a figure-eight pattern. The killing of a large animal, such as an eland, may motivate this kind of dance. When many people gather to help eat and share the enormous quantity of meat, the mood for dancing is aroused. From their black neighbors, the Kung have learned about Christmas celebrations. During this season, the blacks may slaughter a cow or two, and that amount of available food, plus the festive air, invariably stimulate a very large, long dance.

No special equipment is necessary for the dance. Dance rattles (*zhorosi*) are used when available. They are made from dried cocoons with pieces of ostrich eggshell inside, strung on pieces of fiber. Preferably, a pair of rattles is used, one string being wrapped around each of the dancer's calves, though when rattles are in short supply, a dancer may use only one string. Usually several pairs are available at the average-sized dance. As the dancers move around the circle, each step elicits the distinctive staccato sound of the rattles, which accompanies and accents the rhythmic texture of the dance. Most dancers also bring their walking stick to the dance. This stick, which can also be used for digging roots and carrying objects, is carved from a piece of stripped hard wood, usually with a large gnarled knot at the top serving as a handle. They use the stick to accent their dancing steps or, especially when fatigued, to support them as they continue to dance.

In their curing efforts, healers may use plant substances which contain num (Marshall, 1969). These plants are ground to a powder, mixed with marrow or fat, and put in an empty tortoise shell, several inches long. Healers place a burning coal into the mixture, wafting the smoke, which carries num, toward the patient.

Clothing for the dance is the normal everyday wear, though a special personal touch may be added, such as a feather in the headband, an extra headband, or a hat.

Typically the healing dance moves through different stages. When there is to be a dance, a dance fire is begun in the central open area of the camp late in the afternoon as the sun disappears from the land. The women who are to sing and clap the healing songs come together informally and gradually. They sit side by side in intimate physical contact, legs intertwined, shoulder to shoulder, forming a tight circle around the fire. The dancers, both men and women, start to circle around the singers. Other smaller fires are begun slightly away from the dance fire. Persons not singing or dancing sit in little groups conversing and joking around these peripheral "talking" fires.

At the start, there is a lot of warm-up activity. The mood is casual and jovial. Many of the dancers are adolescents trying out and showing off their new dance steps. Then, almost imperceptibly, the mood intensifies. The singing and clapping become more spirited, the dancing more focused. Most of the healers at the dance are now dancing; the adolescents have either retired to the periphery or begun dancing in a more serious manner. Joking and socializing continue. The atmosphere is earnest, but not somber.

As midnight approaches, with the flickering fire illuminating the singers and dancers, a healer or two begins to stagger, then perhaps one falls. They may shudder or shake violently, their whole body convulsing in apparent pain and anguish. The experience of kia has begun. And then, either on their own or under the guidance of those who are more steady, the healers who are in kia go to each person at the dance and begin to heal. They lay their fluttering hands on a person, one hand usually on the chest, the other on the back, pulling out the sickness, while shrieking earth-shattering screams and howls known as *kowhedili*, an expression for the pain and difficulty of this healing work. Then they shake their hands vigorously toward the empty space beyond the dance, casting the sickness they have taken from the person out into the darkness.

Such healing may go on for several hours. During this time the healers plead and argue with the gods to save the people from illness, demanding that the spirits of their dead ancestors, the *gauwasi*, not take a sick one away. They plead while they are laying on their hands; they plead as they stop dancing for a moment. They turn their heads toward the sky, yelling to the spirits to let the people alone: "What business do you have here tonight! This man is not ready to go. He wants to remain with those who love him."

Gradually a calm sets in as the dance moves into the early morning hours. Some dancers sleep for a brief period; the talk is quiet, the singing soft. The dance is resting. But the dance awakens again before dawn. The atmosphere picks up as sleeping forms rise and come toward the dance circle. The singing becomes stronger, the dancers more active. Another period of healing usually occurs as the sun begins to throw its light and warmth on the persons huddled around the dance. Before the sun becomes too warm, the kia and healing subside, and the singing gradually softens, then ends. The dance is over.

People slowly, comfortably move off to their camps. During the day after the dance most things take place as if in slow motion. Some persons rest quietly, acknowledging the fatigue of their sleepless night of physical and emotional exertion. Others visit a bit, their mood relaxed and humorous.

The Kung say that kia comes from activation of an energy that they call num. Num was originally given to the Kung by the gods. Though experiencing kia is a necessary prerequisite to healing, it is painful and feared. The cause of kia – the activated num – is said to boil fiercely within the person. Some at the dance avoid kia; others experience kia but fail to develop it so that it can be applied to healing. Even among the healers, not all heal at every dance.

Those who have learned to heal are said to "possess" num. They are called *num kausi*, "masters, or owners, of num." Num resides in the pit of the stomach and the base of the spine. As healers continue their energetic dancing, becoming warm and sweating profusely, the num in them heats up and becomes a vapor. It rises up the spine to a point approximately at the base of the skull, at which time kia results. Kinachau, an old healer, talks about the kia experience: "You dance, dance, dance, dance. Then num lifts you up in your belly and lifts you in your back, and you start to shiver. Num makes you tremble; it's hot. Your eyes are open, but you don't look around; you hold your eyes still and look straight ahead. But when you get into kia, you're looking around because you see everything, because you see what's troubling everybody. Rapid shallow breathing draws num up. What I do in my upper body with the breathing, I also do in my legs with the dancing. You don't stomp harder, you just keep steady. Then num enters every part of your body, right to the tip of your feet and even your hair."

The action and ascent of num are described by Kau Dwa, another powerful healer: "In your backbone you feel a pointed something and it works its way up. The base of your spine is tingling, tingling, tingling, tingling. Then num makes your thoughts nothing in your head."

Num is an energy held in awe and considered very powerful and mysterious. This same energy is what the healer "puts into" people in attempting to cure them. For once heated up, num can both induce kia and combat illness.

As Kung learn to have some control over their boiling num, they can apply the num to healing. They learn to *twe*, that is, to "heal" or "pull out sickness," or simply "pull." Kau Dwa describes how one can heal while experiencing kia: "When you kia, you see things you must pull out, like the death things that god has put into people. You see people properly, just as they are. Your vision does not whirl." The purpose of kia is reached. Healing results.

During kia, the Kung experience themselves as existing beyond their ordinary level. As Kinachau puts it: "When we enter kia, we are different from when our num is not boiling and small. We can do different things."

Kia itself is an intense, emotional state. Emotions are aroused to an extraordinary level, whether they be fear or exhilaration or seriousness. The Kung also practice extraordinary activities during kia. They perform cures and, as part of their effort to heal, may handle and walk on fire, see the insides of people's bodies and scenes at great distances from their camp, or travel to god's home – activities never attempted in their ordinary state. Moreover, they experience themselves as beyond their ordinary self by becoming more essential, more themselves. Toma Zho, perhaps the strongest healer at Xaixai, speaks of this increased essentiality: "I want to have a dance soon so that I can really become myself again."

Through kia, the Kung participate in what Westerners call the "religious-spiritual" dimension. Transcending themselves, they are able to contact the realm where the gods and the spirits of dead ancestors live. Sickness is a process by which these spirits, helped by the lesser god, try to carry off the sick one into their own realm. The spirits have various ways of bringing misfortune and death, such as "allowing" a lion to maul a person or a snake to bite one, or a person to fall from a tree (Marshall, 1969). But the dance is where the spirits are most likely to bring sickness.

Sent by the great god, the spirits are strong but not invincible. A struggle takes place between two groups of loving relatives, those still living and those already dead. Each group wishes to have the sick one for themselves, and neither the realm of the living nor that of the spirits is seen as bad. In their ordinary state, the Kung do not argue with the gods, such is their respect. But in kia, healers express the wishes of the living by entering directly into a struggle with the spirits and the lesser god.

When a person is seriously ill, the struggle becomes intense. The more powerful healers sometimes travel to the great god's home in the sky, bringing the confrontation directly to the source of illness. The Kung say the healer's soul makes that journey at the greatest risk to the healer's very life. Healers undertake such a terrifying journey because they want to rescue the soul of a sick person from the god's home and bring it back to their own camp. On their return, these powerful healers may describe the god's home, at times in great detail, as well as recounting their own struggle for the sick one's soul. If a healer's num is strong, the spirits will retreat and the sick one will live. This struggle is at the heart of the healer's art and power.

Kia can be viewed as an altered state of consciousness, enhanced to the degree and quality of transcendence. As the Kung's sense of self, time, and space are being significantly altered during kia, they experience a feeling of ascent. One healer says, "When I pick up num, it explodes and throws me up in the air, and I enter heaven and then fall down." Others during kia feel that they are "opening up" or "bursting open, like a ripe pod."

The education of men and women healers differs, but the differences are more matters of form and structure than process and experience. Essentially, the training of both sexes is the same, especially the process of receiving num. One of the most striking things about the Kung education for healing is that it is an aspect of normal socialization. Most males and more than a third of the women try to become healers. Long before persons seriously try to become healers, they play at entering kia. A group of five- and six-year-olds may perform a small "healing dance," imitating the actual dance, with its steps and healing postures, at times falling as if in kia. Through play, the children are modeling; as they grow up, they are learning about kia. Furthermore, education for healing occurs within the context of the family, the major vehicle for socialization. The primary source of information about kia, as well as the experiential teacher of kia, is likely to be in one's immediate family, or a close relative.

But this strongly supportive context for healing is not enough. To become a healer, a Kung must first seek num. With men, this seeking usually starts at the age of approximately twenty. The young man becomes a student and for several years expresses his search by going to as many dances as possible, perhaps two or three a week. With women, the age of seeking is more variable, the search briefer. But num is not "put into" someone who cannot accept it; students must be willing and ready to receive the num which can evoke the experience of kia. They must learn to "drink num" (*chi num*), a phrase used by the Kung to describe the process and act of learning to heal, especially the experience in which kia first develops into healing.

Socialization for kia and then seeking kia are preparatory phases in the education for kia. At the heart of this educational process is the experience of kia itself. While the Kung maintain a conceptual clarity about what happens during kia, they speak of the experiential mystery at the time of kia. This is especially the case with one's first kia experiences. At its core, the education is a process of accepting a kia experience for oneself. This is very difficult, because kia is painful as well as unknown. It is greatly feared.

Along with feelings of release and liberation, kia brings profound pain and fear. In describing the onset of kia, healers speak again and again of the searing pain in the *gebesi* and sometimes in the pit of the stomach. The word *gebesi* refers to the general area between the diaphragm and the waist, especially toward the sides. The term is also used to refer to two specific organs, the liver and spleen. A healer recalls his first experiences with num: "Num got into my stomach. It was hot and painful in my gebesi, like fire. I was surprised and I cried."

More than physical symptoms are involved. Kau Dwa makes the further dimensions of this painful fear explicit: "As we enter kia, we fear death. We fear we may die and not come back!" This fear of death without an experience of rebirth evokes its own special terror for the Kung, as it has for persons in every culture. When potential healers can face this fact of their death and "willingly" die, the fear of num can be overcome, and there can be a breakthrough to kia. The knowledge or conviction of being reborn or coming alive again is helpful, if not essential. Wi, an older healer at Xaixai, describes this death and rebirth in kia: "Your heart stops. You're dead. Your thoughts are nothing. You breathe with difficulty. You see things, num things; you see spirits killing people. You smell burning, rotten flesh. Then you heal, you pull sickness out. You heal, heal, heal. Then you live. Your eyeballs clear and you see people clearly."

Various aspects of the dance support this critical passage. Potential healers can receive support and encouragement from a number of people – first, their teacher, who has agreed to train them and give them num. This teacher, perhaps with one or two other healers, will probably be the one who tries to put num into the student during a dance.

Num is usually sent by means of invisible arrows which are felt as painful thorns or needles. Teachers shoot these arrows of num (*num tchisi*) into the student, sometimes by snapping their fingers, always trying to regulate the number of arrows and the intensity of the num they carry.

A younger Kung talks about these arrows and this passage into and out of death: "In kia, around your neck and around your belly you feel tiny needles and thorns which prick you. Then your front spine and your back spine are pricked with these thorns. Your gebesi tightens into a balled fist. Your breathing stops. Then someone rubs your belly and the pricking stops, and you start to breathe again."

The Kung must give up what is familiar – their familiar identity – to enter the unknown territory of kia. They must experience death before they can be reborn into kia. Kia remains an experiential mystery; it demands a truly frightening passage into the unknown.

A number of other people provide support and protection. They may give the students physical support when the onset of kia makes them shaky, or lead them to others whom they can heal. These guardians also protect the students from harming themselves or others. For example, the students may want to get closer to the fire to help their num boil up. But when they try to put their heads in the fire or throw hot coals in the air, someone at the dance usually leaps up and restrains them. Another supportive and at times inspirational group is the women singers. By singing and clapping the healing songs, they stimulate the num to boil. The intensity of their singing can help to determine and regulate the depth of kia. Finally, the entire community is present at the dance – friends, family, neighbors – all of whom participate to some degree and, by their presence, offer support.

As the students continue to dance through the night ever

more seriously, their num may begin to boil, and kia becomes imminent. At this point, another critical phase in the educational process occurs. The aspiring healers try to regulate their condition. When they feel kia coming on, they involuntarily draw back from and at times actively resist this transition to an altered state. Others help them to overcome this resistance and to strike a dynamic balance between the oncoming intensity of kia and their fear of it. If their kia is coming on so fast that their fear escalates and prevents them from experiencing the kia, the teacher may make them stop dancing for a while, or drink some water, or lie down – all to "cool down" their too rapidly boiling num. The num must be hot enough to evoke kia but not so hot that it provokes debilitating fear. It is never a question of merely putting num into the students; the correct amount is critical. Experienced healers are encouraged to go as deeply into kia as they can, provided they maintain enough control over the num to use it for healing.

Throughout this work at the dance, there is extensive physical contact between the students and those who are helping them. Much of the students' sensitivity to these subtle balance considerations comes from this intimate contact. The physical, emotional, and psychological aspects of support are inseparable.

The Kung speak of "carrying" in describing their healing. Carrying can refer to the concrete physical support offered at a dance to those seeking kia as well as to the general process of helping a student learn to heal, as in the idea that experienced healers must "carry the students." Carrying also can signify the general effects of a healer's work. Powerful healers talk of how their efforts are "carrying the camp" or keeping the camp healthy.

Drugs are not used on any regular basis to induce kia. However, an indigenous drug may be used on occasion, especially by the women. If the students are having considerable difficulty reaching kia, they may be given a drug at the dance, as a training device, to mitigate their intense fear and bring them closer to the kia state. The drug experience itself becomes a preparation for kia, since both experiences are altered states of consciousness. As with other techniques used at the dance, the dosage and timing of the drug are carefully regulated by the teacher. The drug is supposed to help the students, not catapult them into yet another unknown and potentially frightening altered state.

There are specific and sometimes idiosyncratic signs that people are approaching that threshold of fear or kia. Bodies shake. Eyes are glazed or downcast. Faces appear impassive. The signs must then be interpreted. The fear can be so intense that the students must sit down, or the fear may be such that, if they stay with it, they can overcome it and enter a kia state. These signs are used not only by the students themselves but also by those helping them. If, for example, the singers sense that someone is ready to go into kia, they may intensify their singing and clapping to give the student an extra push.

The subtlety of this balancing response is shown in the case of one young Kung who is new to kia. He has a look of tremendous fear as he dances. The singing, clapping, and dancing in general are at a high pitch of intensity. Kia is threatening to overwhelm him, and he runs away from the dance. But instead of letting him stay away from the dance, two persons go and take hold of him, one from the front, the other from behind, and physically bring him back to the dance. The three of them then continue dancing in the circle, remaining in physical contact, as the singing reaches a new level of intensity. They bring the fearful one back to what he most fears, but they are now physically with him. He is able to go through his fear and into kia. The approach to each potential healer depends on his or her own history and present readiness for kia.

As kia occurs at a dance, the atmosphere becomes more electric and the dance more focused. One person going into kia is usually a stimulant for others. At one dance where there are fifteen dancers, twelve of them already know how to enter kia. I try to imagine what would happen if all of them were to go into kia at once. Certainly the process of education for kia would be severely strained. But no more than two or three are in kia at any one time. What happens is a process of kia management. The more experienced healers hold back their kia until those who need more help are either under control or able to function in kia. Rarely are there people in a state of kia who need help and cannot get it.

The teachers are Kung healers. During their non-kia state, they remain ordinary persons rather than intimates of the gods or chosen instruments. They do not demand from students either obedience or a long apprenticeship. The period of learning is focused within the dance itself. The emphasis is on experiential education. The core of teaching lies at those points when kia is about to occur. The teachers are with the students at the threshold of this experience, trying to help them over their fear and into kia, then guiding them to use that kia for healing.

Though originally issuing from the gods, num now passes regularly from person to person. Teaching is primarily by example. The teachers have been there before. They may or may not experience kia at the same time as the students, but certainly they have experienced kia many times before.

The principal dance form is the Giraffe, so named because giraffe healing or num songs now dominate in it. Gemsbok and eland songs have also enjoyed a popularity in this dance form, and at times have lent their names to it. But the Giraffe is presently the central form of healing dance among the hunting-gathering Kung and is the focus of this book.

The more experienced healers do not always need a full Giraffe dance to activate their num. Severe and especially chronic illnesses usually precipitate small healings which can hardly be called a dance. One or two healers can kia and heal, supported only by their own singing of num songs and perhaps by the singing of several women. The actual dancing may be minimal: perhaps a few steps, done mostly in place.

With some chronic conditions, small healings can occur every night of the week and over long periods of time. A wife or husband often treats an ailing spouse in such a manner. Certain experienced healers can also heal themselves while sitting alone at night and singing num songs. If the healer's spouse is present, the two may sing to and for each other, healing themselves and each other.

Richard Lee (personal communication) has described one such healing. An old woman healed her husband nightly for almost a year. Diagnosed by visiting Western doctors as having cancer, her husband lasted much longer than they had expected. She "fought the battle almost single-handed." Sometimes only her daughter would sing with her. The woman's message to her husband was clear and consistent: "Your dead father is trying to take you away. Those who are still alive have been mean to you. Your dead father is going to deprive them of you. You've been good all your life. I begged your dead father to give those who are still alive another chance to be good to you. Your dead father agreed, and spared you tonight."

There are two other dances in the Dobe area where kia and healing occur, the Trees and the Drum, of which the Drum is the more important. In the Drum dance it is the women who sing and dance and experience kia. Other than the man who plays the drum and who may also experience kia, men are not generally participants. There is much less emphasis on healing in this dance as compared to the Giraffe, and the healing that does occur is more restricted to the active participants. The experience of kia, however, is quite similar in the two dances.

Whereas the Giraffe occurs everywhere and at all times, the other kia dances are more local and infrequent in their occurrence. Whereas the Giraffe is open to the entire community, uniting the community as it unfolds, the other kia dances exclude some persons. Whereas in the Giraffe, men and women contribute equally to the activation of num through their different but overlapping roles, in the other kia dances the contributions of men and women are differentially valued, their roles more sharply divided. Whereas in the Giraffe kia is experienced in order to heal, in the other dances kia is often not transformed into healing energy. The Giraffe is the dance in which healing energy becomes most deeply a part of everyone's life.

Other important rituals involving dance are *choma*, the male initiation camp set up for boys from the ages of approximately fifteen to twenty; and the Eland dance, which marks the girls' first menstruation. Dancing at choma also brings on experiences of kia. Choma and the Eland dance may each occur only once every several years. Certain persons may on occasion enter kia while playing one of the musical instruments which are a continual source of pleasure for the Kung. In the Kung manner with such instrumental music, they are playing primarily for themselves, not performing for others. There are also numerous little dance patterns and dance-games, most including singing, which are performed by the older girls and women when the mood strikes them, for their own pleasure and entertainment, and for the pleasure of any others who may be watching (England, 1968; Marshall, 1979).

Herbal medicines and a healing massage are also used by the Kung, but these are supplementary treatments, usually reserved for less serious or more localized ailments. Neither requires a healing dance or the experience of kia for its use. Only when such treatments fail to work does a small specialized kia healing or a healing dance become appropriate. Plants which contain num, or medicinal plants, number more than 15 (Lee, 1979; Marshall, 1969). They may be used by people, healers and non-healers alike, for minor curing efforts and protection. Apart from the dance, persons may rub charred bits of such plants on their skin to cure an ache or pain, or bring luck in hunting. Abrasions, cuts, and infections are routinely treated with medicinal salves.

"Aches and pains" and especially a general "tiredness" can also call for a massage. The healing massage involves forceful manipulation of large areas of the body, concentrating on the shoulders, back, and stomach. The massagers rub their sweat onto the one being healed and periodically shake their hands off into space, expelling the patient's sickness. This behavior is similar to the healing behavior in the Giraffe dance. Massage can also be a preparation for healing in the Giraffe. As the healer Kana puts it: "We massage each other to get out the sickness. We also massage to make a person ready for the healing num of Giraffe."

Knowledge of herbal medicines and skill with massage are not necessarily possessed by the same person, nor are such capabilities limited to or even possessed by all healers. Koto, for example, who has never entered kia, is considered one of the best massagers.

The traditional Kung approach to healing is integral to its context in the Kalahari. Woven into the Kung's hunting-gathering life-style, the dance seems to highlight it. Time is definitely available for the all-night dances. Community is at the dance, and the dance establishes community. Everyone is welcome at the dance. Parents teach children about num. In a real sense, it is the community, in its activation of num, which heals and is healed. What Westerners might call the "sacred" and the "profane" merge playfully and dramatically at the dance: the raucous sexual joking as the dancers move toward kia; the dialogue between the healer and the spirits, first pleading, then insulting. And there are no restrictions in the access to num. In egalitarian fashion, all receive healing. Num is shared throughout the community. It is not meant to be hoarded by any one person; perhaps it never can be. There is no limit to num. It expands as it boils. As one person reaches kia at the dance, others are stimulated to follow. One Kung becoming a healer does not mean another cannot become one; the reverse is true, especially when the two are closely related.

The Kung do not seek num for its own sake. They seek its protection and enhancement for the individual, the group, and the culture simultaneously. The healing approach does not undermine the execution of everyday responsibilities. The healer is a hunter or gatherer who also happens to heal. Healing remains harmonious with the different levels of Kung existence. Its effectiveness depends on this context.

The question of whether kia-healing "works" depends to a large extent on who asks it. When asked by someone with a contemporary Western scientific orientation, the question usually has a rational, materialistic emphasis. Such a person usually wants to know what specific illnesses are cured, how rapidly, and how completely. If asked by a Kung, the question would have a more holistic meaning. Num is energy, one form of which can be translated as "medicine." For the Kung, healing deals with the whole person, in all aspects and situations. Healing is directed as much toward alleviating physical illness in an individual as toward enhancing the healer's understanding; as much toward resolving conflict in the village as toward establishing a proper relationship with the gods and the cosmos. A healing may be specifically directed toward one of these focuses, but the healing in fact affects them all. For a Kung, the question would be: Does healing "heal," rather than just "cure," and does it heal "sickness" as well as "illness"?

Although the Kung word for "heal" and "cure" is the same (*twe*), as is the word for "illness" and "sickness" (*xai*), the context of usage creates distinctions. "Illness" means a more specific or delimited disease with symptoms, usually manifest. As the Kung see it, all people have sickness in them, which on occasion flares up and is expressed in an illness. This does not mean that every Kung is an ambulatory disease-ridden patient. Rather, each Kung has the potential for illness. When the Kung offer healing to all at the dance, whether they have a manifest illness or not, they are healing sickness, providing in part what Westerners would call "preventative" treatment.

"Healing" is the generic term, including in its meaning, "to cure." The Kung criterion for a cure is that someone with an illness gets better, usually with the relief or disappearance of symptoms. A supplementary criterion is that the healer sees the cause of the illness coming out of the patient. A cure does not occur with every healing effort.

When confronted by illness, the Kung healer uses num to bring the protective powers of the universe to bear on the patient and, as one possible though not necessary outcome, relieve her symptoms. A specific illness is only a manifestation of some imbalance in the whole individual as she exists in her total environment. A healing seeks to re-establish the balance in the individual-cultural-environmental gestalt. One expression of this new balance might be a cure, the relief of symptoms. But the person being healed can also die, and a new balance can still be established, a healing accomplished. A healing dance may increase group cohesion during a period of tension within a camp, even though the patient for whom the dance was held dies. As the Kung say, sometimes it is proper for the spirits to take a person away. The healers, in exhausting their resources in this struggle with the spirits, confirm the correctness of the larger relationship of the community and the gods.

The full range of what in the West would be called physical, psychological, emotional, social, and spiritual illnesses are treated at the healing dance. Nearly every Kung, and many of the neighboring blacks as well, can describe how the healing dance has cured someone. Sometimes the reported cure is dramatic. For example, someone who has been clawed by a leopard and "given up for dead" is healed and recovers miraculously. More often the cure is undramatic. Someone who complains of "chest wheezing and coughing," who is experiencing respiratory congestion from what would in the West be diagnosed as chronic emphysema, is healed and then is able to go about his day in a normal way. A woman who is described as "so weak she is dying," probably with advanced tuberculosis, receives intense healing and has a little more strength the next day. A young woman comes to the dance for healing because her "milk is not coming properly" to her nursing baby. The next day her milk returns. Another woman receives healing at the dance because her lip has become increasingly infected and swollen. After several days, the swelling and infection subside. A healing dance is held for a young healer who complains of "tired blood" and shows signs of great physical and psychological fatigue. At the dance he regains his strength, in part through his own dancing and healing. Or a woman gets relief from the discomforts of her pregnancy. Two families from different camps are in conflict over an upcoming marriage between two of their young people. Accusations of stinginess in regard to some of the gift exchanges required before the marriage fill the air. During a healing dance attended by the two families along with the rest of the camps, the tensions subside, though the conflict is not resolved to the total satisfaction of either family. After spending the night in the intense intimacy of the healing dance, the people will speak of how good it is to be together. The Kung refer to the healing dance as *num chxi*. The sense of *chxi* is "to gather together to sing and dance" (Biesele, personal communication).

Although the Kung try to heal the full range of illnesses, they are not unreasonable about the limits of num's healing powers. When, for example, the Kung suspect that Goba sorcery is the cause of the illness, they do not attempt further healing. Goba refers to an unfamiliar black person, in practice someone who is not recognized to be either Herero or Tswana. The Kung believe that Goba sorcery is too strong for their num.

In certain instances, after the Kung have tried as much healing as they can, they willingly admit that their num cannot deal with the illness at hand. This is the case with a boy who breaks a food taboo and is considered "crazy" because all he can say is, "Nothing. Nothing." He becomes extremely thin. Many times he receives healings. But his condition continues to deteriorate, and finally he dies. As the healer Gau puts it: "Sometimes you get someone who is ill who wants to die, but you heal him and heal him and he lives. Other times you heal him and he still dies."

The Kung are extremely pragmatic about terminal illness and death. When a person, especially an old person, is in the final throes of a fatal disease, the healing efforts usually intensify. The immediate family works on the dying person each night. But the Kung do not see num as reversing a situation which is supposed to be. Wi, one of the older healers, expresses a common Kung understanding: "Sometimes you heal and god helps you. Sometimes you heal and heal and heal, and you lose the person."

Whereas I witnessed each of the "undramatic" cures I described here, I have no first-hand data on any dramatic cures, such as the sudden healing of profound physical damage. Also, within the period of my research in the Kalahari, I could not establish the degree of experimental control that Western science demands as validation of cures, whether dramatic or ordinary. The required outcome study would have to account for the fact that most diseases are self-limiting; they heal on their own, almost regardless, and sometimes in spite of, specific treatments. Such a study would be difficult to undertake, given the small size of the Kung groups and their pattern of moving about the Kalahari. The fundamental questions of what is "healing" and what is a "cure" remain.

There is also other evidence on the effectiveness of the healing dance. A practical and pragmatic people, the Kung use things that they believe work. They have been exposed to other systems of treatment, both African and Western, yet they continue to rely on their healing dance. Antibiotics may be used in conjunction with a dance, to provide extra protection or to deal with diseases particularly amenable to Western medicine, such as gonorrhea. Antibiotics are also used sometimes in conjunction with or instead of indigenous medicinal salves. Although contact with Western medicine is still limited, the pattern of that contact is clear: the Kung integrate elements from other treatment systems into the tradition of their dance. The prevailing mode of healing remains num, though the Kung attitude remains realistic. As Gau says: "Maybe our num and European medicine are similar, because sometimes people who get European medicine die, and sometimes they live. That is the same with ours."

Moreover, the neighboring blacks turn to the Kung healing dances for help, coming to the dance with an attitude of respect uncharacteristic of their general domineering attitude toward the Kung. The Hereros in the Dobe area say that num is strong and powerful. In the Ghanzi area, where several black groups live in close proximity to the Kung, their respective healing systems are often in direct competition. The Kung approach to healing is valued and sought after by these black groups.

The younger Kung are not giving up the healing dance but continue to work toward becoming healers. Young adults speak like the older ones. They express a strong belief in num and great respect for its healing powers. Gau, now in his mid-thirties, is an impressive figure. Though still young, his views are highly respected by his fellow Kung. His feelings about black and European intrusions into the Kalahari run deep. He wants to establish Kung rights to the land they have always hunted and gathered, in the face of the overgrazing cattle of their pastoral neighbors. Yet with all his fervent orientation to contemporary political and economic affairs, Gau is one of the most promising healers. "Num is our way," he says.

4 At a Healing Dance

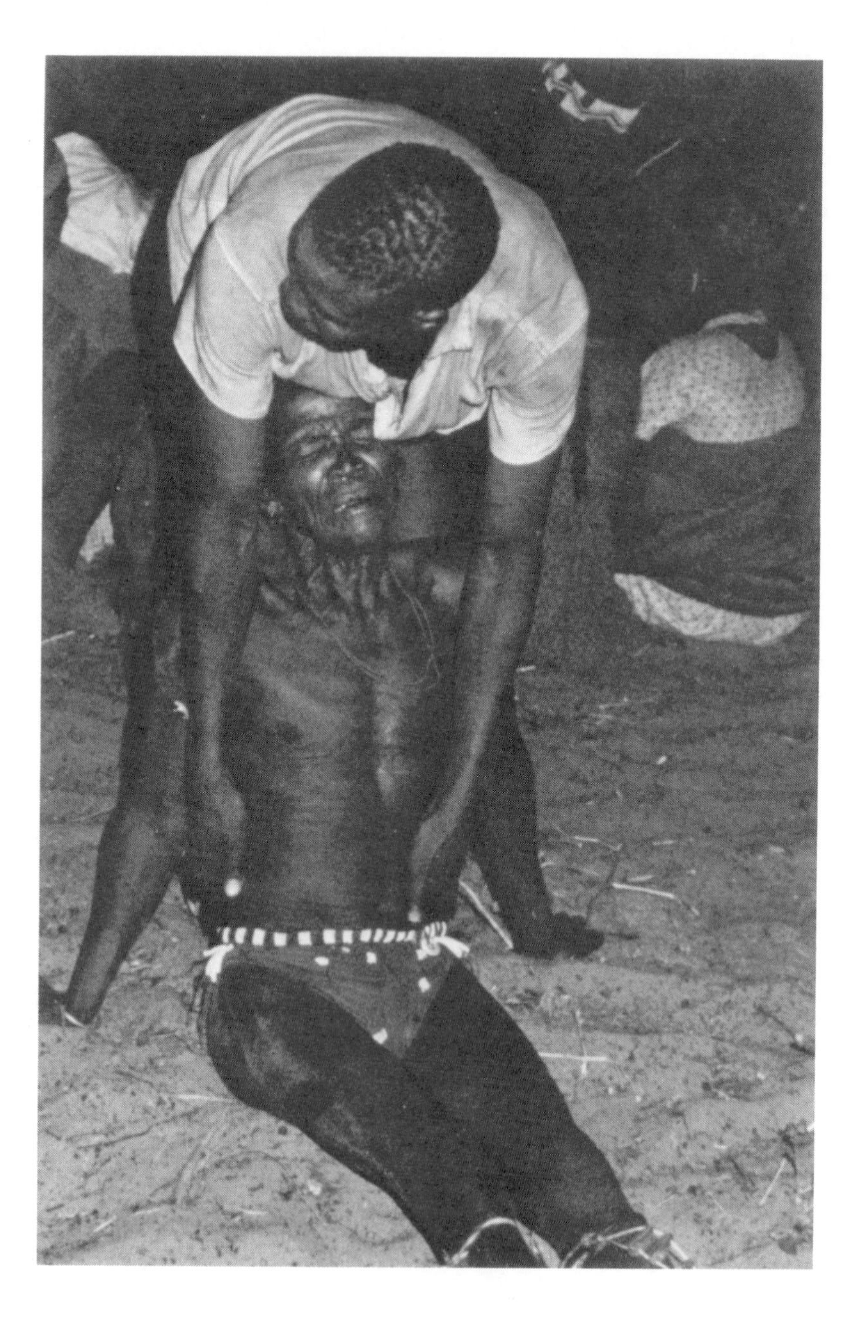

TOMA ZHO mentions it that long, sun-baked afternoon, during the lazy banter of just lying around, between our methodical movements into newly emerging shade areas. He says his camp has decided to have a dance tonight. He has been talking to persons from some of the other camps; they think they will come too. He is not extending an invitation. He just mentions there will be a dance, and that in itself was the invitation. Persons are never excluded from a dance.

Toma Zho, a healer in his late fifties, is a complex and controversial figure at the Xaixai water-hole. He is not enthusiastic about everyday responsibilities, neither getting food nor raising the children. His two wives take an active, competent role in those areas. Toma Zho loves to joke, and he spends many hours in animated, dramatic jesting with others. His imagination roams as he constantly changes the pace, moving swiftly from the serious to the comic.

A young Xaixai man seeking num says of Toma Zho: "He is the biggest healer at Xaixai. He is big, big! There are others who do num, but they are far behind him." Toma Zho easily and confidently makes a similar evaluation of himself: "At Xaixai, I'm the only one with strength."

Toma Zho is considered one of the three most powerful healers at Xaixai, if not the most powerful, but he is also controversial. Some say that the way he approaches kia is not quite right. His access to num is unpredictable. Unlike other experienced healers, he cannot be counted on to pull sickness at a dance. This unpredictability is not so much because he fears num as because he is struggling to change his usage of num. Toma Zho is now more of a traditional healer, oriented toward healing in his own camp. He wants to be more of a professional healer, oriented toward heal ing persons in the general Dobe area, Kung and non-Kung alike, and receiving payment for his cures, especially from non-Kung.

Page 58: Kinachau being worked on in kia

Being the only Kung at Xaixai who has two wives increases Toma Zho's social importance. It is easy for him to say that there will be a dance at his camp. Both his wives are good singers; his sister, whose hut is across from his, is a very strong singer and healer; his oldest son is a healer; Bau, who lives two huts from his, is one of the most powerful female healers in Xaixai; and many other women in the camp are eager and lively singers. Toma Zho's camp "knows how to dance."

When I reach his camp for the dance tonight, people are still sitting around their individual cooking fires, though eating seems mostly over. The atmosphere is comfortable. Some people then lie down or stand to stretch; others clean up around the cooking fire, putting away their few utensils. The sun disappears for the day.

9:30

Several women in the camp begin to make a wood pile at the edge of the open space into which the little huts face. Soon a small dance fire has been lit near the middle of the space.

10:05

Three of the women who started the dance fire are joined by two others. These five begin singing num songs around the fire. They form a rather large circle, unusually far from the fire in the middle. It is as if they expect a large turnout and are starting big, leaving spaces for the many who will come.

10:15

One or two women sing at a time, a bit sporadically, joined off and on by others around the fire. Soon all five sing together and continually. Almost immediately, one or two young boys begin to dance, sporadically. They do a few steps, sometimes around the women in the dance circle, sometimes away from the circle, facing toward the women. The five individual voices form a chorus, and every so often one will improvise on that chorus. Four adolescent boys now dance around the singing women, beginning to make a rut that will be the dance circle. None of these four has experienced kia; none actively seeks kia. They practice fancy footwork, stop dancing and unexpectedly start again, teasing each other: "If you keep dancing that way, your balls will fall off!" To those just coming toward the light of the dance fire, they call out: "Where have you been? The dance is almost over!"

Most people in the host camp, plus many from the surrounding three Xaixai camps, have come to the dance area; there are now two other fires on the periphery of the dance fire. Around each fire are approximately six persons, mostly old or middle-aged. Another ten persons, mostly young or middle-aged, are milling around the area of the dance. About ten youngsters are playing and talking in another area, on the periphery of the dance circle.

10:30

Now the dance is mobbed. The four young adolescents are joined by four other dancers. There are still no healers in the dance circle, nor persons likely to experience kia tonight. The singing circle is so filled with nearly twenty women that it can no longer be contained. Some of the women who are singing sit two and three deep, leaning toward the fire. Legs cross under and over each other, shoulders and arms touch and rub. The singing circle bulges here, dips in there, and moves with the strong rhythm of the clapping. The atmosphere is intense. There is much conversation and milling about.

11:30

The dancers express and support the women's clapping with their strong, stomping dance steps, accentuated by the shaking sounds of the dance rattles around their ankles. A few of the dancers sing with the women, coming in to punctuate their dancing, rising over the women's voices to influence the direction of the song. The songs have taken hold. They have a definite start, introduced perhaps by one or two women singing a short melody. The conversation, which springs up naturally at the end of each song, fades as more and more women join in the singing. Then the song comes together as all the voices form a full, connected sound. Songs go on continuously for five minutes or so, building in intensity and volume toward the end, lifting the dancers into more serious dancing, and then ending, sometimes sharply, sometimes gradually.

11:40

Individual dancers still walk around after a song ends and the co-ordinated group dancing is over. They try to maintain the momentum of the dance, to keep the num which is starting to warm up from cooling off. It is as though they are looking forward to the point where their num will boil and kia will come. One mumbles to himself, "My sweats are hot, my sweats are wet." Another teases the women: "When will the singing begin? Is this a dance I am at?" The women join in animated conversation, gesturing wildly, laughing, calling out in delight: "This is the way we people are meant to dance." "This dance is good, because our singing is strong and rises up to the heavens."

The possibility for kia has now been introduced. Among the ten dancers, who are all men, there are two very experienced healers, Toma Zho and Kinachau; three fairly experienced healers, Gau, Dau, and Kana; and one learning to be a healer, Bo. Like his nephew Toma Zho, Kinachau is considered one of the three most powerful healers at Xai-xai. There the similarity ends. In his character and approach to num, Kinachau is quite different. Though nearly seventy, Kinachau remains alert and lively, even sprightly. He retains much of his physical capacity, walking briskly to the water-hole, carrying heavy loads of water, and continuing as a skillful hunter. Despite the undisputed power of his num, he does not try to build up his reputation in the interest of becoming more of a "professional" healer. He orients primarily to his own camp, dancing and healing there with consistency and regularity. In his quiet way, he provides others with strong healing.

Gau is in his late thirties, tall, handsome, and proud. He

moves with confidence, his posture erect, his chin strong and jutting forward. As a central figure at Xaixai, where he lives with his wife and seven-year-old son, he already wields considerable social and political influence, which is likely to increase as he grows older. He is sharp and intelligent. Gau has experienced kia at the dances for nearly ten years. His num is strong, yet since he is still young, others' num is said to be stronger. But all agree that Gau's num will continue to grow.

Dau is more controversial. In his mid-thirties, he is unpredictable. One time he is outgoing, laughing broadly with others; another time he seems withdrawn and moody. He has little social or political power. Dau and his wife have a little girl barely one year old. As Dau is controversial, so is his num. Some persons criticize Dau because he dances and pulls so flamboyantly; they question whether his num has real strength, because "when he is in kia, he runs all over the place, and that's bad." Others say that Dau's num is strong. Dau himself expresses both an overconfidence and a slight lack of confidence about his num.

Toma Zho's oldest son, Kana, is also in his mid-thirties and, like Gau and Dau, received num more than ten years ago. But whereas Gau is proud and Dau is controversial, Kana is inconspicuous. Still not married, he exists in the shadow of the aggressive, energetic late adolescents who are his companions. Everyone acknowledges that Kana's num is strong, but otherwise no one finds anything outstanding in him, whether positive or negative. At a dance he does not require much care from others. He just goes about his kia-healing as if it were business as usual. The way Kana first received num, however, is quite unusual. He did not fear it or struggle with it; he just accepted num because he felt it was his lot to be a healer.

Bo, not yet twenty and unmarried, is on the verge of becoming a healer. He has experienced kia a number of times in the past two years but has yet to pull out sickness. He pursues num eagerly. Bo is strikingly handsome and strong, a skillful hunter. His face is fresh and expressive; his eyes dart about with curiosity; his smile comes easily. He runs about with the other adolescent boys yet is especially shy and tender.

There is now a tremendous amount of action around the dance fire and in the areas nearby. Conversations and physical movements are animated. The men are dancing close to each other, moving as one body, some actually touching the person in front, an arm on his shoulder or waist. The dancers are calling to the singers, individually or together: "The singing is strong!" "We need your voices!" "Pick up the singing, louder!" The dancers call to each other: "This is a night for strong num." "Oh, my father, help me tonight!" The singers call out to the dancers: "We have just begun to sing!" "You there, have you not yet learned to dance?" And the singers laugh to each other: "Tonight we will not move, not even to take a piss. We will stay in our places and sing and clap until dawn." "Tonight is a night for our singing to climb into the skies!" At the many little fires in the area of darkness ringing the central fire, persons are talking, sometimes calling out: "Where are the dancers? When you little ones get tired, we will come and show you how our people are supposed to dance!" All the while the singing, clapping, and dancing increase in intensity.

11:45

Toma Zho sits down after having danced for less than five minutes. Several of the girls and women are now dancing in front of the men, some facing into the dance circle itself. Several men dancers give things to their wives. Dau, having begun to sweat profusely, takes off his shirt and hands it to his wife in the singing circle. Gau takes off the feather he has in his hair and gives it to his wife to hold. These seem to be signs that the dance is getting more serious and the dancers are getting down to the "business" of num.

Kinachau's dance movements are spare, sharp, and effortless; his body seems almost weightless. Sometimes he does not travel around the dance circle but moves in place, with light, strong, rhythmic steps. Hovering over the ground, hands up in the air, elbows bent 90 degrees, accenting the beat, he is like a giant water bird readying for a landing on a shimmering lake surface.

The atmosphere becomes more exciting, electric. The word passes around the singing circle and to some of the dancers: "Till dawn, till dawn! We will sing till dawn!" Women at the peripheral fires get up to dance a few turns. The singing and dancing seem to have an irresistible effect on all those in the area.

Kinachau is sweating; his face is beginning to take on a pained appearance. He starts to tremble, his legs quivering. His movement around the circle is becoming unsteady. He calls out, "Am I in kia so soon?" He stops dancing for a moment to put on a pair of dance rattles, then jumps back into the circle eagerly. He does not complete one full circle. He swoons and falls softly into the sand just outside the dance rut. He has entered into kia, sharply and quickly.

Kinachau sits up and remains sitting for several minutes. His look is glazed, and his body trembles spasmodically. He returns to dancing and, after three full turns around the circle, goes over to one of the peripheral, "talking" fires and begins to heal. As he pulls the sickness from each person, Kinachau's whole body shakes roughly and his legs tremble violently, the tendons sticking out. His jerking hands quiver rapidly over each person's chest, one hand in front, the other in back. Then he goes back to the dancing, in the middle of a song that the women are almost shouting. The mood of the dance has become more electric, almost agitated. Kinachau again returns to healing, now among the singers. He shrieks out the characteristic deep howling sounds which express the pain involved in pulling out sickness. Suddenly he stops. The singing stops. It is not clear which stopped first. Kinachau wails at the top of his voice: "You women! Have you left me now?" Several women call back, "No, we're still here," and immediately another song is begun. The singing is strong. Kinachau's healing resumes.

Midnight

Thirteen persons are now dancing, five of them women. There are so many dancers that no space in the circle is empty; a solid line of dancers moves around the singing women. After more healing, Kinachau dives for the dance fire. He pushes his head toward the blazing logs, plowing the sand up in front of his hair. Just as his head touches the flames, his hair smoking, he is dragged back by two women and held tightly. They massage his head and chest, taking sweat from his armpits and their own, rubbing it over his neck and chest. Another woman gingerly shakes some live coals in her hands, drops them, and then rubs her warm hands over Kinachau's belly and head. One of the dancers kneels down next to Kinachau and shouts to the women: "Start singing! Get this man going again!" A num song immediately fills the air, and the dance comes alive again.

Two women continue to work on Kinachau. He sits up, and begins to heal the two women, groping toward them, resting his head on their shoulders. The women hold him, dragging him back whenever he lunges toward the fire again. Kinachau finally becomes quiet, breathing slowly, regularly. He looks alert and steady. He carefully unwinds the dance rattles, which have slipped from his calves to his ankles. He seems to have returned to his ordinary state.

12:20

Toma Zho begins to dance again, joining those who have been dancing continuously, among them Gau, Dau, Kana, and Bo. Debe, Toma Zho's twenty-year-old son, has also been dancing most of the evening, but not continuously. He has never experienced kia before. He dances earnestly but stops often, sometimes abruptly, sitting down outside the dance circle to rest. Right before he stops each time, he has a look of fear, and especially after a period of strong dancing, the fear turns into anguish. After sitting a while, the fear seems to diminish, and he resumes dancing. Everyone at the dance knows that, like all young seekers of num, Debe stops dancing to cool down the num beginning to boil within him and causing him pain.

12:30

There are now six dancers who at any moment could kia. Gau is leading another dancer around the circle, Gau in front, the other clinging to his waist. Both move around the circle unsteadily and stiff-legged, at times wandering out of the dancing rut then finding their way back, as if groping in the dark. Some of the singers and other dancers begin to watch those two more carefully. The singing and dancing go on. Gau now walks around alone, moaning, breathing heavily.

On the other side of the circle, Debe is enjoying his own dancing. He talks and laughs with the women singers and goes over to some of those sitting around the periphery of the dance fire. He sits down and lights a pipe. He seems very far from kia. Gau falls down flat on his stomach. Several people begin to work on him: one massaging and rubbing his body, along the back up to the shoulders; another rubbing his own forehead around Gau's head, blowing sharply into each of Gau's ears. Gau is in kia. Young Bo continues to dance. He stops and rubs his ears vigorously, as if the sounds of the dance are getting too intense. He becomes wobbly and has a somewhat blank stare; he seems to be starting to kia.

12:45

Toma Zho works on Gau, who is still flat on his stomach. Toma Zho rubs his hands over Gau's entire body, concentrating especially on his chest and head. Toma Zho then leads Gau, who is very unsteady, to the fire and bends him over it. For a few seconds, they hover, the fire several inches from Gau's face, and then spring back. Toma Zho leads Gau back outside the dance circle and sits him down. He leans over Gau's back, their bodies in full contact. Toma Zho rubs Gau's sweat over both Gau's body and his own. His hands return continually to his own and Gau's armpits and chest, where the sweat shines in the firelight. Toma Zho has assumed both the protector and the teacher roles toward Gau.

Debe stops dancing, walks out of the dance circle, and sits down away from the dance fire, the firelight flickering dimly across his body. He looks scared. He is teased by some of his peers who are also sitting outside the dance circle: "Hey, Debe! Why don't you dance? Are you scared of the num?"

1:00

Bo bolts out of the dance circle, racing around the dance area. Everybody jumps up. The women reach for their infants, drawing them close, covering them with their arms. The singing stops. The dancing stops. Conversations on the periphery of the dance stop. It is suddenly quiet. The stillness is immediately broken by Bau, who has been singing with intense concentration all evening and shouts: "Look at Bo! He is in kia! Look after him. What's he doing! He may puncture his eyeballs on a branch or hurt himself. Why doesn't someone go and help him. What's the matter? Who's going to help him?" Bau's voice is loud and concerned, more authoritative than anxious. The other singers join in, yelling all at once, expressing their concern.

Several men have already begun to race after Bo. They chase him into the darkness and leap on him. They restrain him, then bring him back toward the fire until they are just within range of the firelight, though still outside the dance circle. They push him down in the sand, physically restraining him as he struggles to run. Debe and another man sit on him, one near his head, the other near his feet; he still twitches and shakes violently from his kia. Toma Zho begins to work on Bo, rubbing his hands and body over Bo's body, while Bo remains flat on his stomach in the sand, still restrained by the others, his body gradually trembling with less violence.

Gau is still in kia. He walks stiff-legged and unsteadily, his face masked in a blank stare. Unexplainedly, he yells: "Do I get a knife? Do I get a knife?" Then, with intense, sobbing moans, he pleads: "My father, help me! Help me, my father!"

1:15

Kana has been wandering around the dance circle for the last several minutes, like a sleepwalker. One of the dancers points to Kana and says, "He has entered kia."

Kana and Gau come together, as if accidentally bumping. They sink to their knees together. Toma Zho kneels behind them and rubs their shoulders while they hug and hold each other, moaning loudly in anguish. Then Gau falls down with a thud, flat on his stomach. Kana crawls over to Gau and crawls the entire length of his body, starting at his feet and ending at his head. While Kana is crawling, he cries out: "Give me water. Where are you? Where are you?"

Kinachau joins Debe, who is still sitting on top of Bo, and helps him hold Bo down. Kinachau rubs Bo gently, talking softly, trying to calm him.

1:20

There is a tremendous variety at the dance now. While Kana and Gau are still in kia, some of the adolescents have begun to dance again, joking, trying out fancy steps. Kana and Gau moan softly, their mood serious, even pained. The adolescents dance, their mood light, even cheerful.

1:25

Gau is now sitting down. His wife comes to him and lights a pipe of tobacco for him. He starts to smoke. It seems he has come back into an ordinary state of consciousness: his eyes no longer have the blank stare, and he is conversing normally. Kana gets up and begins to dance again.

After a brief but intense period of dancing, Kinachau is again experiencing kia. He systematically heals each of the singers. Then he walks right across the fire. Two women hold him as he goes through the fire and guide him away from it. They seem concerned over him and lead him around the dance as if he has no clear sense of direction. Kinachau's kia continues, interspersed with periods of healing. In a few minutes he runs around the outside of the dance circle, then dashes off into a dark corner of the camp. Another dancer runs after him. Within a minute he is carrying Kinachau back toward the dance circle. Kinachau's body is stiff, his feet dragging, his heels making little furrows in the sand. The other dancer sits Kinachau down near the dance circle, and he and Toma Zho work on Kinachau, rubbing him, holding him, giving him short drinks of water. Soon Kinachau is sitting, resting wearily off beyond the strong light of the dance fire.

The singing and dancing at the main fire continue, the voices enthusiastic, the songs growing in rhythm and volume as each nears its end. Bau has been a mainstay from the start of the dance. Her singing is strong, her head lifts up, her mouth pointing to the sky. Her mood is intense; her eyes mainly closed, she moves with the music, talking little. Already past sixty, Bau remains vigorous, one of the most powerful healers at Xaixai. Like other Kung women, she has not danced much in the circular dancing rut. Once, about an hour ago, she danced a few turns around the fire, apparently inspired by one of those special moments in the dance when singing and dancing peak to unimagined levels of intensity. Now, still singing strongly, she starts to sway. She falls over, completely limp, into the arms of the singer who sits next to her. She moans softly and begins to gasp for breath. Bau has entered kia. The dance continues.

1:45

Ten persons are now dancing, bunched together, moving almost in unison. Kana has begun to heal, moving from one singer to another, placing his fluttering, quivering hands over the area of the chest, one in front, the other in back. He shrieks and moans alternately, drawing his hands away from the person, shaking them vigorously into the darkness surrounding the dance fire. Without warning, Kana goes to the fire, reaches into it, and picks up two burning sticks. Three of the singers pull him back and shake the sticks out of his hands. Sparks fly out of the fire and several women yell in alarm, jumping back. The singing is maintained by the women who sit on the other side of the fire.

Gau, Dau, and Bo are all dancing. Each is experiencing kia. Gau seems to be coming out of kia: he looks around more attentively, talks more coherently. Dau seems to fluctuate in his experience of kia: his look of withdrawn anguish alternates with a smile. Bo seems deeply into kia: his eyes are blank, focused on the dance rut as he moves around, his expression pained. Bo is joined by two other young dancers, and the three move around the circle as one, dancing the same steps, moving up and down at the same time. Bo is in the middle, supported and at times carried by the other two.

1:55

Toma Zho and Gau are now sitting on the periphery of the dance fire. They converse with each other and several other men in low voices. The talk is ordinary and relaxed. Toma Zho and Gau seem back to their normal states. Still in kia, Bau remains collapsed in the lap of the woman next to her. She moans loudly several times, her pained sounds mingling with the singing.

Kana continues to walk around in a state of kia, like a tightrope walker. He is healing people who are sitting at the little fires on the outskirts of the dance fire. He does not shriek as he pulls the sickness, but just presses his hands in the area of the chest, flutters them, and moans. He then goes back to the central dance fire, picks up several reddish-orange coals, and rubs them together in his hands, then over his chest and under his armpits. The sparks fly. He drops the coals back into the fire just as the singers begin to scatter.

There is still a variety of moods at the dance, not only among the dancers and singers but especially around the small fires and among the small groups on the periphery of the dance circle. Socializing, quiet joking, teasing, and concentration on the dance all mingle among the still forms of the few adults who have already fallen asleep. The young children sleep together in bunches underneath blankets, wrapped up in each other's warmth.

2:10

Bau is healing each woman in the singing circle. Her hands flutter rapidly and lightly over each chest and upper back, one hand in front, one in back. She holds each singer firmly for a moment and then embraces her, rubbing the woman's upper body with her own hands and head and body, all the while moaning in a low, deep voice. She goes deliberately from one singer to the next, giving an extra embrace before she moves on. Kana continues to heal those on the periphery of the dance circle.

2:30

Kana comes over to Toma Zho sitting on the sidelines. Toma Zho has not been dancing for nearly three-quarters of an hour. He gives some tobacco to Kana and they begin to talk. Their conversation is filled with long pauses. They talk of ordinary matters in an ordinary way: "Do you have any tobacco?" "Hey, let me try your pipe." Kana lights his pipe. The sleepwalking, distracted quality of his kia state is gone. He seems back to a relatively ordinary state. Bo, Debe, and several others are dancing now. Toma Zho has just entered the circle. He dances a little, five or six steps, then stops, then begins again. He has not yet danced seriously during this dance.

2:35

The excitement of the dance abates somewhat, and the number of singers and dancers decreases. Dau still dances intently, steadily. Toma Zho continues to dance in a casual, sporadic manner. A small group of nine- and ten-year-olds bursts into laughter and play. Curling up together, they had just about settled down for the night's sleep when a blanket was pulled off someone, and a foot ended up in someone's face. After a few animated exchanges, they slowly settle down again, the blankets once more coming together, to form a continuous covering.

2:50

Dau's expression is deadly serious as he dances; his body is tense, bent at the waist, leaning stiffly on his dance stick. He giggles in a rapid burst, uttering hardly intelligible words, remaining tense. The singers sense something; they waver between reacting to his half-words as a joke or as the pained gasps and grunts of kia. Dau laughs again, and a grimace quickly wipes out the grin. He has just stopped dancing. He staggers out of the circle and falls down stiffly, his body making a smacking sound as it hits the sand. He lands flat on his stomach. It is confirmed: Dau is in kia again.

Dau begins singing the num song that the women are now singing. He sings in a low, pained tone, interrupted by moans and cries, still flat on his stomach, his body stretched out and twitching violently. One of the young dancers stops dancing and comes over to Dau. He helps Dau to stand on his rubbery legs. Wrapping both of Dau's arms over his own shoulders, the young dancer leads the staggering Dau back to the dance fire, his own usually lively dance style now heavy under Dau's weight. Every so often Dau manages a few dance steps. Otherwise the young dancer drags him along. All the while Dau continues to sing the num song with the women, his moans interrupting and accenting his singing.

After several times around the circle, Dau seems more in control, more able to walk on his own, and he starts to dance again. He goes toward the singers and begins to heal. His hands flutter rapidly and tensely over each one's forehead and chest. As he lays on his hands, he wails painfully, and as he shakes his hands away from the person he heals, he shrieks violently. He now goes to the dancers and moves behind one of them. The dancer stops, moves slightly outside the dance rut, and Dau heals him. Dau goes to another dancer and heals him in the dance rut, the other dancers dancing in place until Dau moves on. Dau comes over to Toma Zho, who has been dancing for several minutes, and heals him. While healing Toma Zho, Dau talks to him, alternating words that tumble out so fast as to be unintelligible with groans that burst out so deeply as to be other-worldly. He is making the sounds of kia.

All the while Dau heals, he talks to himself, though the words are not vocalized. Only vague, one-syllable responses like "eh" can be heard. The responses suggest an internal dialogue that remains deep inside him. At times, he looks into the sky, where the spirits live, or out to the dark edges of the dance area, where the spirits who have been attracted to the dance may be lurking. Dau calls out, admonishing these spirits. He becomes belligerent: "You spirits cannot take anyone from this dance. I, Dau, will fight you." He pleads: "This one I have just healed. Can't you see he is still so young. He is not ready to go. Can't you see that?" And he jokes wildly: "The spirits are all gone! The spirits are all bombed out of their heads!" Dau goes to the peripheral fires and heals there, then back to the central dance fire and starts to heal some of the singers again. After healing one singer, he retches, but no vomit comes out. Gau and Bo have joined the four other dancers. Toma Zho sits down outside the dance circle.

3:00

Dau is still healing. The young dancer leads him around again, and they go systematically from person to person, leaving nobody out, healing first the singers, then the dancers, then the others who have come to the dance. The young dancer remains behind Dau, holding on to him as Dau heals. With the start of each new num song, they break away from the healing and both dance on the edge of the dance circle. They dance in place and then create their own little circle, the two moving as one, firmly holding each other. After less than a minute, they go back to healing.

3:10

The pace of the dance gradually slows. Some of the dancers are sitting around the peripheral fires, relaxing, some with a blanket over their shoulders, talking softly. Others are lying down, facing into the fire, resting. Others, wrapped tightly in a blanket, have fallen asleep.

3:20

It is clear by now that there are enough persons at the dance to keep it going until dawn. As some who have danced for a while take a rest, others already rested return to the dance circle. A few, like Dau, Bo, and Gau, who began to dance early are still dancing.

3:35

More have gone to sleep. Debe and another young man yet to experience kia are the only ones dancing. Their dance steps and postures are elaborate and dramatic compared to the steady, simple, straightforward way most dancers travel around the fire toward kia.

4:10

The singers are tired. About half are resting, a few with their eyes closed. The singing circle is close-knit, the resting women held up by the shoulders, arms, and thighs of their neighbors. The songs continue, the melodies carried more and more by one or two soft, solitary voices. There are no persons dancing.

4:30

Debe has just gotten up to dance again. He dances sporadically, without strain, enjoying this quiet opportunity to practice his steps without being under the eyes of his peers who have teased him about his fear of num. Most other people are either lying down or sleeping. A few sit and converse in hushed tones, smoking slowly. The atmosphere at the dance is now in sharp contrast to earlier in the evening when the air was electric with the activation of num.

5:00

Five other young dancers join Debe in the dance circle. After all of them have completed several turns around the singing women, Debe sits down. The others continue dancing casually.

5:10

Nobody is dancing now. The women in the singing circle are engaged in soft conversation. Every once in a while one or two sing, sometimes together, sometimes alone. A full num song does not form. Around one of the small fires several men are also singing bits of the num song, more to themselves than for the dance.

5:15

Almost imperceptibly the atmosphere becomes more alive. Six men, among them Gau and Bo, have begun dancing.

5:30

Toma Zho joins the dancers.

5:40

Orange color infuses the far sky, low across the open space. The dance acknowledges this beginning of day with increased activity. It is as if the dance is waking up. People stir around the talking fires, and dark shapes covered by blankets move and rise up as bodies. The singing picks up; it becomes more lively as the women sing more energetically. The women yawn, then stretch and raise their voices, looking up into the brightening sky. Kinachau comes into the dance circle and joins Toma Zho. They dance hard, beginning to sweat, a pained look coming over their faces. They work toward kia, and the singing stimulates and confirms this. The songs are loud, vigorous, and excited, intensifying in pace and mood as they come toward the end, and then closing sharply and abruptly. The next song starts almost immediately. One woman shouts: "We are strong this morning. We have sung until dawn. Our songs are here to greet the morning." Other women join in, exchanging proud comments on their tenacity and strength.

Two adolescents join the dance and begin a little clowning, playing at their dancing. At the same time, Toma Zho again intensifies his efforts. His hard dancing moves in and out and around their playful movements. For the first time at this dance, he puts on the dance rattles. As he goes back into the dance circle, he joins in the singing of the num song which rises loudly into the lightening sky. One can now see all the people in the dance area. Toma Zho's voice stands out, accenting the women's voices, transforming them into a chorus that carries his solo singing. He faces straight ahead as he dances around half of the circle. Suddenly he breaks out of the circle, stands in place, and continues to dance, leaning toward the fire, his arms up in the air. He becomes a large, impressive figure, hovering over the dance. Then he returns to the circle, dancing in the rut again. He repeats this sequence several times. Toma Zho dances hard but always gracefully, intensely but always beautifully.

Kinachau sits down. The focus of the dance goes clearly to Toma Zho, who is sweating over his entire body as he dances strongly around the fire. He is beginning to have a glazed, fearful expression. He starts to stagger and stumbles slightly. He is now quivering, tensely and rapidly, especially in his legs. He walks around the dance area, without apparent direction, stepping on a low bush. Kinachau goes over to him and leads him back to the circle.

5:55

Toma Zho continues to dance seriously. He sweats more profusely and begins to become stiff-legged, a bit unbalanced in the way he moves.

6:15

More persons wake up, as if to become an audience for Toma Zho. Several others begin to dance, including Gau. But Toma Zho's quiet, intense, almost preoccupied presence colors the entire dance.

7:15

Toma Zho continues to dominate both the dancers and the singers, more actively now. He instructs the singers about which songs they should sing and their tempo. They are singing for him, to heat up his num. He is the only one working hard toward entering kia. Dau is also dancing seriously, looking straight ahead, stomping hard on the ground, but he does not seem to have much energy left after his long night of dancing and kia. The other dancers slip into the background, following Toma Zho's lead and supporting his pace. Soon some quietly sit down and watch him from the sidelines. No one else has taken charge of the dance as Toma Zho now does.

Singing loudly, at times without the women, Toma Zho jokes with the singers. At the song's end, he staggers, loses his balance, and falls down. Toma Zho has started to kia. He rises slowly, resting on one knee. As the next song starts, Toma Zho is dancing once again, with renewed vitality. His face and hands are dripping wet, soaked with sweat.

8:15

A song has just ended, and everything seems to stop. The women stop singing and Toma Zho stops dancing. A major decision now has to be made. Should the dance continue into the day, or is this the time to end? Toma Zho has a brief discussion with some of the women who were singing. Two sides emerge during the discussion. A hard core of singers are ready to continue. Feeling revitalized by the dawn, they are singing as strongly now as earlier in the evening. With the exception of one woman, they are from Toma Zho's own camp. They are ready to continue singing for Toma Zho if he decides to go on dancing into the morning, or even into the full heat of the day.

On the other side are many more singers who want to stop. They say Toma Zho is only in the early stages of kia, that it will be well into the day before he is through. They feel it will be too difficult to provide food and water for those at the dance who get hungry and thirsty. This larger group also says that, as the day comes on, the heat will be too much, even if the dance moves into the shade of one of the large trees. They carry the decision. Toma Zho turns to the women who have been singing all night and says, "That's it for the day." His tone is one of resignation.

Toma Zho remains at a high level of excitement as he goes on talking with others at the dance. Still wiping the sweat from his eyes and mouth, his gestures and conversation are animated, though he is in control of his body and his conversation is lucid.

8:30

As the decision to end the dance is passed on to all in the area, people start to collect their blankets and other belongings and slowly leave the site. Some remain, talking or just sitting around. They stretch and yawn as they meet the early morning beginning of a day.

9:00

The deep rut made by the dancers rings the dying embers. Otherwise the dance area has returned to its normal uncluttered, unpopulated condition.

5 Kinachau, a Traditional Healer

SATISFIED with his role as a healer oriented to the camp and not seeking a reputation that would allow for a more professional status, Kinachau's approach to num is straightforward and traditional. In this he offers a contrast with Toma Zho. Their behavior at the dance expressed this contrast. Whereas both had been thrown down by their boiling num, Kinachau alone was able to pull sickness; num, it seemed, had "defeated" Toma Zho.

I seek out both men to learn more about that dance and the workings of num. Toma Zho is not immediately available, so it is with Kinachau that I begin. I walk toward Kinachau's hut and, greeting him, sit down with him. Richard Lee joins us, and we begin a conversation, talking about the enlarging of the well and other recent events at the camp.

After a while, I ask Kinachau if he would be willing to tell me about num. With a warm, coy smile he says: "Yes, I know about num. Yes, I can tell you about that." He has given me the signal to start.

"Kinachau, who are the powerful healers here at Xaixai?"

He smiles again, more warmly and coyly. "Me!" he states emphatically.

"Is there anyone else?" I wonder.

"There is also Toma Zho and Wi," says Kinachau. "The others I don't know properly." He pauses for a moment and, in an off-handed manner, adds, "Oh well, there's also Gau."

"Who is the first and foremost healer?"

"The outstanding ones have all died. Today we are children, and I don't know which of us stands out."

"Kinachau, do some persons have more num than others?"

"I used to have a lot," he replies, "but today I have a little." Kinachau has turned to the characteristic Kung disclaimer, but he is prepared to talk more about kia.

"Could you tell me about the dance where both you and

Page 80: Kinachau

Toma Zho were thrown down by num, but only you pulled sickness?"

"Didn't you see the dance?" he asks.

"Yes, I saw it, but I don't think I understand some of the things that happened there. Was it a powerful dance?"

"It was heavy," he reflects.

"Was the pulling strong?"

"I pulled strong," he says, "because if the dance had been light, I couldn't have pulled strong." Kinachau points out the fragmented quality of my question with his string of organically related answers.

I pause briefly, trying to learn that lesson, but realizing it cannot be learned by trying, I continue. "Was there anyone who was sick that you worked on especially hard?"

"One old man was sick," replies Kinachau. "It was his insides and stomach that were sick. And all the people here at Xaixai, their flesh had little things in it, so I removed them. Num teaches you how to recognize sickness and remove it from others. When you are pulling out the sickness, you see properly. You see little things, like twigs." Kinachau stops briefly, then adds. "Little things, things sent by god that are troubling people. You see and you pull." Kinachau seems to collect his thoughts for a moment and then goes on. "Your eyes are open then because you have to see the people. However, the fire is shimmering. Looking at the fire makes your eyes tremble, but you turn away because you want to see people so you can heal them."

"When you're in kia," I ask, "how do you 'see' people?"

"In kia, you have to know who are your own people," Kinachau replies, "and who are strangers, so you can give your own people special treatment." He quickly adds in the form of a correction, "We pull everybody. We look for what's wrong with a person, so that we can remove it. When we pull, we go from person to person at the dance, and even if we don't see anything wrong, we pull. But in other cases, we see something specific and we pull strongly to remove it."

"What else do you see during kia?" I ask.

"During the dance," he says, "when you look out beyond

the fire, you see things. It's light, not dark, even though it is nighttime. You see camps; you see at a distance in the night. You see actual things, persons and objects. When the healer talks at the dance and says, 'Go away,' he is talking to bad things that are hurting those he is pulling."

"Do other healers see these bad things?" I wonder.

"No," he responds. Then he stops for a moment and, in a tone suggesting a public statement, adds: "I don't see anything. It's a lie that we healers see anything."

Our talk has reached one of those moments of understanding which takes time to settle in. After a silence, I continue on. "Kinachau, if I dance and dance and dance, even though I am not one of you people, could I kia?"

"Yes," replies Kinachau thoughtfully. Then he says, "I'd teach you." His pipe, made from an expended bullet cartridge, is empty, and he stuffs it with tobacco, lights it with a borrowed match, and draws several deep breaths of smoke.

"When you were pulling me at the dance, what did you see?" I ask.

Kinachau responds thoughtfully: "When I came to you, Dick, I said to myself, 'This is one of my own people who has come to us, and I put my hand on him so that my other people over there, the spirits of my ancestors, could see that he was one of my own people and therefore would fear to harm him.' And something else. When I stuck my hands in the fire and then pulled you and Lee, it was to show the spirits that you two were my *very own* people who are in my heart, and what I was doing was begging them not to harm you."

"Kinachau, the way you know me today, is it different from the way you knew me before you pulled me at the dance?"

"No," he says. "I see you now just the way you were then because you're not sick. I don't see anything of sickness in you today, and I didn't see anything in you when I pulled you. What I did do was to demonstrate to the spirits that you are a person who means no harm, that you are one of us."

I feel Kinachau's protective concern strengthened in his restatement. We begin to focus more on Kinachau's kia during the dance. "How did you know when you were starting to kia?" I ask.

"I felt num in my stomach," he reports. "I felt it rising. I felt it shiver and shiver."

"When you started to kia, Kinachau, what did you say?"

" 'Now I am in kia,' I said to myself. 'Has num already killed me? How else can it be that my flesh is like this, so painful and hot?' "

"How do you know when to start pulling?" I ask.

Kinachau makes it simple and obvious. "I had already danced num and num had already entered me, so I pulled. This is the num that our ancestors, our elders, have given us. It was they who started it among us. They distributed it to us, and now we can do it."

"When num enters you, what happens to your heart?" I ask, hoping to get another perspective on kia.

"Oh, help me out," Kinachau appeals with a good-natured humor. His face assumes a perplexed expression, and he seems to be searching for some response. "How do I answer a question like that? Since it's the elders who gave num to us, num does the same thing to us that it did to them." He hesitates momentarily, then in a confident tone continues. "You breathe hard and fast, your heart is pounding. You run around because the num is shaking and agitating you violently. So you run around with it until it cools down, until you feel that you can lay your hands steadily on those that you are going to pull."

"Do some healers pull before they are ready?"

"In some cases," says Kinachau, "the shaking of num is so strong that it completely overwhelms the healer. In such a case, another healer has to come over and make the num lie down; the other healer has to remove some of the num and make it sit properly, until the first healer is better. Then when that first one is cooled down, he is steady enough to go around and heal."

"At the dance, as you walked through the fire, the singers were supporting you. What was happening then?"

"People were helping me dodge the fire because my num was shaking me, and I might have stepped on them or splattered fire on them. Also, they held my legs so that they could lead me straight out of the circle, so they could straighten me and lead me out."

"Straighten you?"

"I was straight, you see there is no hump in my back," observes Kinachau, "but my path was crooked."

"People were also picking up live coals, putting them in their hands, and then rubbing you with their hands. What were they doing?"

Kinachau takes on a more serious demeanor. "I was dead, and they did me so I could live. I wasn't breathing." Kinachau demonstrates that state by holding his breath for a long time. "I wasn't breathing. I was dead according to the custom of this num." Kinachau remains silent for a moment, then goes on. "I don't know who rubbed me with their coal-warmed hands. It was only later, when I was pulling, that I opened my eyes. I didn't know who had made me come alive. All I knew was that I was alive."

Kinachau has reached a level in his talk as intense as the dance itself. It seems like a time to talk about Toma Zho's kia experience. "Kinachau, could you tell me about Toma Zho's experience at the dance? What did he do?"

"Toma Zho danced and danced," says Kinachau. "At first he didn't see the singing, and it was only after dawn that he saw it and began to dance strongly. Then finally the num took hold of him and shook him around. Then num entered him and entered him and made him do what he did."

"What did Toma Zho do?" I wonder.

Kinachau looks at me directly and in a soft voice says: "Toma Zho is my nephew. He and I dance much together. He has his type of num, and I have mine. Our types of num are different. It was his thing, and it's for him to tell you." Kinachau's diplomatic response is not at all unexpected; it expresses a characteristic Kung manner of speaking in public. Yet our talk has developed an intimate quality, and I intuit that Kinachau is willing to continue.

"Was Toma Zho all right, or not quite all right?"

"He was all right," responds Kinachau.

"Why did the women stop?" I ask.

"They stopped because the sun was so hot, and they saw that this dance was going to be a long thing that might take all day. Furthermore, we know the num is hot and the sun is also very hot, and the two heats could be very bad for Toma Zho, so bad in fact that it might make him spend the whole day bothering people, or it could actually kill him. I mean *really* kill him! And then his soul would leave his body and crawl down a hole, and this would be terrible, and I for one am not prepared to follow his soul down the hole and retrieve it. Look, there are many types, many ways of relating to num. He has his type and I have mine." Kinachau had taken my questions as an invitation to speak with unusual frankness about Toma Zho.

"Could you have moved the dance to the shade?" I ask.

"That is a good idea," he says, "but the women didn't want to."

"If you went to the shade," I wonder, "would it have been all right?"

"No," he states emphatically. "It would have been just as bad, because even in the shade, you'd be much hotter than during the nighttime."

"If you agreed and moved to the shade, couldn't you have had a good dance? Haven't there been good dances held in the shade during the daytime?"

"Sure," he says. "Wi and I are the same type of healer, and when dances take place in the daytime, we can pull and pull and finish properly. But I can't speak for Toma Zho because he has his own type, and I was very surprised to see what he did." By his tone, Kinachau implies it was not a pleasant surprise.

"Why were you surprised?"

"Because there are types and there are types, and I don't know Toma Zho's type." Kinachau seems a little evasive.

"Do you agree with Toma Zho's type?"

"No, I don't agree. It's bad," Kinachau answers simply.

I am not prepared for such a direct statement. "What do you mean, 'It's bad'?"

"It's bad because of the things that Toma Zho does."
"What would be an example?"
"Toma Zho was going to pull people," says Kinachau, "but perhaps he got –" Kinachau breaks off in mid-sentence and concludes: "Toma Zho failed in that and just quit. It's bad that he entered kia and then was just dead, dead, dead, the death of kia, whereas others of us get up and go around and pull while we are experiencing kia."
Kinachau has finished. Silence remains for several minutes. The sun's intensity is beginning to lessen and our talk is drawing toward its own close. "Kinachau, do you pull sickness from yourself?"
"Yes," he replies in an unassuming tone. "I get the tortoise shell and put a coal in it and let the smoke go all over my body. I drink the smoke and tremble all over and pull myself. And then I sleep, and by the next morning I wake up feeling fine." He demonstrates how he pulls himself on the stomach, the chest, and the head and neck.
"Who else pulls himself?"
"All do it."
"Do you sing to yourself when you pull yourself?"
"Yes, I sing a num song."
"And are you alone?"
"I'm all alone."
"If there are others around, will they bother you?"
"It is good to have a quiet evening."
"Is your wife there?"
"If my wife were there, she would sing with me."
"Kinachau, during the dance you pushed your head into the fire –" Toma Zho's greeting interrupts me. He has just come into the camp, seen us, and called out. We invite him to join our talk. The atmosphere shifts quickly, but after an initial uneasiness, we all felt comfortable sitting together.
With one of those wordless understandings, Kinachau and I continue. Toma Zho lights a full pipe and listens intently. "Kinachau, you pushed your head into the fire," I say. "What was happening then?"
"My num was doing it to me. I wasn't thinking of anything because num made my thoughts nothing. But I

looked into the fire and saw the fire quivering, and I said, 'What's this, why is the fire doing this?' So I just tried to get rid of it."

"Kinachau, after you went into the fire, you were being worked on by Toma Zho and given water to drink." I look toward Toma Zho, making an attempt to bring him into our talk.

"I drank the water," reports Kinachau, "and lived."

"How much do you have to drink?"

"I was very hot and wanted to cool down so I could live, and one cup is enough."

"Could you drink too much?" I ask.

"I wouldn't," he says.

"At one point in the dance, Kinachau, you had been dancing very intensely, and it seemed you were in kia. Then suddenly the women stopped singing. You cried out to the women, 'Have you left me?' Could you tell me about that experience?"

Kinachau responds quickly. "I said that to the singers because suddenly their voices stopped, and this was because my ears had become almost deaf. So I asked them, 'Have you left me?' And when they said, 'No, we haven't left you,' then I was very happy to hear that."

Kinachau's description mellows the atmosphere. By not placing blame on the singers, he has removed most of the judgmental quality that lingered on from our talk just prior to Toma Zho's arrival. A new phase is about to begin, where Kinachau and Toma Zho and I can all speak together. "If num is so painful, why do people seek it?" I ask.

Kinachau responds, "God gave num to us." He pauses and thinks for a moment. "I seek num because I am a man, and this num is something that can save your life. So that I sought it in order to remove my own sickness and my people's sickness."

"Any other reason?"

"Just that reason, to remove sickness."

"Were you sick when you first sought num?" I ask.

"No, I wasn't sick at that time."

I look to Toma Zho, who seems eager to speak. "Why do you seek it, Toma Zho?"

"I don't know why we seek it," he replies. "Not everybody seeks num. There are some who, when they are sick or when they are asleep, dream of god. And god tells you he's giving num to you, or he simply puts it into you, so whenever you go to a dance, it makes you experience kia. In a big sickness you may start crying out and moaning all night through. Then the next morning you find you're better and you've already got num."

"When you go to a dance, do you have to kia even if you don't want to?" I ask the question of both men.

Toma Zho replies first. "Yes. What happens is you say, 'I'm just going to dance,' but you find num coming up on you anyway. If you fear it, you have to get out of the dance circle and sit down and try to get it under control and let it dissipate. Then when the num is down, you can come back in the dance. But sometimes num just comes right up on you and there's nothing you can do about it. Num grabs you and throws you up in the air."

"That happens to me also," says Kinachau.

Toma Zho speaks further. "Some days I can handle num. Other days I don't want it, and if it starts, I can control it and not kia. Other days it overwhelms me and throws me."

I feel Toma Zho has been talking about the dance when num had thrown him down and he did not pull, and I want to hear him speak of it more explicitly. "Toma Zho, could you tell me about your dancing and your kia?" I ask.

Toma Zho responds by describing that difficult experience. It is apparent that he too wants to speak of it. "At the dance," he says, "I refused num. I did not want to kia. So all night I danced, and whenever num came up, I stopped dancing and got out. But after sunrise num overwhelmed me; it took me and threw me down. I was in kia. I wanted to keep on dancing without entering kia, dancing on into the cool morning, but num threw me. If only I could get the women to sing I would dance right now. I'd like to get the dance going right away, but the women said they were hungry and wanted to collect mongongo nuts. So they will collect nuts, and when they have full stomachs, they will start the dance up again."

I am struck by the contrasting perspectives of Kinachau and Toma Zho. For example, the dawn brought the "cool morning" for Toma Zho and heralded the heat of the day for Kinachau. But I want to follow Toma Zho in the unfolding of his story. "Is it good to stop where you stopped in the dance?" I ask.

"It's all right," replies Toma Zho.

"Is it very painful?"

"It's all right," he continues, "because if you're not seeking num and it still throws you down, you say to yourself, 'So that's what my num is doing even though I don't want it,' and you say, 'It's all right, it's my own thing, how can I be mad at myself?' "

"Toma Zho, why did you go to the dance if you didn't want num?"

"I like to dance," he says.

"How did you know when to stop? How did you know when your num was coming up?"

"I felt my body getting very hot, so I said, 'I better step off to the side and cool off, because it would be bad for this to come.' "

"Why bad?"

"It would be bad because I wanted to dance and if num starts you, you spend all your time pulling sickness from others, and I wanted to dance. Since I came back from Ghanzi, I haven't had a chance to dance because we haven't got the people together. And since there was no one really sick, I said, 'Tonight I just dance.' "

Again, the differing approaches of Toma Zho and Kinachau stand out, but we do not speak openly of them. More tobacco passes around to Toma Zho, who stuffs the empty bullet cartridge pipe and lights it. Then the burning hot pipe passes around the circle, Toma Zho and Kinachau each drawing deeply, their rib cages rising up and down. The focus shifts slightly. "Do you pull together with another healer?" I ask.

Kinachau responds first. "If there's a dance on, I kia and

pull illness from others. If someone's ill and there's no dance, I go to the ill one and I pull him until he gets better. If I find the illness defeats me, if the illness is big, then I go to another healer and say, 'Let's pull together on this person.' I might put my hands on, pull, and take mine off, and he might put his hands on, pull, and take his off, and I might put mine on. We would both put hands on the sick one. I might do the belly and he the head. We would pull together, but only when one of us has a difficult case."

"Do you ever feel that when you pull with another, the other will ruin the healing?"

Both Kinachau and Toma Zho reply with almost the same phrase: "There are times when we pull with another healer and we say, 'He's not doing it right.' "

A quiet period follows. We sit, relaxed. "Your own num, how does it make you feel?" I wonder.

"Good." Kinachau is emphatic in his response.

Toma Zho joins in, also enthusiastically. "Your own num makes you feel *very* good! Your heart is happy and sweet."

"Yes," Kinachau affirms immediately, "that is so." A broad smile spreads over his face. "My heart is happy because I am num's owner." Kinachau stops and lowers his head, his voice now soft. "But today I'm old, and I'm not happy because I'm losing my num." There is no sadness in him.

"How do you know you're losing it?" I ask Kinachau.

"It's age that does it," he says, "it comes with age. My num used to be heavy, and now it's a little on the light side. I've got backaches; that's what's doing it to me and making my num lighter. Others are very old, like Wa Na, but hers is a different type of num. She isn't ill. Her num keeps her going."

Into the ensuing silence of our conversation, the fading sun brings the expected message. Time has run out. We part in the customary manner as each of us has things to do before the day's end.

6 “The Death That Kills Us All”

THE ACTIVATION of num into kia, followed by the application of kia into healing, is a process based on the experience of transcendence. The word *transcendent,* when used to summarize what happens to the Kung during kia, means an experience characterized by a certain level of profundity in perception and knowledge, rather than an experience that is just more intense than what is customary or expected. Transcendence is more accurately an enhanced rather than simply an altered state of consciousness. As such, it has great potential for understanding and growth (Bourguignon, 1979; James, 1958; Katz, 1976; P. Lee, 1977). That potential begins for the Kung with num.

Num is the basis of the healing dance. Though the word *num* has been translated by others as "medicine," I believe that translation is too limited. Certainly one of the things num is is medicine. But its meaning seems far broader, more profound. A clearer translation is "energy." But it is better to retain the Kung word *num* and try to arrive at an understanding of the phenomenon by considering what the Kung have to say about it.

There are many referents for num, and the limits to these referents are purposely ambiguous. Num, for example, refers to medicine, sorcery, menstruation, and power. It appears in many different things, both human and inanimate. Its effects are varied, both beneficent and maleficent. But in whatever form or function, num is consistently felt as strong. As with other strong phenomena, the word *num* itself carries the power of num.

The Kung believe that some num, such as that of the great god Gao Na, is especially strong. Gao Na created num, giving it his own power. He does not govern its functioning but can at any time stop it from functioning. Gao Na's num is so strong it can be dangerous. As one Kung puts it, if Gao Na were to come "near" to ordinary men, perhaps 100 yards away, his num would kill them (Marshall,

Page 92: Kau Dwa healing

1969, p. 351). Only the most powerful of healers can approach the great god during their healing efforts and bargain with him to save a patient. Ordinary healers can deal only with the lesser god, Kauha, and the spririts, as they seek to save sick ones from being taken away.

Referring to its strength, the Kung call num a "death thing" and a "fight" (Marshall, 1969). These two expressions are often used for anything strong or dangerous. The sun, for example, is also a "death thing" and a "fight." Healers in kia must not point their finger fixedly at anyone, especially a child, because a "fight" might go along their arm, leap into the child, and kill her.

Num is said to be "invisible," though it can be "seen" and "picked up" by those experiencing kia. Otherwise, num is known only by its action and effects. It is located only by its existence in a particular form, whether it be a person, a song, or a bee. Num is not personalized or personified. No one can possess it exclusively nor control it completely. Num's "invisibility" enhances its power.

Num, this primary force in the Kung's universe of experience, is at its strongest in the healing dance. It resides in the healers, the num songs, and the dance fire. The concentration of num at a dance far exceeds that generated in any other time or place of Kung life. Num is at its peak when the num songs are sung with the most abandon and enthusiasm, and when the healers in kia heal with the most intensity and depth.

The num in the healer must be activated for it to become a healing energy. The Kung say the num must *gam* or "rise up." The singing of num songs helps awaken the num and awaken the healer's heart (Marshall, 1969). The Kung feel that their hearts must "awaken" or "open" before they attempt to heal.

The num becomes stronger as its becomes hotter. The singing and the physical exertion of the dancing help heat up the healer's num. So do the various ways healers bring themselves into contact with the fire, whether rubbing live coals in their hands and over their chest, or pushing their head into the fire. As the healer's num is heated up to boiling, it vaporizes and, rising up the spinal column, induces kia. At that stage, the num is at its greatest strength for healing.

The Kung word meaning "to boil" refers not only to boiling num, but also to the boiling of water on the fire and the ripening of plants (Lee, 1968). There is thus a strong symbolic association between boiling num, boiling water, the meat cooked in that boiling water, and ripened plant foods. Just as the num, which is dormant when cold, reaches its peak of available strength when boiling, so water becomes powerful when hot, and plant foods become nutritionally potent when ripe. The Kung sometimes go one step further and, in a joking manner, extend the boiling concept to females who have reached menarch. They say that such women are now "ripe" for intercourse and impregnation.

Kia is the experience of boiling num. Kia has been translated as "trance," which is misleading. The word *trance* is used to describe a variety of altered states of consciousness, including possession, hypnotic, and meditation states. Its use remains ambiguous and inconsistent. So again, I prefer to keep the Kung word *kia* and let what the Kung have to say about kia lead to an understanding of that phenomenon.

Kia is not a unitary, unidimensional, linear experience. Kia is an altered state of consciousness, which at different times in different or the same persons may function at different levels, may capture different degrees of meaning, and may express itself in different forms of behavior. For the Kung, kia refers to certain kinds of thoughts, feelings, and physical actions.

I remember my initial surprise while attending my second dance. There is Kinachau, having just experienced an apparently profound and agonizing kia, sitting down with his wife and commencing a routine conversation about the lack of tobacco in the camp. How could he talk so "normally" so soon after his profound kia experience? Then I recall how one can "move into" and "out of" an altered state of consciousness, or at least through different "levels" of the experience. Kia, too, shows different faces, and at some points the healer in kia can talk coherently. Kia has permeable boundaries. A healer can pass into and out of the state, returning to so-called normal discourse or activity at different times during his kia experience.

I hesitate to use the phrases "into" and "out of" kia, or "return to" normalcy. Kia is not a state that begins definitely and at a discrete point, nor does it end that way. Healers work themselves into kia, and it is much easier to say whether at any one point they are in kia or not, than to mark the point at which they enter kia. Healers come out of kia more like a glider than a machine which can be turned off by a button. They may float gradually back to their ordinary state, or like the glider, they may be caught up in an unexpected burst of song and sail off again into a deep kia.

Again, to speak of "levels" of kia, or to refer to an "intense," "profound," or "deep" experience of kia, is somewhat misleading, for the Kung do not propose sharp boundaries between levels of kia. But there are indications that a particular experience of kia is more or less intense or profound. Generally, the hotter the boiling num becomes, the more intense the kia it brings on. One experienced healer says: "When we fall in kia, our num is very hot, as hot as it gets." Another healer puts it this way: "You feel your blood becomes very hot, just like blood boiling on a fire and then you start to heal" (quoted in Lee, 1968). Still another way the Kung express this variation in intensity is to say that when their num is "heavy," the kia will be strong.

Having one's num hot and heavy is enough to make one's kia "intense." But it is not necessarily enough to make one's kia as "profound" or "deep" as possible. Being able to apply the kia to healing makes it profound. For when the num is hot and heavy, a person can be overwhelmed by it; fear then dominates rather than the clear perception necessary to see the sickness and heal. The kia in that case remains only intense. The effectiveness and power of the healing efforts determine the depth of the kia. For example, traveling to the god's home to rescue the soul of a sick person is possible only when the kia is deep.

The Kung do not emphasize discrete stages of kia or a necessary succession of stages that all healers must experience. At any one time, healers can go immediately into a deep kia; at another time, they may go through a more extended build-up period. Generally the more experienced the healer, the more intense and deep is their kia at a dance. Yet during the first experiences with boiling num, when the num and the utter fear escalate in response to each other, the kia can be especially intense. Dau speaks of this when he first got num: "I was very surprised when num came to me. It made me cry out in pain. I cried out: 'What's this pain in me? What's come over me?' "

The heating up of one's num brings on certain painful and frightening changes, which are expressed in a physical, emotional, and cognitive way. Fear dominates during these changes. If the fear is met and overcome, if healers transcend the fear by dying, then they can accept these painful changes rather than being dominated by fear of them. They can transform these changes into vehicles that allow them to heal. The experience up to this point of transcendence, or transformation, might be called "beginning" kia. Many of the Kung have had such experiences of beginning kia. Most of the men and perhaps one-third of the women have danced and sought num. Among those who seek num, perhaps 75 percent of the men and almost all the women experience beginning kia. But among those who seek, perhaps one-quarter of the men and three-quarters of the women go no further. They do not transcend their fears, nor transcend themselves. They do not become owners of num, and they cannot heal.

Experiences that include the moment of transcendence and the subsequent application to healing may be called "full" kia. It is in full kia that one can heal. More than half the adult men, or more than half of those males who seek num, and perhaps 10 percent of the adult women, or almost 25 percent of those females who seek num, experience full kia. They are called *num kausi,* "owners, or masters, of num," namely healers. These healers experience beginning kia in their early contacts with num; beginning kia is in a sense a preparation for full kia at some later dance. Also, at any one dance, beginning kia usually occurs as a prelude to full kia, even for the experienced healers. The kia experience itself has its own internal development.

In beginning kia, one typically sweats profusely and moves about stiff-legged or perhaps staggers on wobbly legs. Kinachau says: "Your footing gets bad, your legs become rubbery. You feel very light; your feet don't touch the ground properly. It seems that you don't have any weight on the ground holding you steady. You have to work to keep your balance. You can lose control over your body because you feel as if there are no bones in your body." The body trembles, especially the legs, and one has a blank, glassy stare. Any or all of these physical manifestations may occur while one is moving about in the area of the dance. One's perception is "congested"; one's thoughts "whirl." And fear dominates.

There is fear of the hot, almost boiling num which creates great pain and confusion. Dau speaks of these effects: "What happens in kia is that it hurts in the gebesi, the pain is great on the sides and in the stomach. Your belly and spine quiver. Your vision becomes funny in that when you look at people or the fire, you will see the fire as if it is way above the ground or at eye level." Another healer describes the effects this way: "I see all the people like very small birds, the whole place will be spinning around and that is why we run around. The trees will be circling also" (quoted in Lee, 1968, p. 11). There is also fear of the unknown and of the potentially frightening experiences to come, which will herald full kia.

Dau describes what it is like to be in beginning kia: "You can tell a person who is fearing num by the expression of pain at his gebesi. You see a person grimacing with stomach pain. Now look at me for example. The pain sometimes gets too strong for me and I have to sit down, and when it subsides, I can get up and dance again. We will massage and feel our gebesi, not to bring the num up, but to keep the num down so that we can dance."

Nai talks about beginning kia from a different point of

view. As she sings at the dance, she is looking for those in beginning kia. She is ready to offer them support if they need it. I ask her how she can tell if someone fears num. "Num hurts, you know," she replies. "Those who are new to kia leap up to heaven and then fall down and dive into the fire and scatter the coals all over us singers, and we leap up brushing the coals off ourselves and say, 'What is this man doing? Does he fear num? Look, he's going to murder us with the fire.' Then he sprays the coals, and he climbs into the trees. Then he might go and pick things up in his hands, and we might help. We have to take them away from him and say, 'What're you doing?' His face is also blank; his eyebrows might be slightly raised, and his eyes might close and open." Nai demonstrates by staring blankly into space, her eyes bulging, and then gradually her expression becomes like a frightened or pursued animal.

The dynamic that moves one from an experience of beginning kia to full kia is being able to "die." This dying should not be reduced to the Western concept of psychological death or ego-death. Nor do I find evidence that the Kung call this dying a "half-death." For the Kung, it is simply dying. This dying and attendant rebirth are the central expressions of transcendence in Kung healing. When persons still seeking num experience this death, it signifies their capacity for full kia and healing. It is said that they have finally "drunk num." They then embark on a phase of active dancing and kia, trying to gain more and more experience in applying their boiling num to healing. When established healers experience this death, it may signify their entrance to a very deep, full kia.

Often a particular form of dying marks the passage from beginning to full kia. Dancers usually fall to the ground. They may crash down suddenly after running around wildly, or they may slip to the ground, their feet becoming like soft rubber. Lying on the ground, their body is sweaty and clammy. It usually twitches and trembles, sometimes in violent spasms. There seems to be much physical tension in the body, and sometimes it is as rigid as a board. At other times the body is limp, almost lifeless. Either the eyes are closed tightly or, if open, the eyeballs are often rolled up into the head, only the whites showing.

While in beginning kia, the healers' soul or spirit remains in their body. As Kinachau says: "The soul is inside, not traveling around. It's there. It's small, but it's there." During the death of full kia, the soul leaves the healers' body through their head. The soul goes to encounter god and the spirits of the dead ancestors. It pleads for protection for the Kung back at the dance. The Kung say that healers are in great danger at this time. Their soul might wander away or be taken by the spirits. Then they, too, would die and become a "spirit of the dead."

When healers are in this death, the others at the dance focus their attention and energy on protecting and caring for them. The singing may become more enthusiastic and intense. Others work over the person in death, trying to cool down their num, healing them, and calling out for their soul to return.

There are different things healers can do while in full kia, each an expression or application of a transcendent experience. They may handle, contact, or walk on the dance fire without being burned. Describing something like X-ray vision, they may predict the sex of infants in utero or describe the location and shape of a sickness inside someone's body. They may see at a great distance, enabling them to warn persons of lions lurking out of sight or to describe people's activities in a far-away camp. Even those working on healers, affected by the latters' kia, may themselves handle hot coals in their supportive efforts without being burned.

Healers in full kia may obtain special information, for example, about the appropriateness of an impending marriage. They may also have what could be called "out of the body" experiences. (Tart, 1969). These experiences may be both elaborate and extended, as are the trips to god's home. Healers may have direct contact with god in the form of a conversion experience, where god himself gives them num.

The Kung believe that a few of the most powerful healers

of the past could transform themselves into lions, who stalked the desert in search of human prey (Lee, 1968). Lions do not ordinarily attack man, and sometimes the Kung hunters may even drive a lion away from its fresh kill in order to scavenge the meat. On the several occasions when a lion has attacked a man, therefore, the Kung say that the attack was made by a human healer turned lion. This ability to become lions is the only one attributed to the healer that is not benevolent.

The primary application of full kia is in healing sickness. Healing itself is a transcendent experience. Healing becomes possible through the healers' ability to go beyond their ordinary self into kia and, in kia, to allow their num to work against sickness. Full kia becomes a transcendent experience with definite applications in daily life.

During full kia, the Kung certainly transcend themselves. They have experiences and do things beyond their ordinary capacities. But most important, they "see" things with a clarity and understand with a depth beyond their ordinary states. This enhanced perception and knowledge come from their contact with the spirits and gods and, in particular, from their working with num.

The word *kia* is also used to refer to other states, such as those associated with the consumption of alcohol and the smoking of tobacco. Being drunk is seen by most Kung as a "bad thing." Kaha, a strong healer from Kangwa, remarks that a person who is drunk does not "know people. You start off talking nicely but then can't finish." The Kung way of smoking, which involves a series of rapid, deep inhalations, can lead to a tobacco kia. As Kau Dwa describes it: "You can achieve kia from tobacco if you're dying for a smoke. Tobacco diffuses throughout your flesh, but it is not num. It is not num. It is tobacco. It's like an arrow that fires into your chest and kills you. If you take tobacco only, you will not pull sickness. Tobacco is just like a food you might eat." These other kia experiences involve alterations of consciousness but, more important, do not result from the activation of num and are not applied to healing. Alcohol and tobacco kia are viewed primarily as sources of pleasure or release. The kia of num remains distinctly, uniquely significant.

Healing is what ties kia directly into the Kung's everyday life. Healing is the function for which the pain of kia is endured. This healing must be understood in the broadest sense of protection and enhancement for the individual, the group, and the entire Kung people. Healing is a give-and-take process. Those who put on the dance, especially the singers, give the healers the setting in which their num can be activated. In return, healers give to all the healing power of that activated num. Healing seeks to maintain a balance in the Kung's universe of experience. The healers go forth into active contact with the spiritual realm, struggling with the spirits and gods over issues of sickness and death. The character and outcome of these continuing struggles do much to establish the texture of the Kung universe.

The healer struggles with the gods because it is from them that sickness comes to people. The great god Gao Na, the creator and controller of all things, is said to create sickness and, according to his own will, to send sickness to his people, the Kung. The actual sending is through the lesser god Kauha and his messengers, the *gauwasi* or spirits of dead Kung. An experienced healer from Dobe describes this act: "Kauha is the owner of sickness. He holds it in his possession and shoots it out [into a person] when he wants to kill [that person]. The healer's job is to draw sickness out [of the person] and send it back to Kauha, who must receive it and keep it until it is sent out to kill another. Kauha is very bad. He possesses terrible purposes" (quoted in Lee, 1963–1974).

Sickness is more an existential condition or level of being than a particular illness or symptom. Everybody has some sickness, and so everybody who is at a dance is given healing. In most persons, this sickness remains incipient, neither serious nor manifested in symptoms. In some persons, the sickness is actualized into what Westerners would call an illness. Persons who are ill get especially intensive and extensive healing. Num is for prevention as well as treatment.

It is at the healing dance that the issue of health and

sickness is dealt with most directly and forcefully. For it is there that the spirits, attracted by the beautiful singing and dancing, hover in the surrounding darkness, waiting to shoot their arrows of sickness into people. It is there that the healers can confront these spirits and battle with them to save the people from sickness and death. The very performance of a dance calls for such a confrontation.

Theoretically, kia-healing is appropriate for all kinds of what Westerners would call physical, psychological, social, and spiritual sicknesses. In practice, healing is withheld in certain cases, for example, if the sickness cannot be understood or diagnosed. The cause of the sickness may be something the healer is not able to handle. Koto describes the cure of a Herero, Mr. Thomas, who lives at Xaixai: "When Mr. Thomas was struck by lightning and died, his body was carried back to his village. Wi was called in, and Wi pulled him and pulled him. We had all given Mr. Thomas up for dead, and then he opened his eyes and lived. But the first Kung to be called in was Kinachau and he refused. Then they called in another, and he refused. They both said, 'We don't know this sickness, it is not from our place.' "

Since the sickness must be drawn out by healers into their own body before they expel it into space, some healers are wary of having an unknown sickness enter their bodies, even temporarily. What would happen if the sickness did not leave them? Such a question is usually not raised with recognizable illnesses, but it is with unknown ailments. When the sickness is diagnosed as being the result of Goba witchcraft, then a healing is usually withheld. Goba witchcraft is in one sense a label for sicknesses the Kung cannot understand or heal.

A young healer from Nokaneng, who has been told to stop dancing because his num has "killed his father and uncle," comes to Xaixai in part to visit relatives, in part to be cured. He is completely lethargic in physical appearance, extremely depressed. When I speak with Toma Zho about him, Toma Zho becomes thoughtful and reflects for a moment before saying: "I don't know about that young man from Nokaneng. He's sick, but I don't know what he's sick from. I haven't been to him."

"Has anyone been pulling him?" I wonder.

"No." Toma Zho looks perplexed. "And I don't know why nobody's pulling him here at Xaixai. I don't know why."

I too am puzzled. "But he's pretty sick, isn't he?"

"Yes," says Toma Zho. "I've heard around that he's sick. But he's been to dances. He went to our dance the other night."

"That's right," I say, "but nobody pulled him there. Why did Kinachau pull others at that dance but not him?"

"I didn't see. I didn't see that dance," Toma Zho replies simply.

I then ask Kinachau about the sick healer. Kinachau expresses sincere bewilderment. "I don't know what's wrong with the one from Nokaneng," he remarks. "He just arrived. I went over there to see him the other day, but I didn't heal him. The num in me is no longer strong." This characteristic Kung disclaimer ends Kinachau's response.

I am still puzzled why such a sick person is not healed more immediately and extensively. It was only later, after talking with Kau Dwa, the healer who lives at Kangwa, that a possible explanation emerges. "Yes, I know that man very well," says Kau Dwa. "He came off the truck at Kangwa a few months ago, almost dead. I pulled and pulled and pulled him. Then I said to him, 'Look, don't stay in this place. Get out of here. Go down to Xaixai and ask for num.' "

"What's wrong with him?" I ask again.

"We don't know. I don't know. Maybe the Gobas gave something to him. I think it's some kind of gun the Gobas have that they can shoot into you. So perhaps it was the Gobas who gave him that disease. He also had a hunting accident. He was hunting with a rifle. He shot a wildebeest in the right haunch, and the wildebeest turned on him and gored him in the thigh and then gored him in the stomach."

"When you pulled him, what did you see?"

"I saw nothing. I just saw blood in the places where the wildebeest had gored him."

The Kung do not feel that kia-healing is omnipotent. The

healers lose some of their battles with the spirits. Persons die. And often a person dies in the hands of a healer, who up to the end has been trying to save him. Upon such a death, healers may acknowledge the outcome of their struggle in words such as: "The sick one must go now. The spirits have taken him for their own."

Kashay talks about when he was "given up for dead": "There was the time I was very sick, so sick that I was given up for dead. This disease absolutely ruined my feet; they were limp, as limp and pale as dead flesh. I was deathly thin. They were dancing for me. They brought me from my camp to the dance. Toma Zho danced over me until the sun rose. I was so sick I couldn't sleep. My eyes were closed but they were full of visions of ancestors. Toma Zho pulled me and pulled me and pulled me until the sun rose. Then I was taken back to my camp, and I said, 'Is today the day I'm finally going to see some sleep?' I lay down, and to my great surprise I fell into a sound, good sleep. And I woke up saying, 'I'm saved.' "

The actual process of healing has three main aspects: "seeing properly," "pulling out the sickness," and "bargaining" or "battling" with the gods and spirits. Seeing properly allows the healer to locate and diagnose the sickness in a person. Wi, an old experienced healer, speaks of Dau, who is still comparatively young in kia: "What tells me that Dau isn't fully learned is the way he behaves. You see him staggering and running around. His eyes are rolling all over the place. If your eyes are rolling, you can't stare at sickness. You have to be *absolutely steady* to see sickness, steady-eyed, no shivering and shaking. You need a steady gaze. Your thoughts don't whirl, the fire doesn't float above you, when you are seeing properly."

Dau acknowledges that he is not a *geiha,* that is, a "completely learned" healer: "A geiha is a person who really helps people. He is someone whose eye-insides are steady. He can see people properly. I heal people, but I can't see them properly." In seeing properly, not only does one see where and what the sickness is, but also, with that "absolutely steady" stare, one starts to treat the sickness.

Proper seeing can become even more general. A healer

can begin to see into and beyond many material manifestations. "Invisible" elements of the dance become "visible." Wi talks about this aspect of kia: "You see the num rising in other healers. You see the singing and the num, and you pick it up. As a healer in kia, you see everybody. You see that the insides of well people are fine. You see the insides of the one the spirits are trying to kill, and you go there. Then you see the spirits and drive them away. You see the spirits being selfish. You see them trying to take the person away for themselves." Others describe how they can see at a distance, or see what the gods want to tell the Kung. This enhanced dimension of perception and knowledge strengthens the healer's powers.

Proper seeing is a transcendent function and is itself a transcendent experience. The literal, physical act of seeing may or may not be involved. The eyes may be open, they may be closed; it is not crucial. The experience remains one of enhanced perceiving and knowing.

Sickness is pulled out as the healers bring their vibrating hands close to or in contact with a person. When there are no manifest symptoms of illness, the healers' fluttering hands generally move lightly and sporadically over the person's chest and head. When particular symptoms are present, the laying on of hands becomes more focused on the symptom area. Healers put their num into the other person, and at the same time pull the sickness out of the other and into their own body. This is difficult, painful work. The sickness is then expelled from the healers. They shake their hands vigorously toward the darkness which fringes the dance, throwing the sickness out away from the people and back toward the spirits hovering nearby. The Kung word *twe* refers to both the process of pulling out sickness and the physical actions, such as the laying on of hands, which accomplish this process.

Sweat (*cho*) is a most important phenomenon in healing (Lee, 1968). As the sweat first pours out of the healer during kia, it is the visible expression of the boiling num within, a sign of kia. The Kung equate sweat with the steam rising from boiling water and with the vapors that rise up the spine as num boils in the pit of the dancer's stomach. This sweat then becomes a critical element in the pulling out of sickness.

The Kung believe that activated num is exposed on the surface of the healer's body in the form of sweat – mainly at the forehead, the small of the back, the chest, and the armpits. Sweat is rubbed onto and into the body of the person being healed. The rubbing is usually focused on the area of illness, when such is specified.

The laying on of hands is the typical healing behavior. Some healers do only that. Others also try to maximize body contact between themselves and those healed. Kau Dwa, for example, at times wraps his arms and legs around the one he is healing, his chest against the other's back or chest, his head rubbing all over the other's upper body and head. Sometimes Kau Dwa lies down over a person, lengthwise or crosswise. He seems to want to spread his sweat all over the person and to increase the points through which the exchange of his num and the other's sickness can occur. By enclosing the one being healed with his own hot, vibrating body, even though he often is not physically touching him, Kau Dwa establishes a kind of healing-energy field.

But even the simple laying on of hands is quite physical, direct, and penetrating. "When I lay hands on a person, I take sickness into my hands. Then I shiver from the sickness, and then I throw it away." As Wi speaks these words, he makes a strong holding gesture, forming a cup with both hands when he says, "I take sickness into my hands." The process of locating and removing sickness is sometimes accompanied by the healer's treacherous journey into the patient's body.

The pain involved in the boiling of the healers' num, in the putting of that num into the one being healed, in the drawing of the other's sickness into their own body, and in the violent shaking of that sickness out from their body is acknowledged by the healers by crying, wailing, moaning, and shrieking. They punctuate and accent their healing with these sometimes ear-shattering sounds. As their breath comes with more difficulty, until they are rasping and gasping, the healers howl the characteristic kowhedili shriek, which sounds something like "Xai—i! Kow-ha-di-di-di-di!" and usually accompanies the pulling out of the sickness. Some say the shriek forcibly expels the sickness from a spot on the top of the healers' spine. Others say the shriek marks the painful process of shaking the sickness out from the healers' hands.

A person need not be in kia to be healed. In fact, except when other healers or singers in kia are healed, the person being healed is often in an ordinary state. When the kia and healing are not especially heavy, a person being healed may be carrying on a conversation about how uncomfortable he feels in the cold night, or how weak a gatherer someone was yesterday – uninterrupted by the healer's fluttering hands, uninterrupted even by the healer's shrieks.

Beneath these healing behaviors a continuous, nonlinear process is occurring. The putting in of num and the pulling out of sickness are not different acts, nor even clearly delineated stages in the same action. This is particularly clear when healers in kia heal other healers not yet in kia. In the very act of putting num into the others, the healers who are already in kia are not only pulling out the others' sickness but also stimulating them into kia. And as the other healers go into kia, their own newly boiling num contacts the first healers, reintensifying their kia. In this case, the num is put into others to draw out the sickness and to activate more num, which among other things helps draw out the sickness. The healing process is an even more dramatic unity when more experienced healers heal themselves. Their num and their sickness exchange within themselves. Healing is an organized process where a substance called sickness is transformed by a substance called num. It is not a mechanical process where one substance is replaced or erased by another.

The singer Nai talks about how it feels when she is healed: "If my body is feeling bad or having a pain and they heal me, they will *hxobo* my body and make it nice." *Hxobo* means to "cool" or "calm down." The healers speak of having to cool down themselves and their num when num boils too fiercely. In healing sickness, the hot num makes the patient cool. *Deu,* "coolness" or "well-being," is the desired state, being neither too hot nor too cold (Biesele, 1975). The interplay between substances which are hot and cold, or heavy and light, characterizes the application of num to healing sickness.

The goal of the healing is to remove all the sickness, "to remove everything." Kaha talks about how he can tell if he is more powerful than another healer at a particular dance: "I'd sit and look at the other man and say, 'That man isn't pulling. He must be new at num. He isn't pulling. He removes some things and leaves other things.' I see and remove everything. I remove things completely. I would pull everything out, and then your body would feel good." The Kung say that everything is pulled out when the healer "sees all sicknesses leave" the patient.

Kaha and his wife Nukha speak about this process of pulling or removing sickness with pained understanding. For the past several weeks Nukha has been so weak that she has to lie on the sand, wrapped in a blanket most of the day. She has great difficulty breathing and eating, and the ravages of her illness show in her bone thinness. Her respiratory problems have become severe in the last several years, though intermittently she has periods of feeling much better. A visiting medical researcher once suggested she has advanced tuberculosis or cancer, though no definite diagnosis could be made. Nukha looks so close to death that, when her hacking coughs violently shake her frame, it seems they will tear her apart.

For several weeks, Kaha has been pulling Nukha each day, and when she reaches a low point, he works on her several times a day. Kaha says that when he pulls his wife, he sees that "her chest area is full of breaks and holes." Since yesterday, Nukha has taken a slight turn toward health, though she continues to look more drawn to death than life. She is able to rest on one elbow. Today Kaha is sitting by her side, whittling a stick. Nukha motions for me. I go over and express my wish that her sickness will leave her. She smiles a warm response. "I've had this sickness for years," Nukha says. "Look at all these scars." Slowly, very slowly, she turns over and exposes the upper part of her back, lined with little scars.

"These scars on her back are from the sicknesses I've pulled out from her," Kaha points out. "I've been healing her for many years."

"He's been pulling me for many years," Nukha adds, "but the sickness refuses. The sickness started when I was pregnant with her." She points to her late adolescent daughter sitting a short distance away with a small group of other girls, stringing beads. "It started with her birth, and my husband has been pulling me ever since."

"When the sickness refuses like that, what do you do?" I wonder.

"I pull," Kaha replies, the weariness from his concern and his exhaustive pulling invading his voice. "If the sickness refuses, I keep on pulling for a long time. One year I pull and pull, and then she gets up. Another year comes, and I pull again and again."

"What do you see when you pull?"

"I pull little pieces of metal out of my wife's legs and hips, like little pieces of wire. These bits of metal are tying her leg ligaments up. I pulled her dead father's testicles out of her heart. Then I told her dead father not to pursue her anymore."

"Can she see what you remove?"

"No. I tell her what I see." Kaha's response is affirmed by his wife's nodding head. "My wife tells me where it hurts, then I remove things from that place."

My concern for Nukha's suffering takes away my words. We sit quietly. I try to begin again. "Kaha, what happened when you were pulling your wife yesterday?" I direct my words to Kaha, but look at them both, partners in suffering.

"Yesterday I pulled her to take her father's testicle out." Kaha's face is tired, and when he talks of his pulling, the tiredness seems to be expressed more deeply.

"What can you do when you're so tired from so much

pulling?" I am reaching out to Kaha, trying to offer some understanding, not expecting an "answer."

"When you are so tired, you pull," Kaha replies simply.

When somebody is seriously ill, perhaps with advanced tuberculosis or failing health due to old age, loss of blood, or infection through an animal wound, the dance takes on a particularly intense quality. The singing and dancing are strong, the kia profound, and the healing prolonged and penetrating. The focus of the healing is the ill person, who has become what would in the West be called a "patient." The healers return continually to heal the patient and stay with him for long periods. All others at the dance are healed as well, but the healing energy is focused on the patient. Gau puts it this way: "In those dances where no one is seriously ill, we are sometimes playing at dancing. The num is weak. But when there is someone ill, num is much stronger, because we pull and pull him."

When the num is hot and heavy, the pulling power is strong. But healers have off-nights. There are times when their num is weak. Gau talks about a dance which has just ended the night before: "I was thinking that this dance wasn't going to be a good one, because for it to be a good one, you've got to have lots of people singing, and last night we had only a few." When I ask him how his num was that night, he replies: "You mean I've gotten any num? I haven't gotten any num. Last night I did only a little."

There are times when the num is so weak that a healer seems merely to be "going through the motions." I ask Dau if there are times when he heals and does not pull all the sickness out. He reflects, with some sadness: "There are times in num when I say, 'I haven't got anything today.' There are times when I'm weak, when my body feels lousy. I just don't feel right."

"Do you heal during such times anyway?" I ask.

"Yes," he says, with resignation. "I still lay on hands."

In their ordinary everyday behavior, the Kung keep their distance from the gods. Although they tell stories about the gods' stupidity and foolishness, laughing heartily at their human frailties, the Kung do not often speak of the gods, and when they do, they speak in a quiet tone, implying a respect for the gods' power. During kia, the healer may not only talk directly to the gods but also bargain with them, insult them, even battle with them. At stake is a sick person's health or life, and the healers, enhanced by their boiling num, struggle with opponents they normally would not even look at, much less approach.

In their contest with the gods, the healers usually confront Kauha, the lesser god, and the spirits, whom the great god Gao Na sends to carry a sick person away. Kaha, the experienced healer, tells how he chases the spirits away so a sick person can get better: "I cured Tankau. He had a strained back. Tankau's father, who was dead, appeared to me as a spirit and said to me, 'My son must stop digging the well.' Tankau had been digging a well. His father, the spirit, had made him strain his back. Then Tankau said, 'How can I quit that job of digging the well. We need the well.' Then I said to the spirit, 'How can you chase this man from his work?' and I refused the spirit and took out the pieces of metal embedded in Tankau's back. I pulled the pieces of iron out and gave them to his father, the spirit, and said, 'Take these pieces of metal away! Are you stupid? You worked in your day, and now your son follows you. You can't take someone from his work. Go away! Go away!' "

An experienced healer can see the spirits hovering around the edge of a dance; they remain invisible to all others. After diagnosing the source of an illness, healers may plead with the spirits to make the illness go away. They may chant their appeal to the spirits:

> Why do you bother with this [sick] one?
> Go away and don't trouble us!
> We love this man.
> What have we done to you?
>
> (quoted in Lee, 1968)

Though the lesser god and the spirits may inhabit the darkness outside the dance because they enjoy watching the dance, the ever-present danger is that they will also bring sickness or death. The healer's job is to drive them away, thereby preventing sickness from striking anyone. Usually the healers' friendly overtures to the gods or spirits and their appeals for leniency become more assertive: "Get out of here. You are a bad thing." "Go chase yourself. You will not take this child. I will beat you." Often healers yell out insulting and profane phrases to the gods and spirits. They scream at them, calling them "Big penis," or "Elephant-penis," or "You will shit," or "Filthy face," meaning a face covered with excrement (Marshall, 1969). The healer often becomes aggressive, even violent, toward the gods, gesturing menacingly and hurling sticks into the darkness to drive away the spirits.

At times, healers may carry on an extended dialogue with the gods and spirits. Others at the dance can hear only the healers' side of the dialogue, but they know the spirits are speaking to them because they see the healers continually respond and react as if to an opponent – nodding their heads and shaking their fists at the spirits, turning away from them, uttering sounds which acknowledge the spirits' participation in the dialogue. In this dialogue, the mood can fluctuate. There may be friendly overtures, or cajoling, or hostility – all in an effort to counteract the spirits' wishes to take the sick man from the living. Healers usually speak rapidly and intensely, so that their words are almost indistinguishable, seeming at times like mere sounds. Their words are interlaced with groans, shrieks, and fragments of singing, changing them even more into mere sounds.

Another form of contact with gods occurs when the powerful healers risk "traveling" to god's home. The description of that home – a "terrible," fearsome place – and what happens there with god and his family, is often extensive. The animals which inhabit that place, such as leopards, giraffes, elands, and zebras – all god's "possessions" – are detailed, as is the god's appearance (Biesele, 1975). God is a big man with long hair, a horse, a gun, and big boots. Kau Dwa tells how healers climb to god's home and return: "When you go to . . . (God) you climb a thread. You climb a long thread. First you have entered the sand. Up ahead there you emerge again. When you emerge, you begin to climb the thread. And when you arrive at God's place, you make yourself small . . . You come in small to God's place. You do what you have to do there. Then you return to where everyone is . . . and you come and come and come and you finally enter your body again. All the people . . . who have stayed behind waiting for you, they fear you . . . You enter, enter, enter the earth, and then you return to enter your skin" (quoted in Biesele, 1975, II, 163–164). Such threads are said to be used by the spirits to descend to the earth.

During the visit, healers try to understand why the god would want to bring sickness to the people, and they try to change the god's plans to take persons away from the living. The mood on these trips can vary, and healers usually employ a variety of techniques to win their point. But only experienced healers can die to their ordinary selves so completely that they can travel to and exist in god's home. Their num can become so hot and heavy, while their control over it remains so great, that they transcend themselves to the point where they are functioning in the presence of the gods.

Healers must learn other things. They must obey a series of dietary taboos as they are learning to kia and throughout their subsequent experiences with num and healing (Marshall, 1976). They can also learn about medicinal herbs and roots. But these lessons emphasize a cognitive learning, a gathering and retaining of information, which makes them quite different from the lessons at the core of kia-healing. The essence of becoming a healer depends not on learning *about* herbs or dietary taboos, or for that matter *about* num. It depends on learning to *experience* boiling num in kia, and learning to *apply* boiling num in kia-healing. These lessons come out of a transcendent perspective and perception.

The Kung's experience of kia is no less "real" for them than a root to be gathered, or an animal to be hunted, or a conflict to be resolved. The Kung do not rank different aspects of their existence as more or less real than others according to what Westerners would call their "materiality." Especially for healers, who are in direct contact with the gods, both the spiritual world and the Kalahari sands are actual parts of their lives. They try to wrest their living from both things.

This concrete reality of healing is acknowledged simply and repeatedly by the healers. Wa Na talks about the healers who used to travel at night in the form of lions of god; they were real lions, different from normal lions, but no less real. A healer's trip to god's home is an actual trip to an actual place. Num really does exist. It actually boils, and it is painful. For the Kung, there is no philosophical distinction: experiences of healing are simply one other event, concrete and real, in their everyday lives.

When Wi says, "I see the num rising in another" or "I pick the num up," he means that he actually *sees* num and *picks it up*. He goes on to say: "When I lay hands on a person, I take sickness out into my hands. Then I shiver from the sickness and throw it away. I pull the sickness right out at the moment of laying on hands." He means he takes the sickness out *into his hands*. To ask whether he picks up num as he would pick up a stone is to miss the point entirely. When pressed, Wi says there is a difference between picking up num and picking up a stone. But that is when *I* pressed him to make such a distinction. He responds to *my* framework and assumptions and, given *my* set of choices, makes his choice. It is not *his* question, not really a question for him.

This is not to say that the Kung make no distinctions between states of consciousness. They distinguish, for example, between types of kia. Num kia is different from alcohol kia. Num kia has different effects; the Kung value it more. But it is no more real than alcohol kia.

The reality of the unseen is captured in the phenomenon of num "killing" the healer, or of the healer "dying" in kia. I often hear: "You want num? Don't you know it is painful and can kill you?" I learn what those who become healers must know. To "kill" is not simply a metaphor, a statement about the overpowering strength of num, a warning about the difficulty of getting it, a test of one's desire to receive it. Although the Kung distinguish between final death, when the soul permanently leaves the body, and the death of kia, when the soul goes out but then hopefully returns, there is only one *experience* of death, and the experience is what matters.

Kau Dwa is teaching me that lesson as I struggle to maintain my Western notions of reality. "Kau Dwa," I ask, "you have told me that in kia you must die. Does that mean really die?"

"Yes."

"I mean *really* die."

"Yes."

"You mean die like when you are buried beneath the ground?" I am already struggling with my words.

"Yes," Kau Dwa replies with enthusiasm. "Yes, just like that!"

"They are the same?"

"Yes, the same. It is death I speak of," he affirms.

"No difference?" I almost plead.

"It is death," he responds firmly but softly.

"The death where you never come back?" I am nearly at the end of my logical rope.

"Yes," he says simply, "it is that bad. It is the death that kills us all."

"But the healers get up, and a dead person doesn't." My statement trails off into a question.

"That is true," Kau Dwa replies quietly, with a smile, "healers may come alive again."

7 Education for Healing

AS THE KUNG'S healing is essentially an experience of transcendence, their teaching and learning process is essentially an education for transcendence. The education focuses on experiential learning and occurs primarily at the dance itself. Learning to receive num and to bring forth its healing powers is an experiential passage rather than an acquisition of information. It is a dying and rebirth rather than a learning about song melodies, or dance steps, or healing postures. Before this experiential mystery of death, all stand in awe. Both the young Kung seeking their first experience of num and the old experienced healers, whose num is boiling for the thousandth time, fear the death they must face. Both fear passing through a territory of consciousness which can never become known. As their num boils and they are burst into kia, the old ones acknowledge the fearful pain. Although they may say that, when they were young, it used to hurt much more, they rarely say that the pain is no more.

The men learn to heal in the Giraffe dance, whereas the women learn to heal in the Drum dance. Their educations differ in aspects of form and structure, such as the dance steps learned or the phases of their development as healers. But the education of male healers in the Giraffe dance is paradigmatic of the essence of Kung healer education, with its transitions into and out of kia.

The Kung education for healing is an aspect of normal socialization. Kung children play at imitating the healing dance, including dramatic falls into the sand from "kia." Kung grow up going to dances, being around persons receiving num, and later supporting them during kia. Num, though held in awe, is a part of their everyday life, and receiving it is part of what it means to be a Kung – whether one drinks num and becomes its owner, or receives it temporarily while being healed. The Kung grow up with a deep respect for num and unquestioningly turn to it for help and protection.

Page 117: Helping a healer regulate boiling num

The Kung family plays a critical, continuing part in the educational process. A young male Kung is most likely to receive num from his father, or uncle, or other close relative. In a study by Lee (personal communication), 57 percent of the male healers received num from their close kin, 19 percent of these from their fathers; 25 percent received it from non-kin; 9 percent were self-taught; and 9 percent did not specify their source of num.

The drinking of num occurs within a family support system and is deepened into the ability to heal within this same context. A Kung almost always dances at his own camp, and his immediate family is there, singing and clapping for him or he for them; he heals and is healed by his family. The others involved are invariably relatives. The intimacy of the family is enhanced in the terrifying intimacy of kia-healing.

It is within the supportive context of their experienced universe – from the immediate family to the gods – that the Kung seek num. Debe, a young man who has yet to drink num, speaks without hesitation about this search: "We seek num even though it's painful because we can help people. If someone is very sick and almost dead, with num we can bring them back to life. That's why we seek num."

The healer Gau explains why, though all seek num, not all continue to seek it with enthusiasm and dedication: "Num is hot; mine is hot too. Others who say it is not have deceived you. Those without num may look at those who do num and say, 'Why can't I do like that?' Now if I tell them that it's very painful, they say, 'Oh, you're just fooling me. I still want to do num!' But then when they start, they see how painful it is, and then they stop because they fear it. This is how it was with me. I thought they were kidding me when they told me how painful num was. I tried num, and it was so painful that I stopped. And I even stopped going to dances for years because I feared num. Only after I got married did I try num again. This time it again came up in me, but I passed through it, and then num came to me. Now I have num."

Seeking num brings one to the healing dance, the setting where num is both strongest and most acessible. Gau describes this active seeking on the part of his nephew Bo: "I think Bo is going to stay with num and grow with it, because I see that every time there's a dance, he's there, dancing, and not always sitting down. But if I saw him staying away from dances after he had started going to them, then I would say he's going to leave num."

The primary purpose of the dance is to activate num. The fire and darkness, the singing, clapping, and dancing, all contribute to an intense, volatile environment ripe for boiling num. Some dancers open up their hearts and they burst with num; others are forced to close their hearts tight with fear; others go back and forth, reaching nearer to what they must run from, running from what they have almost received.

"When god created this num dance, he created it with a fire in the center. If we let the fire die so that we sing in the dark, then god's arrows will strike us and make our skin painful." This is how Nai, a woman who is an active singer but has never experienced kia, speaks of the dance fire. The fire etches a place in the desert's total darkness; it carves out a circle in the flat, open area of the camp center. It is a circle of warmth and comfort. While camp fires always attract people, especially in the cold Kalahari nights, the dance fire carries a unique emotional and spiritual attraction.

The fire is never too big. Persons like to be near the fire; sometimes the healers want to hold the burning coals, even to go into the fire. A roaring blaze or billowing smoke would force them to keep their distance.

The small fire remains hot, its light flickering. The singers are bathed in warm, pulsating light. The dancers are picked out of the darkness as they move around the fire, the sweat shining on their bodies. In the immense darkness of space, the fire reaches out in a circle. It holds the singers and dancers together and helps transform them for their healing task.

Chuko, an older woman, is moody during the day, sometimes withdrawn, sometimes feisty; but never does she seem particularly special. At the dance, as she sings and heals, she is strong and compelling, a dominating presence. Kau Dwa is totally blind; during the day he has to be led about and walks haltingly. At the dance, as his num boils, he dances enthusiastically and dramatically; he moves quickly and forcefully. He is led around by no one and locates all who need healing. He is a charismatic figure. Just being at a dance can bring about such changes in mood and personality. This is so even at dances that occur during the day, when perhaps there is no fire. But the fire accelerates and intensifies these changes.

The fire creates a special space in which num can boil. But the fire is not just atmosphere, nor is the atmosphere ephemeral. There is num in the fire, and the Kung work with the fire. The fire helps to heat up and regulate the dancer's num. The singers may rub coals in their hands before they work on a dancer who has fallen in kia. The dancers may go to the fire, walk in it, put their heads in it, pick up coals and rub them over their hands and body. But it is not just the fire's heat that helps the dancer's num boil. Healers use the same word, *daa,* to describe both the central dance fire and the fire within their own bodies which heats up the num (Lee, 1968). The fire also helps the dancer kia because it adds its own num to the dancer's num. This makes the fire an especially strong stimulant.

Usually only experienced healers are allowed to work with the fire unassisted, and even they are not encouraged. Nai puts it this way: "If a 'big' healer wants to go into the fire, we would let him, because he is an owner of num. He may kneel and stick his head in the fire and hold it there. We might leave him because we know he would take it out. Other times I might try to restrain him. But the young ones who are new to kia, we won't let them go into the fire. We try to restrain them. We draw them aside and guide them away from the fire." Those learning to heal are said to be confused during kia: "The young ones in [kia] see the fire as if it is above their heads; they step in it because they think they are passing under it" (quoted in Lee, 1968, p. 12). Kinachau puts it this way: "Because num is hot like the fire, it makes you want to jump in. Because you don't know what is fire and what isn't. But only the young ones without brains do this." In fact, there are no hard and fast rules. Kinachau or another experienced healer may go to the fire in apparent confusion and work with it in a less than experienced manner. And if, by going to the fire and picking up a coal, a young dancer will become more ready to receive num, then he is allowed, even guided, to work with the fire.

The Kung do not see working with the fire as extraordinary; they are not surprised that they are not burned. Their explanation is simple: when the num in their body is boiling and as hot as the fire, they cannot be burned when working with the fire. When their num is dormant or cold or cooled down, they can be burned.

Usually, the fire is started informally by any of the women who happen to be in the camp at the time, and it is fed throughout the night by anyone who happens to be there when it is low. But if one wants the dance to be especially strong, one may follow a certain procedure. Nai explains: "To start the fire, an older woman would call us youngsters, 'You girls, get some wood and start the fire so we can sing. Get some wood because you are the young ones.' But if we young ones refuse, she'll start it herself. If you want a good dance, you get an older person to start it. If I start the fire, it might be lousy because I might be coming and going during the dance, and it would be a light weak fire. But if one of the older women starts it, you know she will stick right at the thing and not jump up during the dance, and she'll tend it well." When such a dance continues into the early morning hours, and drowsiness mutes the singing, Nai says that someone might call to the sleepy singers, "Look girls, this big, old woman has started the fire, now you sing properly!"

The singing, with its accompanying clapping, is another strong ingredient in the dance's call to activate num. It is like the life line of the dance, carrying the dancers along in their quest for num. The songs have num, and when they are sung strongly – that is, enthusiastically, with feeling, and especially by many singers – they help heat up the dancer's num. The singing, with all its steady and familiar sounds, helps carry the healer through the terror of death and into the rebirth of healing. If by chance the singers are not particularly sensitive to the atmosphere at a dance, they may inadvertently cut the life line. That is what Kinachau experiences when, at a confused and intense moment in his kia, the song stops and the next song does not begin. In that dreadful silence, he feels lost, abandoned. He calls upon the women to begin singing again. As they begin, he gains the guidance he needs to bring his kia under control.

The actual construction of the songs, and the specific rules governing how they are sung, are of secondary importance. The songs must be learned, and mastered, so that the singer's sensitivities for the dance and for num can emerge. And since the rules of construction and singing are themselves minimal, there is ample room for personal expression and understanding. The women cannot reach their goal of "singing so strongly that the songs rise up to the heavens" merely by raising the volume. First, they must put their hearts into their singing.

The Kung believe that the great god Gao Na creates num songs (Marshall, 1969). He puts num into the songs and gives them to people. Those who receive num songs pass them on freely to others, and songs move from group to group. Over a period of time, a particular song group may dominate an area. The num in different song groups may be considered stronger or weaker, and the group currently thought to have strong num is generally the one that dominates. The Giraffe song group occupies that position at Xaixai, having replaced the Gemsbok song group. Though a particular group of num songs may hold sway in an area, a number of num song groups exist, and songs from more than one group may be sung at any one dance. Also, new songs are being created.

The process of "receiving" a num song from god is more than ordinary composing. In receiving num songs, there is a visionary element. There is often a vision or dream in which the idea or even words are received and then transmitted to others through singing. A person can be profoundly moved as she receives or creates a song which carries num.

An old Kung woman speaks of this experience: ". . . [god] had come to her in the days when she was young and fresh. He had appeared beside her while she was sleeping and had said: 'You are crying for singing. Why do you not get up and sing!' She did get up, and she sang with him, imitating him and learning. He taught her in a kindly way and said, 'Now, do not stay quiet as you used to do. Go and sing. Sing for the people as I have taught you.' She was glad. When he left, she slept again. In all, he came five times to her in this way, in both the cold time and the hot time of the year" (quoted in Marshall, 1969, p. 366).

When receiving a song from god, the person also receives the num of the song. But this is not necessarily the case when songs pass between people (Marshall, 1969). To hear a song and to be able to sing it does not mean that one becomes its "owner." The song must be given intentionally, as must the num of a song.

Those who compose num songs are not necessarily healers. Still, they seem different from those who compose lyrical songs for the stringed instrument, such as the *kwashi,* or those who compose tunes for the hunting bow. They seem "especially imbued with num music, as well as being musically gifted" (Marshall, 1969). Yet as with the healers, those who receive the num songs are appreciated but not accorded any special privilege or status. The songs are for all.

The num songs blend into and color the texture of everyday life. They "are sung everywhere by everybody, more than any other music, to enliven tasks and miles of walking, to beguile hours of leisure, and to delight and soothe babies" (Marshall, 1969, p. 368). The num songs are both spiritual vehicles and beautiful music. The Kung can appreciate their beauty without the danger of releasing their num because they believe that num is activated only during the dance, especially when it interacts with the dancers' num.

The "pulse" is the underlying building block of the num

song (England, 1968). The songs typically move at the rate of seven to eight pulses per second. The pulse rate is equivalent to the "frequency-per-second" measure of a rhythmic auditory stimulus. It is not equivalent to what is commonly called the "beat" of the music, which in num songs is expressed by the singers' clapping and the dancers' thumping steps, magnified by the dance rattles. Although the pulse as a time unit never appears in any one clap line or rattle line, because it is simply too fast, it underlies both the clapping and the dance rattles. The pulse is the building block, and the resultant lines where there are distinct beats, expressed by the claps and rattles, clearly emphasize this pulse. The vocal line or singing is too fluid to speak of it as being broken up in terms of specific pulses per second. The rhythmic quality of the num songs resides in a steady dance rattle line, which marks the beats and subdivides them into double- and triple-pulse beats; several clap lines, generally based on double- and triple-pulse beats; and a vocal line staggered one pulse off the rattle and clap lines. The resultant music is a combination of the various single lines, which would be meaningless in isolation.

The num songs have titles but few if any words. A singer may use a word or two relating to the title or some event of daily life, such as hunger, but syllables dominate, composed mostly of meaningless vocal sounds (Marshall, 1969; Shostak, personal communication). Nor are the same sounds necessarily repeated each time the song is sung.

This technical description of the num songs leaves out much of how they sound. The fundamental rhythm of eight pulses per second underlies a rich musical and emotional experience. The clapping and rattling emphasize the pulse through their steady beat; and the singing, joined by the claps and rattles, improvises on the fundamental structure. As a number of women sing together, the improvisational complexity is enriched to a point where it seems to break away completely from the fundamental beat. The clapping starts to stimulate and respond to itself, the voices start to build on each others' innuendos and challenges. The whole song becomes an exciting event, whose spontaneity and aliveness belie the fact that it has been sung countless times in the camp this year. Although the eight-pulse-per-second structure remains and is periodically emphasized by the beat of clapping and dancing, the particular group of singers and their particular improvisations make it a new song.

The particular length of songs during a dance, as well as the intensity, pace, and tone of the singing, depend to some extent on the mood and enthusiasm of the singers, and to some extent on the desires of particular dancers, but mostly on what is happening in the dance as a whole. One of the strong singers usually starts a song with a few notes to a melody; then she is joined by several others; and quickly thereafter all the women join in. The same strong singer may end the song with a few closing notes, sung loudly above the other voices. Or powerful healers may request a particular song at a particular time because that is what they personally need in working with their num. That is the case with Toma Zho, who loves to dance as the sun rises and wants to dance then to a particular song. Such a dominating healer can also end a song when he feels his num needs to cool down. He might turn toward the singers, bringing his hands down like a conductor ending a piece, or he might just call for them to end the song.

Songs usually last three to five minutes. In between are periods of conversation, animated or quiet, lasting about the same amount of time. When the dance has entered its more serious phase, songs may last as long as ten minutes, and the breaks between are under two minutes. When kia is imminent in one or more of the dancers, a song may be carried on, increasing in intensity until it seems ready to burst the singers' lungs, so as to give the dancers' num an extra push toward boiling. At such times, when kia is in the air, the women seem to be singing for the gods as much as for the dancers. Their voices reach a pitch of ecstasy, sending a current charging into the dance.

The singing gives num to the dance, like the fire and the dancers. It is one aspect of the dance, inseparable from the others. The singing is a life line because it often catalyzes the dance and carries it forward toward kia, especially when the singing is strong and the singers are sensitive to the rapid, sometimes quixotically changing needs of the healers, now for inspiration, now for comfort, now for sustenance. The singers cannot gossip among themselves too much; they must keep their eyes and ears and intuitions trained on the dance and its rapidly unfolding tempo and tone – a tempo and tone the songs themselves have largely determined.

Wi speaks bluntly and definitively from his more than forty years of experience in kia: "It's not good when the women are chattering, because when half sing and half talk, the music is not heavy, it is light, and the one doing num has no strength behind him. But when the singing is strong and rises up toward heaven, then the one doing num, his num boils hot and he can heal better."

Kanka, who has yet to kia, offers this view: "If the women sing strongly, I dance strongly. If the singing is not strong, I don't dance strongly."

Nai, who loves to sing, comes to the dances whenever possible and is known as a strong singer. She speaks about num songs: "We sing so that the men can dance. Sometimes we get very tired. Other times we sing until dawn and on. Sometimes when you have sung for many hours, you fall asleep and your head starts nodding and falling on your chest. Then someone wakes you up, calling, 'Are you sleeping?' You open your eyes and start singing again. Just sitting there clapping and singing, women kia. Or a woman might jump up and follow men around and then kia."

"If many persons kia at a dance," I ask, "is it because the singing is strong?"

"When the healers fall into kia," Nai says, "it is because of num. We don't congratulate anyone. It is the num which does it."

In the dancing, the emphasis is not on style or aesthetics, though the dance is a beautiful, sensitive art form, which becomes more exciting when the individual dancers imbue it with their own expressive manner. As with the singing, the emphasis is on dancing as a vehicle to allow num to boil.

Through dancing, the body moves with control, in time with the steady rhythm of the dance; and through that movement the body becomes hot, sweating, receptive to boiling num.

One must dance naturally and without thought of *how* to dance if kia is to come. If dancers are too intent on perfecting fancy steps or too concerned with how they appear to others, their dancing remains in the foreground and obstructs their ability to let their num boil. The male adolescents who typically dominate the beginning stages of a dance are examples. Many of them are not seeking num; instead they are seeking the admiration of others or just playing around. They try out fancy steps, some so elaborate that they could never keep up with the group of dancers as it moves fervently and insistently around the circle in times of strong singing. They joke with each other. They "parade" around the circle, trying to catch, out of the corner of their eyes, which of the young girls are enjoying their display.

In sharp contrast is the simple, concentrated, seemingly effortless dancing of experienced healers who want their num to boil. As Kinachau moves around the circle, he too dances beautifully, his strenuous stomping managing to be light on the ground. But Kinachau dances with little conscious effort. He adds a new step here or there, or unexpectedly changes the rhythm, accelerating his steps or slowing down his movement. But these creative touches do not detract from his central purpose.

There is a basic form to the dancing, regardless of which num song is being sung. The movements are usually small and controlled, the posture slightly bent at the knees, either erect or leaning over from the waist. The feet are lifted up only several inches, then stomped firmly and sharply into the sand. A sequence of four steps or beats constitutes the basic dance pattern. These four steps may carry a dancer only several inches forward (Marshall, 1969).

Although the dancing may sound routine from this description, it is not. One dancer accents his steps differently during a particular song. Another, very active dancer stamps twice to a beat, while an older person steps gently in place. Still another dancer bends sharply at the waist, his chest nearly parallel to the ground. With these individual variations on the basic form, each dancer expresses himself.

Though the dancing may look easy, it is not. The different phases of the dance affect the way one dances, but dancing is usually strenuous and active. It is hard, steady work for sometimes ten minutes at a time, over long periods, sometimes several hours or more. There are occasionally shorter periods when there is a burst of accelerating activity.

It is with kia that the dancing may become less controlled, and sometimes wild. The struggle with the painful boiling num throws the body into unexpected idiosyncratic postures and rhythms. As dancers work toward kia, they struggle to control the form and pace of their dancing; just below the surface the num is boiling within.

As the dancers work toward kia, their steps become stronger. Their feet pound the ground like pile drivers, sending a sharp pattern of kinesthetic stimulation throughout their bodies. It is almost like "shock waves," as the dancers' flesh and muscles shake rhythmically on their frames and their heads bob rhythmically up and down. The dance rattles tied around the dancers' calves add to the beat, as the seeds within the rattle cocoons vibrate against the dancers' legs. The pounding thuds of the dancers' feet and the crisp, continuing accents of the rattles underscore the dancers' occasional singing and their expressive outbursts, the grunts and moans which show that this dancing for num is hard and difficult work. All these elements enrich the singers' voices to make up what is the dance's sound.

As the dancing gets stronger in this way, the dancers become more ready for num. Their gaze focuses straight ahead or down on the ground, their bodies begin to vibrate rapidly but in a barely noticeable way, and the sweat pours out. Along with these changes in the dancers come changes in the singing. The dancing and singing get stronger together. They both lead and follow each other, preparing the way for boiling num.

As with the mechanics of learning to sing, so with the

mechanics of learning to dance: singing is "taught" very much as one is "taught" to talk; dancing is "taught" very much as one is "taught" to walk. Young Kung learn the dance steps and postures by watching the older dancers and "practicing" the dance steps as part of their play. There is no explicit instruction.

As with singing, the key to num dancing is to have an open heart. Dancing is an expressive art form for the Kung, but the expressive beauty the dancers bring to their num dancing is secondary. In the healing dance, one dances first to activate num; the pleasure of beautiful dancing is a bonus. Teaching one to sing and dance with an open heart, so that num can boil is essentially an emotional, psychological, and spiritual teaching.

There is another, less tangible ingredient which flows between, around, and within the fire, the singing, and the dancing, weaving them together. This might be called the "emotional atmosphere" of the dance. It is a dominating force, extremely influential in the activation of num. The different ingredients of the dance stimulate and respond to each other, forming a gestalt which is more than its parts. This emotional atmosphere fluctuates in pace and intensity over different dances and during any one dance. Experience and sensitivity are needed to guide this atmosphere toward healing.

In one dance, for example, two men are moaning and shrieking their kowhedili. These expressions of healing stimulate their kia. The moaning and shrieking continue after the singing has stopped. The men moan out: "It is hot, hot. Help us with this pain," and then they sing along with the women as the num songs begin again. What may have appeared as linear causal links between specific elements in the dance quickly evaporate into a process in which all parts reciprocally affect each other.

Sometimes when kia is not imminent, the atmosphere is unexciting, routine. The dancing and singing seem perfunctory and listless. There is a lot of casual conversation. The emotional atmosphere is permeable. The concentration of the singers and dancers is easily broken; they are often distracted. The dance doesn't seem to "come together" or "take off."

But when num is boiling, the atmosphere becomes exciting, unpredictable. Emotional sparks begin to fly, and sometimes, suddenly, they catch fire. A dancer starts to tremble and then suddenly howls into the sky: "Oh, my father, I need help. This num has got me. This num is throwing me down." Immediately the singing leaps to a new level of intensity, almost before the dancer has uttered his cry. The dancers stomp harder, almost fiercely, as if they have anticipated or ushered in the lonely, painful howl. When the emotional atmosphere is as charged as this, the dance is on the track toward kia. Even outrageous sexual jokes from the bystanders do not deflect the dance from its course. Such jokes become just another part of the dance, incorporated during the rush to kia.

When there is no clear and compelling reason for a dance, the decision to hold one depends on the mood of the people. It then becomes a question of marshaling interest and support for the idea. Someone asks another person if he would be willing to have a dance at his camp. The other person says: "Not tonight. Who would collect all the firewood?" And so another host camp for the dance must be found. Once the site has been settled upon, someone may come over and say: "I hear there will be a dance at your camp tonight. That's good. We will be there. My camp will come." And the word spreads in this informal way. When some critical "mass" has been reached and arrives at the camp, the dance can get underway. Making the decision and gathering the necessary support are subtle processes. How these processes unfold helps establish the emotional atmosphere.

Gau describes how a dance at his camp was started and supported in such a way as to undermine its very strength: "It wasn't such a good dance last night. The people spent a lot of time eating, and so we started late. Then Dau's gang from the other camp came over and formed the mainstay, while many of the people from our own camp didn't participate. Even before we ate I was thinking this wasn't going to be a good night, because for it to be good, you've got to have lots of people singing, and last night we had only a few. Dau's gang came late; they held up the dance. I had already given up on them. I had said, 'No dance tonight,' and then they came and we started after all." Gau's own ambiguous attitude was yet another factor in creating an emotional atmosphere that detracted from the strength of the dance.

Dancing in one's own camp, with one's immediate family singing and dancing alongside, creates an especially supportive atmosphere. Gau says it is easier to kia when he is dancing at his own camp: "You can really put your heart into it when you're in your own camp. They're your own people there, and they'll give you water. But you might go to a strange camp and they might deny you water." Gau always pays special attention to his wife, one of the stronger, more enduring singers, and she pays special attention to him. Her eyes often follow him around the circle as she sings, and he looks to her often for assurance, increasingly so as kia approaches. He says her voice stands out for him among the women.

Young Debe says he is more comfortable dancing at his own camp than at his father-in-law's, with whom he has a traditional Kung avoidance relationship: "When I dance at my own home, I can dance stronger, because I'm not ashamed. When I dance at my father-in-law's, I'm ashamed because my father-in-law sees everything that I do."

Not only is the combination of persons important, but also the attitudes they bring. Whether a particular person attends a particular dance is not always a foregone conclusion. Especially in dances where there is no acute illness, persons in other camps, even though they may hear the singing, may choose not to attend. Their attitude toward the dance may keep them away. "No one has come to give me num, " Wi says to me. "You're the only one who has asked thus far about my condition, even though I've been feeling badly for almost a month. My spleen bothers me, it doesn't let me eat. I didn't go over to the next camp for a healing during the dance last night. My heart refused to go."

"Did those at the dance know you were ill?" I ask.

"Yes," he says, "but I replied, 'Today my heart doesn't like to dance.' My wife didn't go either. Our hearts didn't like it so we didn't go."

"Did anyone from the camp which held the dance ask you to come over?"

"No, but someone from my camp went over to the dance and came back and said to me, 'There's a dance over there. Come over.' But I said no." Wi is expressing many feelings about that dance when he says his "heart doesn't like to dance."

The emotional atmosphere is also expressed in the different moods or qualities of the dance, and the transitions – sometimes abrupt, sometimes gradual – into and out of those moods. There is, for example, the transition between light, fragmented, even desultory singing, and strong, exciting, sensitively orchestrated singing. The dance develops from a gathering with the *potential* for num into an arena of boiling num.

A more generalized emotional atmosphere is also at work. Sometimes there is a lot of dancing at a water-hole or camp, maybe two or three dances in a week. Other times, there is a paucity or even absence of dancing, not even one dance a month. It is clear that in the former case the idea of dancing is "in the air." Chance remarks tell the story, such as "We at Xaixai are strong singers," "The people of Xaixai can dance every night and past every dawn," or "My finger is infected, but I can still sing tonight."

In the periods without dancing, little interest is expressed in dancing. All types of excuses are offered, such as "How can we dance tonight? The women are weary. Tomorrow they must collect mongongo," or "This heat is too much for us. If we were to dance, we would fall from the heat." Sometimes a very delicate balance exists in a camp, and when the mood shifts in several persons, dancing either springs forth or becomes dormant.

Growing up as a Kung produces certain characteristics: a belief in the power and efficacy of num, a familiarity with the dance, a realization that num is at its peak strength at the dance, and a seeking of num in the dance. Because of these beliefs and expectations, the Kung can respond to the dance so that it not only alters but also enhances their consciousness. If the dance did not exist within such a deeply supportive context, the environment could lead persons to block out its stimulation, or could provoke distorted altered states, such as confusion and what in the West is called "anxiety." In fact, most of the Kung, as they seek num, do at one time or another close off the stimulation of the dance. Their fear becomes too great. Moreover, confusion is characteristic at different stages of healing. Num can overwhelm experienced healers as well as those who are inexperienced or still seeking num. But the unusual feature of the Kung approach to healing is that so many remain open to the dance's stimulation, and for so many confusion is a prelude to healing. Even those who, out of fear, have given up their search for num generally come to the dance, letting its environment affect their consciousness, though now more subtly and less intensely.

Not every Kung becomes a healer. The environment of the healing dance does not propel every healer into healing. There are individual predisposing factors that may explain some of these different responses. Healers have certain characteristics that seem to encourage their search for num and their openness to the dance environment itself.

But the fact of num heating up to the boiling point remains critical. That fact must be met and accepted. The passage into some unknown territory of the mind and heart must be recognized and made. The fear and pain of that boiling num, the terror of that passage, is faced and overcome as individuals die to themselves. From the death of the individual Kung personality, the rebirth of the Kung healer must come. The essence of the educational process becomes: How can persons learn to receive boiling num without being overwhelmed by its fear and pain? How can persons learn to control their boiling num so that they can apply it in healing? And how can persons be encouraged to receive hotter num, to die to themselves more completely, and to be reborn into a stronger kia? The Kung do not formulate the issues of education in this manner, but such questions touch on the fundamental dynamic in their education for healing.

That education focuses on learning to recognize and cross experiential thresholds, which mark transitions into and out of kia and healing. At the dance, certain educational techniques and processes come into play, each dealing directly with that threshold. There is the process of putting in and receiving num. There are also the different ways in which singers and other dancers help healers deal with their emerging num.

Underlying all these processes is the idea of regulating num. Healers are encouraged to have their num boil as hot as they can handle, and yet still apply that boiling num to healing. They are encouraged to go as deeply into kia as they can or want, as long as they can then pull sickness while in kia. This balancing does not have to occur every time a healer experiences kia. But the emphasis is on a marriage between the depth of kia and its control. If there is no application to healing, kia becomes of little value.

What one learns is closely tied up with how one is taught. What one is trying to learn is to activate, accept, and regulate one's boiling num. What one is trying to teach another is this same activation, acceptance, and regulation. One is trying to accept and regulate one's own num; others are trying to help one do so. Self-regulation of num and helping others to manage their own num are two sides of the same coin. Each releases the healing power of num.

Putting num into someone for the first time; working on someone who is in the throes of an intense, uncontrollable kia; helping a healer cool down her boiling num or cooling down one's own num; leading around a healer in kia so that he can heal others – all these are ways in which num is regulated. All are expressed in a similar set of behaviors, including physical support and contact, rubbing and massage, and the use of hot and cold substances, such as sweat, burning coals, and water.

Toma Zho describes the putting of num into a student seeking kia: "When the dance starts, I say to the student, 'Today, I'm going to dance num with you.' For example, we're at a dance together, dancing. I come over to him and say, 'Tonight I think I see some for you. When you do it, you'll see it.' After the student experiences kia, I rub him and rub him and rub him. That's how I do it. I teach him how to pull sickness, which is how to control num. We can do it three or four times, and maybe on the fourth time if I can see the student doing it, then I carry him around, I take him from person to person, and he pulls sickness through me. There are different ways of doing this. In one way, I pull the student I'm teaching, and then the sick one, and then the student, and then the sick one, and then the student, and all the things go into me. In another way, the one I'm teaching holds on to me around my back and hangs over my shoulders, and I pull, and the stuff goes through my body to his. And in another way, the one I'm teaching is in front of me, pulling, and I'm behind him, working on his belly as he works on the sick ones. The num comes through my body into him."

As the num is being put in or activated, care is given to putting in certain amounts and to managing it in certain directions, so that it becomes usable for healing. The "putting in" and "regulation" of num are essentially one process.

When healers are experiencing difficulty in kia, the regulation of num becomes particularly critical. When people are experiencing the death of kia, others who may also be in kia work assiduously on them, holding and rubbing them, and also holding and rubbing each other. The num boils strongly during that death, and it sometimes takes several persons, in their collective effort, to regulate it. As they are trying to cool down the num of a person in death, their own num, through contact with the one in death, is sometimes heated up. In fact, working on another is a way of helping to activate one's own num. When num boils violently, its effects spread to those in close proximity.

Nai speaks of the work the singers may do: "We singers help a person in kia because his soul is separated from him, and if we don't rub him, num will kill him. We rub his gebesi in order to calm down the num, because when he experiences kia, the num comes up his sides along the spine and it drives out his breath. Then you can't see his breathing. And if you don't see his breathing, a person is dead. First we rub our hands on our own hair. Then we rub our hands on his belly in a motion from the upper center of his body down the sides, in a direction opposite to the rising num. After we do that, he goes kowhedili, and then we know his breath is coming again, because he is driving it out with the kowhedili."

Regulating the depth and control of num has internal and external expressions. As the dancer struggles to regulate his num, resources at the dance are marshaled to assist him. During periods of difficult kia, the dance focuses on regulation. When, for example, the singers feel that too many persons are in kia, they direct their help to the specific problem at hand. Nai explains: "What we singers try to do is to help. We go and pick up a live coal and rub it in our hands, and then we rub our hair and heads and then our armpits. Then we rub the body of the one in kia until his gebesi bursts, and he starts to kowhedili. Then we leave that one and go to another healer in kia and repeat the operation until his gebesi burst. Then when the healers start to move, they can take care of each other and pull our sickness."

If all the healers have fallen in kia, help is still available. Nai again explains: "Then we sing strongly so that the music goes up. Then others who haven't fallen can work on those who have fallen. They can put their souls back into them, so that those who have fallen may start to cry and live again."

There are many at the dance who can help guide a person toward kia. Central among these helpers is the teacher, the one who has agreed to "put the num in." The teacher remains central, even though not everyone seeking num has an explicit relationship with a teacher, and others beside the teacher try to help by putting num in. Although the teacher functions most extensively in relationship to a person still seeking kia, the student, the teaching function also emerges at dances between experienced healers. When such healers feel their own num is weak, they may ask another to work on them, to help them activate their num. Those who teach the young Kung to kia are usually those who are called upon for help by their more experienced colleagues.

The relationship of the teacher to the young person still seeking num is in a sense a paradigm for the teaching functions. The close familial relationship of teacher to student is a critical factor. They are in constant and intimate contact, throughout the day, not just at the dance. A father teaching his son may say before a particular dance: "Tonight, I'm going to put num into you. Tonight I'm going to dance you." He also works directly on his son at the dance. But this should not obscure the countless times the father is teaching his boy how to meet his fears and face the unknown just by virtue of their being and doing things together, whether on the long, dry marches, or in hunting, or in stressful social interactions. When the teacher's family ties with the student are less intimate, the boundaries of the "teaching" are only slightly more marked.

It is important to live near one's teacher. This increases contact during the day and ensures that teacher and student will be at many dances together. When the teacher is not a close relative, this physical proximity is often missing.

Twikumsa is a quiet, serious man in his early thirties who has yet to receive num, even though Bau, a strong and experienced healer, is his mother. "Are you seeking num?" I ask.

Twikumsa hesitates for a moment and then, with something less than conviction, says, "Yes, I like num, and I'm seeking it."

"Who is your teacher?"

"The man who wants to teach me is Kamto. He is not here at Xaixai now. I asked Kamto to teach me. I said to him, 'Kamto, help me with num.' "

"And then?"

"But then, later – " Twikumsa becomes more resigned, "he left me and started living elsewhere. And so today at dances when I start to feel pain, I sit down."

"Are you looking for another teacher?"

"No," Twikumsa replies, "I don't want anybody else to teach me. The only other teacher I know is Toma Zho."

"If Kamto doesn't come back, would you ask Toma Zho for num?"

"If Kamto doesn't return and I still want num, I'll go to Toma Zho."

"What about your mother, Bau? She has num."

Twikumsa speaks definitively: "My mother has num, but she doesn't help me. She doesn't give me num, but she always pulls me when I'm sick."

"Twikumsa, do you believe you will get num some time?"

"It's not only if your body is right that you do num," he responds. "For example, it may be that people refuse, as today Toma Zho refuses to give me num. Because people can refuse."

"Are you still seeking num?" I ask.

"At first," he says, "when num gave me pain and I feared it, it was stupid to fear it, because today I really want it and I don't have any people to teach me. I don't see anyone today to help me."

The teacher's physical proximity does not guarantee that the student will get num, nor does the teacher's absence guarantee that num will not be received. Twikumsa's own fears of num, and doubts about his ability to handle it, seem to be factors in his situation. But having one's teacher nearby helps.

It is very difficult to say when a teaching relationship begins or ends. As learning about kia is part of socialization, in one sense it begins at birth and ends at death. Students usually ask a healer to give them num or are offered num by a healer. But the start of a teaching relationship is in practice more gradual. After some work together, the teacher-student relationship is more firmly established. When students are "completely learned," they presumably no longer need a full-time teacher. But the idea of being "completely learned" is a matter of judgment; even the teacher and student may disagree.

Receiving num for the first time is only the beginning of a long educational process. Certainly there is an exceptional quality to these first contacts with num, and more so to those times when one is said to have "drunk num." But num usually must be put into someone many times before that person comes to "own" or "master" num. Wi, an old, experienced healer, describes how a young healer might act. Though he might claim to be "completely learned" or "all finished," in the next breath he would say, "Give me a little more, put your hands on my stomach." Wi would respond to such a request by doing it.

The desire or need for an extra input of num seems ubiquitous. Old and experienced healers are no exception. Experienced healers may ask others to put num into them once again, whether it be at a dance where they feel their num is weak, or during a period when they feel their num is weak or absent. Wi talks about this: "I might go to Tsaa and say, 'I haven't got num today. Give me a little.' Or at a dance I would say that. Now Kinachau is one I can always ask for help. I say, 'Today I haven't got anything. Help me.' And Kinachau always puts his hands on me and rubs me. Then I start to shiver, and I feel it going into me, and I say, 'Yes, it's coming up in me.' I also work with Toma Zho, who says to me, 'Today I haven't got anything at all. Let's you and I dance together. Maybe if you have something, you'll give it to me.' And then Toma Zho and I dance together, and I lead him around, and num comes up inside me and bursts. When num comes up, it's burning. And Toma Zho says, 'Wi, you've got some num. I'll put my hands on your stomach to get some.' There are other times when I say to Toma Zho, 'My son-in-law, I am sick. Come and do me. Come and carry me over.' Then Toma Zho comes and bursts num open so that we both can have some. He takes me over and does me until I get num. Then I go back to my camp saved."

8 Career of the Healer

WI PROVIDES an overview of the "career" or life-long development of the male healer: "The num of the young man is very painful, like fire. The old ones, the ones in whom the num has become weak, their num is light because they have given most of it to younger ones who are now struggling with the pain of it. The middle-aged man has power, pulling power, more so than the old man."

The two most relevant variables in determining male career patterns are age and experience with num. Age is more than mere chronological (natal) age; it also signifies the readiness for various life responsibilities. Age and experience with num interact. There are several key phases in the development of the healer: preseeking, early, middle, late, and old-age. However, these phases only highlight aspects of the career. The life-long development of the healer is one continuous process, and it does not unfold at a constant rate nor in a linear direction.

With notable exceptions, there seems to be a general age limit for beginning to seek num. Boys are not encouraged to seek seriously before their middle or late teens. In the preseeking phase, they may dance at the evening dances as early as nine or ten years old, and on occasion a young teenager may dance quite a bit for extended periods. The general feeling among Kung is that num would be too painful for such young persons. Practically all of them will eventually seek num, more or less seriously. Even at this early stage, signs of future development as a healer can be perceived: "That youngster will some day drink num. He dances with his heart in it." But for most boys, it is too early to tell: "I cannot say about that one. He is still too young. And he only plays at dancing."

During the early phase, from the late teens to the mid-twenties, most males seek num. They go to dances and dance for the express purpose of receiving num. In the late teens the search may not be very serious. The emphasis re-

---

Page 141: An aspiring healer

mains on dancing as an expressive, artistic mode or an opportunity for self-display. The search for num becomes more active and serious after several years of dancing. But for some, the search is serious from the start.

Among those actively seeking num, there are many possible outcomes in this early phase, and they unfold in a dynamic manner. A person seeking num may or may not subsequently kia. If he does, he may or may not subsequently learn to pull sickness.

Young Debe is typical of one seeking num who has yet to kia. His fear keeps him from the taste of num: "I have felt the pain of num and I fear it. I double over from it. I feel the pain anytime during the dance, not just when they are putting num in. I am afraid. I am afraid of the pain. My fear of kia is like being afraid of the fire. Num is hot, hot like fire. If you stick your hand in fire, it hurts." Most young Kung who have yet to experience kia are like Debe. They still actively seek num, going to dances and dancing hard, but often they sit down when their fear overwhelms them. As Wi says: "The young ones fear num and cry out. They cry tears. They cry out, 'It's painful. It hurts.' "

A minority of young Kung who have yet to kia essentially stop seeking num. Though they may dance, they do not dance often or strongly. It may be said of such a person: "He hasn't got it because he doesn't put anything into his heart. He just dances. He's just going to live." More important, these Kung do not see themselves as active seekers. In a sense, they have given up hope of receiving num; they believe the pain is too much for them. Kanka is one such person. "We all seek num," he says, "we all want to pull sickness. I sought it but wasn't given it, so I don't seek it now. I was seeking num so if my wife was sick, I could pull her, and if my child was sick, I could pull her. When people danced, my teacher and I went to dance, and we danced together. Then he rubbed his sweat into me. I felt those thorns, those thorns. Then I shivered. I stopped dancing and my insides were shivering. Then I was afraid and I stopped. I was afraid of the pain."

"Did you tell your teacher about the pain?" I ask.

"I didn't tell him," Kanka continues. "I just hid when the dancing started. I said to myself, 'That's painful.' When people started up dancing at other times, I stayed back at my hut. I didn't come to the dances. When people asked why I didn't come to dances anymore, I would say that I was too tired. My teacher taught me properly, but it was myself who felt the pain."

Young Kung in this early phase of seeking may or may not kia. Even those like Kanka, who have apparently given up on num, may at some later point come back to the dance and drink num then. In any case, experiencing kia is one of the crucial points in the career of a healer.

Bo is in this early phase of seeking. He has already experienced kia. The pain he has felt during kia makes him cautious, but despite his disclaimers, he is considered to be an active, almost avid seeker of num. He goes to all the dances, dances strongly, and goes into kia often and intensely. Bo talks about his seeking num: "The husband of Kore, now dead, first gave num to me. I didn't feel or think anything that time. I thought I was dying because I didn't feel anything. Now I know a little more. Today I know what to expect a little bit in my chest and gebesi. So today when it happens, I say, 'I'm kia.' At some dances I refuse, and when I feel myself kia, I step out and sit down. I refuse it after I feel myself almost kia, after I feel my flesh tingling in my stomach and gebesi. I stop. I dance, but then I stop if it comes up. But I don't always run from num. I'm still young and haven't pulled sickness yet."

Typically, dancers such as Bo are struggling with their fear of num. Though they may back away, cooling off their num, they continually try to let their num boil. Wi describes the violent style of such young dancers, which seems to express and substantiate their intense pain and fear: "Look at the young ones. At the beginning they shriek and shudder, but they don't have any pulling power. It hurts them, but they can't pull well. Also, they don't see properly. They still haven't learned properly. They do the 'tricks' but they don't have the pulling power."

Racing headlong into the bush, wildly climbing trees, or

throwing around burning sticks – these behaviors express the pain of num and are taken as a sign that the healer still does not have his num under control. These unpredictable, at times antisocial behaviors, though not encouraged, can be tolerated if they are part of the dancer's movement toward healing. Young persons like Bo, on their way to learning to pull sickness, often behave in such ways. Experienced healers, whose healing abilities are proven, sometimes do. But with Dau, who has learned to pull but whose healing abilities are not proven, such behavior is less tolerated. Persons say that Dau's num is not strong, because he does so many "tricks." When someone who is not likely to heal consistently acts in unpredictable, antisocial ways, his behavior is actively discouraged. Very few reach that point. They usually have already stopped or interrupted their search for num. Their fear has become too much to handle.

Whereas experiencing kia is the first crucial point in the career of a healer, being able to heal is the second. One must be able to experience not only beginning kia but also full kia, so one can pull out sickness, in order to be recognized as a healer. Gau and Dau are examples of healers in this middle phase.

Between the ages of approximately twenty-five and forty, the question of whether a person will become a healer is usually settled. The probability of becoming a healer increases until about thirty, then decreases. Of the men who eventually become healers, most do so by thirty-five. If a person has not learned to kia and pull by forty, it generally signifies that he is not meant to drink num. These ages are not absolute nor do they demarcate deadlines of "success" or "failure." They represent a general pattern which does not entail connotations of prestige or stigma.

Those men between twenty-five and thirty-five who are seeking num but have yet to kia occupy a place of particular ambiguity and tension in the development of healers. Some seem like good "candidates" for num. Their attitude toward receiving num is often optimistic or, if cautious, at least neutral. Others seem destined not to have num. Their attitude toward num is dominated by fear. They are often resigned to being unable to drink num. For still others, it is unclear whether or not they will drink num; their attitude is ambiguous.

The more uncertain the outcome, the more ambiguity and tension about receiving num the seeker feels. Some of this tension is also expressed by his teacher and others connected with the search. If he receives num, the tension disappears. If he does not receive num by about forty, the idea that he is "not meant to drink num" becomes firmer. And by the time he is fifty or so, there is usually no ambiguity or tension, and no stigma, simply the statement that num is "against his nature," or that he is "no longer seeking num."

Tuka has just reached forty and has yet to kia. He still more or less seeks num, but he believes that perhaps he is not "meant to drink num": "When I was young, I danced it and danced it and sought it and sought it, but I was refused. God refuses, and I didn't take kia. Kinachau who is my teacher said to me, 'Let's dance and let me give you num.' But god refused and said, 'No, Tuka, you won't see num.' Kinachau is a good teacher. If god agrees, Kinachau can give you num. If god refuses, Kinachau can't give you num." I ask Tuka if he ever came close to kia. "I never felt any pain in my stomach during the dance, because when you feel pain in your gebesi, it means that god has agreed that you will have num. When you don't even feel that, it means god has refused. At first, when Kinachau went into kia, he worked on me. Then when he found out god refused, he didn't do me anymore."

Kinachau is somewhat less definite about Tuka's prospects, though not overly optimistic. It is as if, out of respect for Tuka, his nephew, Kinachau does not want to foreclose irreversibly the possibility of his getting num.

One man, Hotun, who has just received num though he is almost forty and showed no prior inclination for num, causes me surprise. It is as if Hotun has suddenly become a different person in relation to num. Kaha, his teacher, has a similar reaction to mine: "I was surprised when Hotun entered kia. But today he does it, and yet he also fears it."

Kaha recalls his own reception of num: "I too was old when I started and I feared it, but people carried me and caused me to pull sickness. They said, 'Pull, pull.' And so I pulled." The actual age at which Kaha drank num is not clear. But he had an open attitude toward the possibility of Hotun's reception of num.

Although Tuka does not kia, he goes to all of the dances at his camp and many at other camps. He dances through most of the night and into the early morning. He is also one of the more reliable guardians at a dance. He knows how to work on those in kia. He often works on Kinachau, massaging him strongly, holding him near the fire, catching his falling body. In many ways, Tuka is a teacher for his teacher. This interchange of teaching and learning is very much a part of the Kung education for kia.

This middle phase of the search for num is especially dynamic. The definitions of when one is a healer and when one is not are open to question, and the Kung may disagree about any one person's status. But as an overall phase in the development of healers, this middle period is not characterized by ambiguity or tension. Many of those who sought num have already become healers; though the process was painful, the outcome was rarely in doubt. Although pressures are felt by those who come into this middle period still seeking num, the fact that there already are enough healers to meet the needs of the people overshadows the dilemmas of any individual still searching for num. At a dance, the emphasis is more on working with someone whose num is boiling than on putting num into someone who has been dancing for many years but has yet to kia.

To be a *geiha,* a healer who is "completely learned" or experienced, one must be able not only to enter kia and pull sickness, but also to pull dependably, frequently, and strongly. It is this quality of how one enters kia and pulls sickness that becomes crucial in the late phase. Bau, Kinachau, Wi, and Toma Zho are all acknowledged as experienced healers.

Experienced healers are usually in their mid-forties, fifties, and sixties. For perhaps twenty or thirty years or more they have entered kia and pulled sickness at dances. They can be counted on and turned to when the need is great. They are often called upon by other healers to help with especially difficult cases. And they can heal sick ones without a full-scale healing dance. They are usually the ones who teach others and give the young ones num.

Experienced healers are still vulnerable to the vagaries of num. At a dance, they can be overwhelmed by num, feeling confusion and pain, exhibiting "wild" behavior more appropriate to those new to num. For a period of time, they can feel tired or sick, and their num can become "weak" or "nothing." In such cases, healing is less available.

Not all those considered experienced are equally powerful. Some are quite undistinguished. They kia and heal, and do it strongly, but they do not have a reputation for strength. They are more like journeymen practitioners. There is less consensus about their effectiveness. On the contrary, there are healers, like Kau Dwa and Wa Na, who is considered a *geiha ama ama*, a healer of "real" or "greatest power." Indeed, Wa Na is the standard of healing power in the Dobe area.

Old age initiates a final phase in the healer's career. Those who do not have num may continue dancing into their fifties and even be active guardians. But as they get older, it is less likely that they will continue dancing because of the great physical exertion required. And since they have no num to offer, there is not that much pressure on them to continue. But older persons in their late sixties, seventies, and even eighties who are without num usually come to the dance, sitting quietly at one of the talking fires. As they often have ailments, they receive especially intensive and frequent healing. As village elders in a culture that deeply respects age, their presence lends a note of authority and approval.

Koto is an older person who has never received num. Approaching seventy-five, he is respected throughout the camps at Xaixai. It was his wife's family who first claimed

Xaixai as a watering place, and she and he are acknowledged as Xaixai's "owners." He is considered the leading authority on kinship. Koto has never drunk num, but he continues to respect it. Like all Kung, he has unlimited access to it and continues to use it. He feels somewhat nostalgic about his attempts to get num but completely accepts not getting it. Lacking num is not a part of his self-definition. And as he stresses with great satisfaction, he need not himself own num when there is always enough available to him. He speaks of and for the group's num, which resides in individual healers but which, when activated, belongs to all.

"Koto, have you ever had num yourself?"

"What sort of a person do you think I am?" he replies, a twinkle emerging from his serious mien. "I've never had it."

"Why is that?" I wonder.

"I don't know why," he reflects. "I've never seen num. When I was a young man, I used to dance, and the ladies danced in front of me. Oh, they admired me. I got married, and the ladies still danced in front of me and my wife would sing. Now I'm old and I have nothing."

"Did anyone in your family have num?"

"My father did, but he died when I was young. The only one who had num was one of my uncles. But he didn't teach me. He pulled sickness from me, but he didn't put num in me. If he did, I'd have it now."

"And what of your family now?"

"None of my four sons has num. Nor my grandchildren. They are just like their parents. They don't do it." Koto becomes thoughtful and hesitates, then adds softly. "My sister's kids have it though. Kinachau is one of my nephews. We ask different ones for healing. We ask all those who can heal. Who we ask depends on who is at the dance."

"Then who caused you to survive?"

Koto smiles. "I'm surprised we have survived. Perhaps god said, 'These people are just going to live without num while some others will have it.' " Koto pauses briefly, then continues, gesturing boldly. "I'm puzzled by the situation here at Xaixai, at this one water-hole, where certain people drink all the num and leave none for one family!"

"But your family seems in good health," I say. "It is large and doing well. Do you really need num?" My question is framed in mock seriousness.

Again Koto smiles. "Yes, god has carried us through."

As the experienced healers reach their seventies, many "retire" from active healing. A severe sickness can bring them out of retirement. They may heal someone without a dance, or they may go to a dance, take a few turns slowly around the fire, then heal with measured, intense gestures. They are most likely to heal when someone in their immediate family is ill. But for all practical purposes they cannot be counted upon to kia and heal at a dance.

Tsaa, once a strong, experienced healer claims he no longer does num. But it is known that he heals members of his own family in small gatherings, where he and several women sing, or he alone sings. And despite his disclaimer, there is uncertainty among the Kung whether he might appear at a dance and heal again. This doubt goes to the heart of retirement. Retirement is reversible. "Yes, Tsaa goes into kia and pulls sickness," says Toma Zho, "though he hasn't been called out today, so he doesn't pull today. But he still dances. He used to be very strong. And he is strong today. It's just that his chest bothers him. But even today, if the right dance started up, you would see him in it."

Tsaa and I talk about how growing old affects num, and how num affects growing old. "I did num for many years," he says, "but this chest of mine made the num disappear from me, ever since the blood started forming in my chest. When I was young, I was an expert, and you've seen me work. I found that when I danced, my chest hurt me so that I couldn't catch my breath. Then it all stopped. Now I'm completely off num."

"What if one of your grandchildren got sick?" I ask. "Could you heal them? Could you do it a little?"

"I would not do a little," he replies sadly. "I would not do even that. When I try it, my breath fails and I am unable to catch my breath. I stop breathing. It's out of the question. But there are others who could heal my sick child." Tsaa speaks more softly, greater sadness in his voice. "It's awful to have to sit by and look at a sick child and say, 'Why can't I help this child?' If there's a dance in the camp, I sit and look at it with a heavy heart, saying, 'I wish I could dance.'

"But, Tsaa, how do you know that you have lost your num?"

"Well," he reflects, "I can just look at myself and know that I don't have any. I see my chest full of blood and I say, 'Why can't I do num like the rest of them?' and my heart is heavy. When I was a young man, I was the only one who had num, at dances or elsewhere. And now both my dancing and healing are gone."

"Are you seeking help for your chest from other healers?"

"At the dances I get pulled, and I get a little chest massage. My wife also gives me a lot of chest massages and she prepares herbs for me to drink. But I wonder how I can possibly get cured. I don't expect that it will get better. If I got the right num, it might get better, but I haven't seen such yet."

"Tsaa," I continue, "why would a healer decide to give up num?"

"If it weren't for a sickness like mine," he states, "anyone should keep it up until death."

There are those whose num becomes weak as they age, especially as they experience the debilities of aging. Also, as their num leaves them, they become aged. But as Tsaa points out, retirement is not a foregone conclusion simply because one gets old. There are, in fact, a few persons whose num gets stronger with age. While their contemporaries retire, they continue active.

Wa Na is already in her early eighties. Though completely blind, hard of hearing, and slow moving, needing a walking stick, her num is still accumulating strength. She exemplifies the Kung belief that, for some persons, their num keeps them young. In experiencing kia and healing, they stay young. Tsaa talks about Wa Na: "Wa Na still feels healthy. Her body is still holding up. She's fantastic. She's a terror with num. That's a woman. Old as she is, she's still a healer."

The process of educating for healing has typical features. For example, though num originally came from god, men now teach or give num to other men. Also, they usually get num in their mid-twenties, occasionally in their early twenties or early thirties. Certain exceptions to this usual process are associated with powerful num. Special conditions seem to stimulate the appearance of powerful num and to signify its continuing availability.

Toma Zho is considered by other Kung to be a powerful healer. He agrees. When I ask him how other Kung get their num, he asks me: "How do I know the others have num? So they dance and do it. But do they *really* know what they're doing? I don't know. Maybe it's the singing of the women that does it." I then ask him whether he heals with the other healers at Xaixai. "What other healers?" he challenges. "You think there are other healers here at Xaixai?" Toma Zho loves to joke, but he nonetheless meant what he said.

Toma Zho's father had num but did not give it to him. Toma Zho received num directly from god: "When I was about fourteen or fifteen, I was asleep. God grabbed me by the legs and sent me out into the bush at night. Out there, he gave me a small tortoise and told me, 'Leave this tortoise here. Then in the morning get your father to degut it and put num into it, and that will be your num.' And then god took me farther and I was crying in the dark. My father came looking for me and found me crying and carried me back to the fireside. In the morning I said, 'Father, come and see this tortoise. Fix it for me and put num in it, and give it to me because this is what god has given me. Fix it and give it to me so I may keep it, so that when you are dying, I can use it and I'll save you.' But my father refused. He just killed the tortoise, roasted it, and ate it. Then the skin of my father's throat parted, and we could see his windpipe exposed. Then god told me, 'For what your father has done, I'm going to kill him. The thing I gave to you that he ate is killing him.' And I refused and I said, 'My father won't die.' And I took another tortoise with num in it and dropped burning coals into the shell. And then I put the shell to my father's lips and he drank the smoke. The same day the skin above and the skin below came together and closed, and my father lived. Then god said to me, 'See what your father's arrogance has done to him. You tell him to stop that and not to do it again or else I will really kill him next time.' And that's how I got what I have. That's where I started it, and today I carry the people in the different camps. If someone is sick, I go to them."

Toma Zho's early vision and gift of num were both unusual and startling. So were some of the immediate effects. As Toma Zho explains, "I danced only after this experience, and kia came only after this experience; but *right* after!" He adds that twice after the vision, god took him out to the bush alone, and he went into kia. The first kia is a time of especially strong fear. But his two solo, god-induced experiences of kia were different from the usual fear-filled first experiences: "How could I be afraid during these kia? God killed every thought. He wiped me clean. Then he took my soul away whirling. My thoughts whirled."

Xam is a youngster of only eleven or twelve. Yet already there is something special about his relation to num. He is a talented dancer, and he dances more frequently than his peers. Most unusual, he seems already to have experienced kia. In the view of others, he has great potential for becoming a powerful healer. Toma Zho describes a particular dance: "I've looked at Xam and didn't see anything there until recently. But a few months ago we had a dance in the bush, and the boy started crying and was carried around the dance crying by his playmates. He was witless. His father was away. I said, 'This boy's already drunk num.' Then I told one of the women, 'Stop singing, because this boy's father, who is teaching him about num, is far away, and I'm not going to work on him. You're going to give this boy a lot of pain if you keep singing.' Then the women stopped."

Toma Zho tries to figure out what it is that has allowed Xam to kia while so young: "When I see a boy like that, I say: 'What is it that sets him apart? His heart is full, full of dancing.' It's his heart. He loves to dance. When the singing starts, he's not the least bit afraid of people, so he dances full out, and that's what helps him to kia." Where others approach kia with fear and caution, Xam approached it with striking enthusiasm.

In rare cases, healers lose their num. Whether they want to give up their num or are pressured to give it up by others never seems to be clear. More than likely, it is some combination of both. The reasons for losing num are also unclear.

One reason seems to be the death of more than the usual number of persons despite a healer's efforts, especially when those who die are in the healer's immediate family and when they die, literally, in the healer's arms. The assumption is that healers should be able to save those in their immediate family unless they are obviously terminal patients. And if someone dies in their arms, then the healers can be more easily singled out as responsible for the lack of a cure.

Yet when a person dies in the arms of the most powerful healers, like Wa Na, the assumption is usually made that it was time for the ill one to die. Wa Na's strength is not questioned; god's will in taking the ill one is acknowledged. It is only when healers are merely "experienced" or, worse, "inexperienced" that a death imputes shortcomings to their num. A series of deaths can signify that their num is ineffective or even bad. It is then that the healer is asked to give up healing.

Although the failure to save members of one's family seems to be an underlying cause for losing num, the loss is also connected with the breaking of food taboos. The explicit explanation for a loss of num is usually an infraction of the dietary rules which govern those who work with num. Yet there also is some ambiguity and flexibility about the application of dietary rules to healers.

Of the two persons I meet at Xaixai who have apparently

lost their num, one is a young healer, perhaps in his late twenties, who comes from Nokaneng. He appeared at Xaixai in a very depressed state, physically and psychologically. He lies around the camp or moves slowly about. His facial expression is blank, sometimes pained, usually withdrawn. He seems to have trouble taking care of himself. Wi says of him: "He is very sick. It's come from his legs, and it's killing him. He's being attacked by his ancestors." It is said that his father and his wife died in his arms as he was trying to heal them. He was told to stop dancing, because his num was bad. He came to Xaixai, in part to visit relatives, in part to seek a cure.

The other person is Kashay, a warm, jovial man in his late fifties. Though somewhat of a loner, he was once head of an active, important camp at Xaixai. Originally married to a Xaixai owner, he is now a widower. Kashay is unusual in that he prefers to be alone rather than endure "poor company." Though something of an enigma, especially as regards his exact relationship to num, he is liked and respected. According to some, Kashay not only experienced kia and healed when he was younger, but he still does.

Gau, Kashay's stepson, says of him: "Kashay doesn't go to the dances, but when someone is sick, he comes to them. I've been healed by him. I was once very sick, and I was greatly surprised one day when he started to heal me. The women didn't sing. He just came over to me and started to sing to himself and pull me. That was before my son, Xam, was born. I've never seen Kashay pull since that time."

Tsaa offers a different view: "Kashay drinks num, but doesn't heal. Why? Is he selfish? He may have drunk num but he doesn't practice it. I can't tell how strong he is because he doesn't practice even though he's drunk it."

Wi offers another perspective on Kashay: "Kashay's got num but he doesn't dance. Kashay heals all the time."

"Isn't Kashay defeated in num?" I ask. Kashay himself told me that several times.

"No," replies Wi, "he's got it."

"But haven't you heard Kashay say he doesn't have it?"

"He's got it," Wi repeats firmly.

"If Kashay himself denies having num, was he kidding?"
"He's got it!"
"But I've never seen him dance."
"Yes, Kashay has got it!"
Though some still speak of Kashay's num, Kashay himself is unequivocal in saying that he has lost it. At about the time that he says he lost his num, three members of his immediate family died. One might assume that, as a healer, he was working on them beforehand, which could explain his loss of num. But he himself attributes his loss to the breaking of dietary taboos.
"Kashay, do you go to dances?" I ask.
"No," he replies. "I may watch a dance, but I don't join in. I don't dance. I didn't even dance as an adolescent. I'm a person who doesn't dance. When people sing, I sit and watch. Sometimes I'll watch; other times I won't even go over to see the dance."
"Have you ever healed?"
"At first when I healed, it was painful and I feared it. I quit, and today I have nothing."
"How many years did you heal?"
"I healed others for about five years. I stopped about twelve years ago."
"And what made you stop?"
"I ate many things," Kashay explains, "things like the blood of animals. And it made my num disappear. You fear a thing and your fear makes you lose your num. Your fear makes you forget num. We eat things such as *go*, and they make me lose my num. Eating that stuff spoils your num. It makes the num disappear. If you want to save your num, lay off that stuff."
"Do other healers eat that stuff?"
"Other healers eat it. Toma Zho eats it all the time. But Toma Zho is very powerful. He is terrific. He'll dance to dawn. He doesn't fear num. I fear it." It is possible that Kashay's num was becoming weak and that, in seeking an explanation, he was told that eating certain foods was the cause. In any case, Kashay's loss of num remains, like himself, enigmatic.

The career of a healer has a pattern. It is marked by three turning points: the first experiences of kia, the transformation of kia into healing, and the condition of becoming "completely learned." But as with the Kung's education for healing, that career pattern is fluid, and variations often occur. The career of a healer is rarely a linear, uninterrupted sequence of going into kia, healing, and becoming completely learned. Gau's career is more typical. He experiences kia and then abandons dancing for several years because his fear during kia remained too great. Then after his marriage he comes back to the dance, again experiences kia, and this time also heals.

A few Kung apparently receive num without fear, or at least without the intense fear almost everyone reports. Kana is such a person. It is said of him that "he didn't even hesitate but just picked num up." Toma Zho describes him: "Kana did not fear num, and the reason why Kana took it so easily was that he said to himself, 'I think it is my fate, my style to do num. It is my destiny to have num, so I don't fear it. I have asked people for it and they have given it to me.'" A few others claim to have received num directly from god and immediately thereafter to have entered kia. Still others lose their num, even after they have been pulling for a number of years.

There are aspects in almost everyone's career that are open to question, that are matters of judgment. There is not always complete consensus about whether a person experiences kia or heals, and especially about the strength of that kia and the effectiveness of the healing. Whether a person is completely learned and therefore an experienced healer is a matter of subtle judgment.

Toma Zho, for one, tries to convince others that he is not just experienced but that, among those who are experienced, he is especially powerful. He has in part convinced himself. But whether a healer is generally considered especially powerful is determined by more than that person's decision; it is determined, over a period of time, by different people's opinions, observations, and judgments. It is important to know whom healers cure and whom they do not. There is no simple formula to translate that evidence into a judgment about the healer's power. There can be disagreements about whether a person has in fact been cured. More important, since usually more than one healer works on a patient, sequentially or simultaneously, it is hard to give the "credit" for a successful cure to any one healer. The Kung approach to healing discourages individual recognition. To emerge, as has Wa Na, so clearly as a powerful healer, is unusual. At the very least, it is the result of many years of strong healing.

9 Female Perspectives

IN THE GIRAFFE DANCE, men more than women do the explicit healing, at least in terms of the laying on of hands. Yet many important aspects of the educational process and the career line are similar for men and women. These include the process of overcoming fear to accept boiling num and the increase in the power of num with age. Other aspects are characteristic of women only.

Almost every man tries to become a healer, and approximately half of them do. The Giraffe dance is the vehicle through which they learn to heal and in which they apply that knowledge. Approximately one-third of the women try to become healers, and most of them learn to kia, though only about ten percent of them also learn to heal. The Drum dance is the vehicle through which the women learn to kia, and in which some of them heal. About half the women who heal in the Drum also kia and heal in the Giraffe. The Drum dance is both "its own thing" and a preparation for the Giraffe.

But the Giraffe dance is not a "men's dance." It is not so labeled by the Kung. It is the central vehicle in Kung hunting-gathering life through which men and women together alter their state and activate their healing energy for all. In contrast, the Drum dance is more peripheral to the Dobe Kung, occurring less frequently, more unpredictably, and in a more localized fashion.

The conclusions about the Drum dance must remain more tentative than those about the Giraffe. The Drum dance, for example, is still less clearly understood by researchers than is the Giraffe. At least in the Dobe area, the Drum dance is also in a more formative or transitional stage. The dance nevertheless provides important perspectives on healing.

The differences in how men and women approach num are often a matter of form and style. Beneath these differences is an essential similarity in men's and women's ex-

Page 159: Bau falling in kia

periences of num. Kinachau is ambiguous when asked whether women heal in the Giraffe. But when he speaks about num, he is clear and definite: "Men's stuff and women's stuff is all the same!"

The Drum dance is said to have begun before recorded history. Be, an old and experienced healer, says that the Drum began "very long ago." She insists that it is not a "black peoples' thing" but in the very next breath remarks that it came from the black people with whom the Kung traded skins. Before the Drum, "women had no dance; only men had one." Yet "sometimes men gave their wives num so that they could heal them." Be's story, with its ambiguity and apparent conflict, is typical.

The Drum dance is a rather recent importation into the Dobe area, though it may have been going on for a long time among Kung elsewhere. Kung who say that the Drum dance is very old talk about its coming from a Kung area deep in Namibia. But the Kung hunting-gathering culture in that area had already been much influenced and changed by black culture even more than a hundred years ago. Whichever way the origin of the Drum is explained, the black influence is definitely there, as in the use of the drum, the existence of the male head drummer, and the sharp male-female distinctions.

The form of the Drum dance differs from that of the Giraffe. Drum dances occur in the afternoon as well as at night. Usually they last only a few hours. Women stand in a loose, narrow horseshoe shape beside a fire or sometimes around a fire. Depending on the size of the drum, the drummer sits or stands at the mouth of the horseshoe. He is invariably a man, although the Kung say that a woman can do it. Women clap and sing num songs for each other. Several of them may step inside the horseshoe and dance in place, sometimes experiencing kia. The Kung, especially the women, also refer to the women's kia experience in Drum as *tara,* which signifies not only the altered state of kia but particular behaviors which accompany kia. *Tara* means to "tremble" or "shimmy," and the women rhythmically tremble and shake while experiencing kia in the Drum.

There are many Drum songs, all of which may be sung in the course of a single dance. The songs, though structured similarly to Giraffe songs, are a distinct group. Whereas in the Giraffe the men dance in a forward progression around a circle to a main beat provided by clapping, in the Drum the women dance restrainedly or in place to a main beat provided by the drum. When kia is reached in the Drum, its own rhythm, a rapid vibration of the entire body, takes over and dominates the slower rhythms of the drum and the accompanying clapping and singing by the women who are not in kia.

The stages in the Drum dance parallel those in the Giraffe. There is the dancing in place and the heating of the num so kia can occur. With the onset of kia, the atmosphere of the dance becomes electric. Many women may fall to the ground from kia at once, shivering and shaking with the strength of the num. A stage of healing usually follows, as in the Giraffe, including the fact that some of the more powerful healers may travel to god's home in search of the endangered souls who are vulnerable to sickness.

Yet there are significant differences between the two dances. Although the kia in the Drum dance can result in healing, this transition is less crucial than in the Giraffe. There is in fact some ambivalence about the importance, or necessity, of healing in the Drum.

All who come to a Giraffe dance can participate. Not so with the Drum dance. Active participation in the Drum is limited to women dancers and the male drummer. On occasion, a man, usually older and experienced with the num of the Giraffe, may kia in the Drum with almost no preliminary dancing. Others, mostly men, stand or sit around the edges of the dancing place at separate fires and watch. They are observers more than participants. To some extent, they feel left out. Often they clown around, as if embarrassed, not knowing what to do. Among the participants, and especially between the participants and the audience, a clear separation of function exists, dependent on sex.

Women have the primary role in the Drum. They are the

dancers, the healers, the ones who experience kia. It is generally understood that the Drum is a women's dance. Women help each other, teach each other, give each other num. The women who are the instigators of the dance and the teachers of num are highly valued. Much of the work at the dance, activating and channeling num, occurs in the context of female-to-female relationships. About a third of the women dance in the Drum and kia, the likelihood of their reaching kia increasing with age. Many more women kia in the Drum than in the Giraffe. But the percentage of women in the different camps who possess num in the Drum is less consistent than the percentages of men in those camps who possess num in the Giraffe. For example, in the several camps around the Goshe water-hole virtually all of the women have some experience with num in the Drum dance, whereas at other water-holes only a few women possess such num. But the mobility of people among camps means that access to num in Drum is assured for any woman who desires it.

Older men are considered to be the best drummers, though young men frequently want to try. The drummer often experiences kia. For example, Dem enters kia as he drums and, collapsing, has to be disentangled from his long drum by his wife, also a healer. But even if a drummer enters kia, the emphasis remains on his drumming, and not on any dancing or healing he may do.

Male-female contacts are minimized in the Drum dance, in sharp contrast to the situation in the Giraffe. Male sexuality is played down in the Drum, especially as it might be expressed in interactions with the females. The primary male participant, the drummer, is invariably older, and many drummers are described as dreamy and vague. Their sexuality is not a factor. Men in their sexual prime seem to be kept on the sidelines, as watchers. They may do some teasing of a sexual nature, or some showing off, but such activities are kept at a distance from the actual dance. The stimulant of a generalized sensuality, particularly of the cross-sex nature, so dominant in the Giraffe, is less evident in the Drum.

The Giraffe dance is a routine part of everyday life. Not

so the Drum. It occurs more sporadically. Whereas the Giraffe can be seen as an omnipresent part of Kung hunting-gathering life, Drum dances are more localized. The initiation of a Drum dance depends on the availability and location of the drum and drummer. The mood of the drummer and his preliminary activities affect the start of the dance, as well as how long it will continue. But the main instigation for a Drum dance comes from the appearance of powerful women healer-teachers in the camp. Women experienced in the num of the Drum dance travel around to different camps, initiating dances and giving other women num. They function like a "traveling festival," stimulating dances and the activation of num by their very presence.

The Drum dance is not, as is the Giraffe, a central event around which all the people orient themselves and to which they bring their important concerns. The enthusiasm for Drum dancing seems mild compared to the abiding eagerness for the Giraffe. Drum dancing does not express central values of the gathering-hunting tradition, such as sharing or egalitarianism, as the Giraffe does. Moreover, the Drum does not express the wholeness of the human group,as the Giraffe does. The general lack of participation by men is a key illustration of this fact.

The num of the Drum is felt to be similar to the num of the Giraffe, and in this essential way the dances are alike. The activation of num and its development into kia are fundamentally similar processes in both the Drum and the Giraffe. The kia in both dances is an altered state of consciousness of a transcendent quality.

The fear of kia and the need to overcome that fear in order to enter kia are as critically important in the Drum as in the Giraffe. The women recognize that too much fear will "defeat num." They speak of the "great pain of boiling num" and the death that kia brings; a few speak of their fear of visiting "god's camp, the camp of the dead, where there are so many people you don't know." Yet many seek num. They want their teachers to "fix their arrows of num well," rather than to remove them, so they can kia. Gasa, an older healer, says: "You don't fear to do num alone because you don't do it alone. You know you can't. When others are there, I still fear dying. But that num is good because it is our thing." Like a few men who kia in the Giraffe dance, several women say that they were not overwhelmed by fear when num first came. Tinay, who is in her early thirties and is one of the youngest women to be acknowledged as a strong healer, speaks without hesitation: "If I feared num, I wouldn't be doing it. It suits me" (quoted in Biesele, 1969–1971).

As in the Giraffe, the num in the Drum is said to reside in the base of the spine and the lower belly. As num is heated, it travels up along the "backbone." Num travels from the lower back to the shoulders, legs, and rest of the body; it "lifts you up." As in the Giraffe, its ascent to the head is especially important. One of the older women healers says: "When the top of your head and the inside of your neck go 'za-za,' that is the arrival of num."

The num of the Drum dance also affects the participant in a slightly different way from that in the Giraffe. During kia in the Drum, there is a ringing in the ears, and there is felt to be "a hole, two or three inches across, starting at the head and going down through the body." Women speak of this hole with great emphasis. When num cools down, the hole goes away. But as in Giraffe, women also say their "middle feels as if it is full of thorns" during kia.

Kia refers to both a particular state of consciousness and a set of external behaviors that can have more variation. There are differences in the way kia is manifested in the two dances. Generally, women experiencing kia in the Drum, and indeed women experiencing kia in the Giraffe, behave in a more controlled and less dramatic manner than men do in kia.

The rhythmic trembling of women in kia is intense. In fact, their word for kia, *tara,* means the action of lightning. Many women say that they "tremble the beads off" their skin aprons. Tam explains this trembling in kia: "It feels like there is a hole going through your body. You tremble in rhythm; even your crotch trembles. If you reach kia, you call out for water, because you are hot inside. Even if you don't know the songs, you can kia. The num itself tells you how to sing and dance" (quoted in Beisele, 1969–1971).

The ideal in kia is for the woman to have enough control to shiver and shake while standing in place. The Kung say a woman's feet must press the ground firmly in one spot; she should not lurch or fall over. A woman should stand and quiver beautifully, and many women achieve this as they learn to control num. Experienced healers help those entering kia, pressing their feet to the ground so that they can stand and begin to shimmy or vibrate.

Those new to num are often overpowered by it. They fling themselves repeatedly into the air and have to be restrained. They lose control and crash to the ground, inside or outside the group of singing and clapping women. Some then enter the treacherous experience of kia death where their souls leave their bodies. If a woman falls, especially if she loses control and falls awkwardly or violently, her clothing may fly out of place or come undone, exposing her genitals or rear. The other women, concerned for the modesty of those who have fallen, rush to their aid, rearranging their clothing, at times even putting a larger genital apron on them. As Nai says: "What we're afraid of is that one who is in kia will expose herself to the men. What we're worried about is that a woman will fall down in the wrong position. Then we have to pull her rear skirt through her legs and tuck it in front."

Such violent behavior is similar to that displayed by men under the pressure of boiling num. Likewise, the increased control which comes with increased experience of num is an aim in both the Drum and the Giraffe. But the subtle, vibrant shaking of the women's kia, though no less intense, contrasts to the shrieking and howling which is part of the men's kia.

More substantial differences characterize the purpose for which num is heated up in the two dances. In the Giraffe, healing is considered essential to the full or correct expression of kia. In the Drum, kia alone appears to be sufficient gratification for some women. One woman says that kia itself is "sweet and good." Another woman, however, says that if you just kia and don't heal, "you are good for nothing." Most of the younger women expect to learn to heal at some later time; until then, they are content to kia for its own sake. Others are content to kia for its own sake regardless of whether they will eventually learn to heal. Dikau puts it this way: "I haven't been made to heal yet. I'm just a young learner, a small child. I don't want more num. At first I wanted more, and now I don't. Now I just kia for myself" (quoted in Biesele, 1969–1971). This emphasis on the satisfactions kia brings to oneself quite apart from its connection with healing others is not found among those who work with num in the Giraffe dance.

The healing of the Giraffe is available to all. The healing in the Drum extends only to those who are singing and dancing and themselves healing. Those who only watch do not receive any of the healing effects.

The dynamics of learning to "drink num" are basically the same for men and women. They both must face and overcome their fear of death in kia. Around this experiential similarity are important structural differences.

Unlike the men's long and difficult apprenticeship, it takes only a few days for a woman to get num. But the actual reception of num is no less difficult and painful. As with men, women are not merely given num. They must choose to accept it, and in that choice they must undergo the arduous process of allowing num to boil within them.

The age of receiving num in the Drum dance ranges from approximately ten years to the age of a grandmother. The frequency of getting num increases with age, drastically so in the post-childbearing years. The specific time of getting num depends on when the old teacher-healers come through the camps. Most women first receive num from older female relatives, though in a few cases men are the teachers.

Those with "soft gebesi" take one or two days, and those with "hard gebesi" may take three or five days after first being "shot" with the num arrows. Almost any woman who wants to get num can, though there have been reports of some who could not, however much they tried. Of the seventeen Kung women whom Megan Biesele interviewed, only one said that, although she had been shot with num arrows years before, and had danced, she had not yet experienced kia.

As in the Giraffe, power is said to reside in the num sweat and the arrows of num. One woman said the arrows were in the head, while others located them in two centers, in the back and in the side of the neck. Sweat is given by the teacher rubbing her hands under her own armpits and transferring the sweat to the student, either by rubbing her sweaty hands on the student or, in rare cases, climbing on the back of the student so her body sweat gets all over the student.

The arrows are "shot" by the same teacher who rubs her sweat on the student. The teacher snaps her fingers at the student's gebesi, each snap being an arrow. Once inside the person, the arrows multiply or "give birth." The student cannot tell how many arrows she has. They feel like many thorns pricking from inside. Sometimes the powerful healers giving num concentrate on one learner for several days. One woman whose gebesi were soft says that the first day she merely sweated. The second day her back hurt and she began quivering deep inside, and that was when she began to kia. Another, whose gebesi were hard, danced for four days but she only experienced a little kia. On the fifth day, the teachers cooked some gwa for her and she "broke into kia."

Gwa is the name of a plant, whose botanical identification has not yet been made, which is used in connection with the Drum dance. Its roots are cooked and then eaten or drunk. The roots and stem of the plant may also be boiled into a tea with a little thin cornmeal, when that is available. The taste is distinctive, strong, and peppermint-like. Many women report that gwa makes them feel as if their diaphragms were lighter and could flutter. Many throw up after drinking it. Gwa seems to be most important as a ritual element during the initiation of young girls into the dance. As Bau, an experienced healer in both the Drum and the Giraffe dances, explains, "It is only we strong healers who prepare gwa and feed it to the new ones."

Those seeking num may drink gwa at one of several occasions, either when they have not gotten num at first, or when they want to get stronger num from the same or other healers. The teaching process is flexible, varying according to the availability of powerful teachers as well as the availability of gwa and the mood of the participants.

Gwa seems to function for students as a partial aid to accepting boiling num, to help the learner over her barrier of fear. Bau talks about this application of gwa: "When you fix gwa, you cook it in the pot. Then you pound it and cook it. Then you pour out a cupful for one who is still learning, and she drinks it all down, and then one cupful for another who is still learning, and she drinks it down. Then you start singing, and during the singing you carry the students, and then they begin to kia." But gwa is neither a necessary nor a sufficient ingredient in learning to kia or heal. As Bau emphasizes, "If you don't drink gwa and you go to a dance, you can kia from real num." Gwa is not seen as "real num."

The older, more experienced healers may drink gwa when they are teaching others to kia. For them, gwa is just another element, akin to the drum and the singing, which helps to activate num. Bau describes this use of gwa: "When you prepare gwa and cook it, and soften it and drink it, you feel it in your body. It begins to climb up in your legs, and you rub it down. Then you go to the drum, and the drum starts to heat up, and you kia." Again, however, the experienced healers do not see gwa as the "real" num. Bau says: "If you see a sick person and say, 'My num is weak,' you don't then drink gwa to make your num strong. You just have to say, 'No, you have to get another healer.' "

The drum also plays a role in teaching. It helps create an atmosphere in the dance to intensify the student's experience and reduce her barriers to num. Tsaa is said to be a very strong drummer, who "beat the drum's heart" and makes the women "clap hard" and their singing "rise up."

Bau speaks about the drum and kia: "You start by fixing num and settling it. Then they take the drum and make it hot. Then the drum goes on and you kia and kia, and then you heal people. Then you go into the drum again and kia again."

"What does a person do who fears num?" I ask.

"Such persons fear their gebesi and their spine," Bau replies. "Such persons sing, but they don't kia. But we experts, we play with num, and we can kia all night until dawn."

"And if you see someone who fears num, what do you do?"

"When I see the face of one who fears num, I say, ' I'd better heal this one.' Those who fear num have a blank stare on their face, and their eyes are downcast. They sit on the ground and shake and shiver. We experienced ones carry them around and put our sweat into them. We have loosened gebesi. Our gebesi are no longer hard, so we just heal."

"Does the singing get stronger at a time like that?" I wonder.

"Yes, at such a time we lift up our voices. We say, 'This one fears num.' So we bring her in and put her in front of the drum, holding her there. Then she begins to kia, and kia and kia, and then falls down. Then we lay her out flat on her belly and let her lie there. But we big ones, we experts, simply kia the whole night through, and we don't do any of that stuff. What I have described is what the num of Drum does."

When the healing power comes to a woman in the Drum dance, it usually comes when she is older and experienced with num and kia. Most older women who kia also heal. The first trip to the gods' camp is supposed to occur at the time of "being made to heal." The act of being "made to heal" comes as the teacher lays her hands on the student, while the student wraps her hands around the teacher's waist.

There are striking similarities between the way women get num in the Drum and the menarcheal and marriage ceremonies, highlighting the dangerous and transitional nature of num initiation. The ceremony preparing girls for getting num is similar to that which prepares them for their first menstruation or for getting married. In each case, they are washed and fixed up beautifully: ocher and fat are rubbed on them, they are hung about with beads, and new soft skin clothing is prepared and put on them. They must eat most foods ritually with a cleansing agent before they may eat them in an ordinary fashion again. Only after such preparations are they ready to make the transition into num, womanhood, or marriage.

Those beginning to learn about num feel bad and are said to get "thin unto death." They must observe certain food taboos, which again are reminiscent of the taboos that apply to womanhood and childbirth (Marshall, 1976). When these foods are eaten for the first time after the training for num has begun, they must be eaten with a bite of gwa during a special ceremony. The taboo foods include fresh meat of all the animals, both male and female, as well as fresh mongongo nuts, and sha roots. It is best to avoid introduced foods entirely, like milk, bread, eggs, meal, tea, and fish. Honey, too, is felt to interfere with the student's learning to "do num" (Biesele, 1969–1971).

A woman's relationship to the num of the Drum dance is particularly affected by her biological condition. During her childbearing years, her num is activated less frequently, though apparently it may still lie dormant within her. One way reproductively active women work with this num which is kept intentionally "light" is to kia without healing.

During pregnancy itself, the woman's num arrows may be temporarily taken away by her teacher because they are considered dangerous to unborn children. Gasa connects the events of her procreative life closely with num events: "I did the num of the Drum dance first near Maiheto when I was with my family there taking care of Herero cows. I menstruated and then Dem married me, and the two of us did Drum dancing together. We had a baby, and so my teachers took the arrows away. But the baby died after it was named. After that, I did not get pregnant again, so now I want my teacher to give me the arrows again. Last night she gave me one arrow, and it nearly killed me" (quoted in Biesele, 1969–1971). Another woman, speaking of the time before her childbearing, puts it this way: "If you're small when you first get num, you can dance num and really get into kia and just grow along with num" (quoted in Biesele, 1969–1971).

Apparently women can concentrate on their num only when childbearing is over. Each pregnancy interrupts the course of perfecting num. This may be why there are fewer women healers than men, and less emphasis on healing among young women. Women know that they cannot develop their num fully until their childbearing is over. Women are conscious all the time of the current state of their "arrows" and of what they want their teacher to do next about their arrows. In this way too they differ markedly from the men. They are constantly concerned about timing, and about whether it is best for num to grow in them or be removed because of the danger to children and the comfort or discomfort to themselves.

Age and experience are clearly linked with num's power for women, as they are for men. A woman now past her childbearing years, who experienced kia before that period but did not heal, may seek healing power. A teacher can come back to her "to make her heal." When that happens, the woman is no longer a student. She need no longer observe food taboos. The num in her can now actively grow. But perhaps owing to its lying dormant during the childbearing years, it may already be so big that, when activated, it bowls her over. As with men, the num must be brought under control.

Although entrance into the post-childbearing years signals increased intensity of num or in some cases the initial activation of it, the power of num usually leaves with advanced age. Koka, an old woman, reports: "I am too old and sick and thin to heal anymore. My num has left me. Maybe if I get fat again, num will return" (quoted in Biesele, 1969–1971).

But with a few old women, their work with num continues to unfold. Age and experience intensify their power.

They become a *geiha ama ama*, a "real healer." These few women are practically indistinguishable from the few older men whose num has also become most powerful. The Kung emphasis on num, and the unique power of that num, effectively erase all sexual distinctions in healing.

The Drum and Giraffe dances do not seem to be in direct competition. The two dance forms rarely occur simultaneously. Even when they do, they are able to coexist. On one occasion, for example, a Drum dance is occurring within earshot of a Giraffe dance, no more than a quarter-mile away. After a while, the Drum dance gradually ends, but the participants in the Drum did not then go over to the Giraffe.

The Drum is, as the Kung say, "its own thing," but it is also a preparation for the Giraffe. Women learn to kia and to heal in the Drum. The num of the Drum is a "women's thing." Those who only kia in the Drum and do not heal may on occasion also kia in the Giraffe. But most of those who kia and heal in the Drum also heal at times in the Giraffe. In the Giraffe, the women usually kia while they are singing, and at times they concentrate their healing efforts on their fellow singers. A woman's matured num can be activated in the Giraffe, though it was probably received in the Drum. When a woman has num in both dances, her num is said to have added strength. The two nums are said "to marry." A woman's experience in the Drum paves the way for this increased access to a more potent num. Moreover, the women most active in the Drum are often the most active singers and healers in the Giraffe. Men, in contrast, do not add the num of the Drum to their Giraffe num. Very few kia in the Drum.

There is a shift in the Drum dance itself toward the more central healing dance of the Giraffe. On one occasion when a woman who has entered the death of kia in the Drum dance, and whose soul has left her body, cannot be brought back to life, those who have been performing the Drum resort to the Giraffe to bring her soul back. The Giraffe takes over from the Drum. Moreover, in recent years, more men are becoming involved in the Drum, and the singing in the Drum is becoming more like the singing in the Giraffe.

The position of the Drum dance is historically ambiguous, but its assertive female emphasis probably represents some counterpoint statement to the equally valued male and female contributions of the Giraffe. The changes accompanying increased sedentism among the Kung may bear some relationship to the Drum.

If the Drum dance is introduced, or is gaining enormously in popularity in the present transition to sedentism, it would seem to connect the dance to changed economic conditions. Given the greater role differentiation between the sexes and the loss of status for women which accompanies sedentism (Draper, 1975), the Drum could be seen as a possible strategy for coping with new social alignments. Preliminary impressions suggest a higher incidence of Drum dancing where the change to a sedentary life-pattern is more complete, as at Goshe and Kangwa.

But if, as some of the Kung say, the Drum dance is an ancient thing in their hunting-gathering culture, it may be seen as a subtheme which provides an important element in the ongoing dynamic of male-female relations. This interpretation of the Drum would have it offering an arena for reproductively active women to participate in a spiritual ritual without endangering their childbearing function from the Kung point of view, that is, to kia without healing. Preliminary data supports this interpretation: female healers in the Giraffe are generally post-menopausal, whereas fertile but not pregnant as well as post-menopausal women participate in the Drum. More systematic demographic data of this kind is needed to confirm or disprove this interpretation.

In contrast to the horseshoe shape of the Drum dance, the circle is the dominant symbol of the Giraffe, a circle which brings the people toward its center, excluding no one. Women in the Giraffe are more involved in singing than in dancing, and are more reserved in their manifestation of kia. The men are more involved with healing, especially in the form of the laying on of hands. Although the education for kia and the career of a healer differ for men and women, the experience of num for men and women in the Giraffe is essentially similar.

Men and women work together in the Giraffe to release its healing num. There is no hierarchical ranking between male and female contributions to the dance, but rather a complementarity. Singing is as important as dancing. Num is at the dance, and it is activated by both singers and dancers. To see the dancer as a "leader" reflects a Western, individualistic bias. Men and women, in their respective, overlapping roles, work together so that the healing can result.

At the Giraffe dance there is an intense male-female interaction, which seems essential to the activation of num. Although explicit sex is prohibited, sexuality is pervasive. Certain forms of restrained sexuality occur, such as when the adolescent males dance for the eyes of their female peers and the women dance appreciatively in front of the men, but this behavior accounts for only a small part of the dance's sexual energy. More important is the generalized sensuality of the dance, evident in the rhythmic crescendos of singing, the kinesthesia of warm, sweating dancers, the release and abandon of kia, and the deep massage essential to helping another in kia.

The Giraffe dance is a paradigm or mirror of sexual relationships within the traditional Kung culture. The relative leverages of men and women in the dance appear as equal but different. Their interaction with each other is crucial; neither can exist without the other. The role of men as dancers is more flamboyant, paralleling their role as hunters in bringing home the coveted but chancy meat. The women, in performing the music, play the complementary, sustaining role, just as they do in their provision of more reliable vegetable foods.

A dynamic balance exists between men and women at the Giraffe dance. As in relations between Kung men and women generally, imperfections in the balance occur. But the basic respect of each sex for the other's contribution to the dance constantly re-establishes the balance. The Giraffe exists for healing, and both women and men release the

Giraffe's healing energy. "It is good for women to have num," says Kinachau. "If they heal, they can save you! It is the same with the men." Nai, a strong singer in the Giraffe, talks about how women kia and heal in that dance: "When a woman in the singing circle starts to kia, you see her singing and shivering at the same time. Her eyes might close a little and then open. When she is in kia, that is the best singing of all. It's singing with real num in it. We hear that singing and see it. She can still sing while she is in kia. We other singers sit close to the one who is in kia, supporting her so that she won't fall over, but we don't rub her. We give her strength and support her so she won't fall. The men are pleased because it's all the same num, and it came from the men in the first place. The healing in the singing circle is the same as the healing of the dancers."

10 Toma Zho, a Healer in Transition

TOMA ZHO is a healer in transition, trying to move away from the traditional camp approach to num to a more professional status, where his services would be rewarded on a quid-pro-quo basis. At times he seems to want to accumulate rather than distribute his num. His "untraditional" approach colors the way he heals and teaches. When I try to find out more about his way with num, his humor makes that a less than simple but always enjoyable task.

As we sit together in the marginal midday shade, Toma Zho brings forth the walking stick he has carved for me. "If there is a dance," I say hopefully, "and you use that stick and put some num into it, it would be great if we could then trade that stick for something of mine."

Looking directly into my eyes, Toma Zho speaks intimately. "Dick, when I'm looking at you and watching you dance, I say, 'There's a guy that's concentrating on num.' "

"How do you know?" I ask eagerly, partly curious, partly flattered.

"I see you and I think, 'There is a guy who is concentrating on num,' but I don't really know what you are going to do about it. I can tell from the way you dance. You dance well, and you look like a person who is concentrating. Maybe someday you are going to do num." The mood becomes quiet. Several moments pass before Toma Zho continues. "Maybe my stuff used to be good. Maybe I am old now, and maybe it's not so good anymore."

"Do you feel old?" I inquire.

"I feel old," he offers. "I feel myself, I feel old. I'm an old-timer at this job of num, because I have been doing it ever since I was a kid, and now I can dance it and dance it and dance it. And I can dance it and I won't pick up the fire and throw it on people. I just dance it. You have seen other guys dance, like Kinachau. At his age, he's still throwing fire around."

"What about Kinachau?"

Page 177: Toma Zho

"I'm just not sure about Kinachau," Toma Zho answers without hesitation, "whether he fears num or not. He plays with num, but then sometimes I think he fears it. When Kinachau is defeated, he calls me in to help, saying, 'Come on, you try it.' At Xaixai I'm the only one with strength."

"And Kau Dwa?" Kau Dwa is a very powerful healer, totally blind, who lives in Kangwa.

"Kau Dwa's got nothing, because look at his eyes. He's blind. When he poked his eye out here at Xaixai, it was I who saved his life."

"And Wa Na?" Wa Na is an old woman, also blind, who lives about the same distance from Xaixai as Kau Dwa, and who is reputed to have the strongest num in the entire Dobe area.

"Wa Na does it," says Toma Zho with conviction. "But we haven't lived together and I don't know which one of us is better, because she pulls num but I pull god's num, so I think I'm better. At Xaixai, I don't know anyone here who really has it."

The tobacco, an ever-present accompaniment to Kung social gatherings, is being smoked today in Richard Lee's Western pipe, a prized object for any Kung, who usually settles for smoking in expended bullet cartridges. Toma Zho draws deeply, inhaling huge quantities of smoke. The pipe goes around again. Lee is smoking it now. With a mischievous twinkle and in mock seriousness, Toma Zho begins on Lee. "That's my pipe. You're smoking my pipe. Stop it man! Don't just sit there. Fill it up!" Toma Zho's tone softens. "Today when we talk, we'll have nice talk. Today nice talk is coming up." Several minutes pass, then Toma Zho continues as if he has never stopped, thoroughly enjoying his feigned insults to Lee. "How can you just sit there and say that this isn't my pipe? The cuts in my arm, all the way up and down my arm, the cuts in my arm are from killing animals. Now I'm blind and I can't kill anything! Look at all the meat I've killed, it's shown by the scars on my arms. I'm a great hunter. But now I'm blind. Lee, can you in all honesty say you have ever killed anything?" Toma Zho is now playing the game to its fullest.

"What's the big idea of not giving me the pipe? I've been sitting here at Xaixai all these months thinking about it. Look, today you're going to give it over. Today I'm going to have that pipe."

Tobacco smoke fills the air and reminds me of something I want to ask. "Toma Zho, do you know about marijuana?"

"Yes."

"Can you kia on that stuff?" I wonder.

Toma Zho jumps in. "Now wait, listen you guys, I have been told for years and years that European guys never smoke marijuana."

"Who told you that?"

"People around here told me," he replies. "They have been saying around here for years that Europeans never smoke that stuff."

I look at him. "But did you ever ask a European? . . . Toma Zho, I want to ask you again. Can you kia on marijuana?"

"I've heard you can kia on that stuff," he reflects. "I've heard that stuff can be used in kia. For instance, if a fellow fails to find kia, if he fails to get there, he can smoke some. I've heard that it only works that way for a person who has experienced kia before. The guy who already knows kia and then at some later time can't kia might smoke marijuana, and it would make his thoughts whirl like being drunk. I've heard that if you can't kia at the dance, when you take a puff of marijuana and then dance, you can kia and heal."

"When is marijuana smoked?" I ask.

"What I heard," says Toma Zho, "is that a group as small as we are now will sit around and smoke, sometimes with women, and sometimes not."

"Would one go to sleep soon after smoking marijuana?"

"I'm told," replies Toma Zho, "that if it puts you to sleep, you'll sleep with it. But some people sit up with it all night."

"Do some people have sex with it?" I ask innocently.

Toma Zho can barely believe what he has heard. "You mean your thoughts turn to sex when you smoke it? Your thoughts – " His last words trail off as he breaks out into uproarious, uncontained laughter, squealing with delight, nearly falling over. For several minutes the laughter comes on, in waves. Finally Toma Zho contains himself enough to verbalize his wonder. "Let me see if I've got this straight." Laughter seizes him again, and he struggles to continue. "You say that, after you smoke it, you have in mind to do what?" It is almost impossible to answer, for we are all overcome with laughter.

I speak almost incoherently. "You smoke it and then you have sex and your heart and thoughts are great."

"When I was younger," Toma Zho reminisces, "and I used to smoke this stuff, I chased the women, but today I don't have any of it to smoke and my heart is bad." He has now gained a measure of composure and reflects further. "We don't think of these things as going together. Having sex is nice as its own thing, and smoking marijuana is also nice, and it is also its own thing."

"I also have sex without marijuana," I offer.

"Yes," muses Toma Zho, "you can enjoy it that way too." Toma Zho's face betrays his continuing laughter inside.

"You know, Toma Zho, I miss my family very much these days."

"Why didn't you bring them along?" Toma Zho asks.

"My wife and I have a little daughter now, and – "

"Give me your daughter in marriage." His request is provocative, and he expresses it with obvious delight.

"Oh," I say, "but she's just this tall," signifying about two feet tall.

"When she's this tall," he says, signifying about four feet tall, "she'll be ready."

"Who will you give me to marry?" I urgently plead, joining into the new playful struggle.

"Ah, I thought you weren't interested in girls."

"Why did you think that?" I ask, feigning insult.

"I didn't think you were a guy I could put into in-lawship. I thought maybe you were just a young guy who actually had not married yet."

"Oh, Toma Zho," I say, "I have been married for years."

"Well, why don't you get another truck and bring your wife here so we can see her," he joyfully challenges.

At this point Lee, who like myself is about thirty, enters the game again. "Not only is Dick already married and as old as your son, but I am much older than you, Toma Zho."

Toma Zho reacts with dramatic disbelief. "Why, come off it, man! You're trying to tell me that you – " He sputters and gestures broadly. "Don't be ridiculous. Why, I'm old enough to be your father!"

"Don't be ridiculous," Lee responds quickly, "you're my kid brother."

Toma Zho looks again at Lee and becomes slightly reflective. "I might be the age mate of your much older brother." He picks up the pace. "Lee, how can you say you are older than I am? No matter what kind of gags you are trying to play on me, I saw you four years ago when you first came to Xaixai. And I remember saying to myself at the time, 'That Lee is a nice little European youngster.' So, today you've got a long beard. But listen, I knew you before. Come off it, man! Look how my teeth are worn down, they are worn smooth. You're trying to tell me you are my age mate? Forget it."

"Look here," Lee retorts, "your father hadn't even given birth to you when I was here. Because when I was here, I saw your father but I didn't see you. So I'm even before your time."

"Listen, man," Toma Zho shoots back, "I've been around. I grew up in this area, and no one ever told me a story about you or the likes of you coming around. Lee, this may be the first year you have been claiming to be an old man." We all savor this verbal duel, which ends with reciprocating laughter and lusty handshakes.

Toma Zho then becomes quiet and turns to me. "Dick, I know you are a good dancer. I know you are a guy who is interested in dancing and num. I've seen you in action. Someday, Dick, you watch the dancing, and I'll dance and put num in my stick before I give it to you."

"Toma Zho, what if I came to you requesting that you teach me num?"

"If you dance and get num from me, don't you think the police will be after me for giving you num?" Toma Zho responds with mock surprise. "Some people might say, 'What sort of a business is it when a white man starts to kia on Kung num? Surely that can't be a good thing.' The word would get out that there's some crazy Kung up-country who is pouring num into a white man. I know you won't tell, but look, we do our num training in public, and hundreds of people could see you kia."

Lee interjects, "But Dick's already a healer in his own country."

"Well, if Dick is a healer, then what the hell have I got to lose? Let's try it."

"Toma Zho," I say, "I don't know how to kia from Kung dancing. I can have something *like* kia from things in my own country. But I don't know how to do num the Kung way."

Toma Zho reflects on this. "Dick, I don't know if it will be possible to transfer your num into our num."

"You may be right," I observe.

A quiet moment precedes Toma Zho's further thoughts. "Every time I give num to a person, I lose a little of my own. The num comes out of you. And then it can become nothing. You can make it nothing in your own body. You'll lose it all. If you give num to a lot of people you are teaching, you can give it all away. If you give it to one student, then you can still have some. When you give it to no one who is learning, then it will still be with you. They all want some," Toma Zho continues emphatically. "All the children want some num. So if I enter kia while they're in kia, then they all say, 'Oh, gimme, gimme, gimme.' So I stay out until after everybody's finished. Then I go in. That's why I don't kia early in the dance."

"Is it good to kia first in a dance?" I wonder.

"I'm big in num. Do you think I'm going to kia first?" Toma Zho's tone is firm. "You mean you expect that when the children are falling down, I'm going to fall with them? No, I'll still dance. I'm an old, old expert in num."

"Do you mean the new ones are the ones who kia first, and the old ones kia later on?"

"Yes."

"But the other day Kinachau, who is not new to num, entered kia pretty early in the dance."

"Yes," agrees Toma Zho, "Kinachau is not a kid, but Kinachau does it his way. His way is early. I find that I like to dance, and if I kia straight off, I won't get a chance to dance. So I save my kia for the morning. And if the women keep singing, then I'll kia in the morning. If they stop, I'll just stop."

"Toma Zho, do you ever think, 'This young guy looks like he'll drink num. He'd be a good student?' "

"The guys I look for are strong dancers," Toma Zho says. "They are really putting their heart into dancing, they are dancing with a passion. They're the guys I really want to put num into Then there is another type of guy you see dancing. He's up and down, up and down. He's in one turn, sitting at the side the next time. Even if a guy like that asked me, I would refuse."

"Who is like that in-and-out type?" I ask.

"Everybody I've seen is the in-and-out type," Toma Zho says. "People don't dance properly."

"If that in-and-out type of dancer comes and asks you for num, would you say no?"

"I would refuse him."

"Toma Zho, is it good for a father to teach his sons?"

Toma Zho's tone softens. "The nice thing about teaching your own son is that he is in the family. When you die, he can go on healing the people and saving them."

"Are you giving num to anyone now?"

Toma Zho becomes reflective. "I taught someone once. He died many years ago. His name was Hxumi. I taught him, and he danced just like me and entered kia just like me, and anyone who was dead he would save and bring to life. But one day he mounted a horse that had been ridden by many people. This horse went crazy and raced all over the place and threw him. People rushed to get me and said, 'A horse has killed Hxumi.' At first I didn't believe them, so I just sat. But then others said, 'A horse threw Hxumi, but he's still breathing.' So I went to him. And Hxumi said, 'I'm finished. Carry me back to the village and let me die there. So we carried him back. But I didn't heal Hxumi because I saw he was already dead, and he died. And when he died, I said, 'What happened? The one person who danced my style and who got my num, the horse kills. What's the matter?' And I never took another pupil, not even my own son."

"When you look at your two sons, Debe and Tsama, do you think they will get num?"

"My son Debe doesn't kia," Toma Zho replies. "Yes, Debe's still young, but I look at him and say, 'He'll do it someday.' When I see Tsama, I say, 'Maybe he will and maybe he won't.' When I see him dance, he dances like Debe, so maybe he'll do num someday. Maybe they'll both do it."

Just then two young men walk by and greet us. Toma Zho returns the greeting, and as they are walking away, he calls out to them: "Come back! I've got to tell you something." They turn around. "Let me tell you . . . let me tell you." Toma Zho's eyes begin to squint with laughter. "Let me tell you something. You won't . . . you won't believe this." He has to stop, his body convulsing with laughter, tears rolling down his face, his head doubling over into his lap. "Dick here just told me that he and his European friends smoke . . . they smoke marijuana and then do sex. Did you hear that? And then they do sex!" Toma Zho rolls over on his side, unable to support himself any longer.

By now we were all thoroughly immersed in laughter. The two other Kung men struggle to respond. "Marijuana? . . . and doing sex? . . . and doing sex?" Their words barely get out as they slap their thighs. Doubled up, they have to sit down before they fall down. For a while, we all are beside ourselves with enjoyment. The two men finally leave, shaking their heads in disbelief, tears of laughter still wet on their cheeks.

"You guys have forgotten about that pipe of mine." Toma Zho's finger shoots out toward Lee's pipe, as he returns effortlessly to the challenge. "That pipe is obviously a pipe of a senior person, an old man, a mature person. How can kids like you be walking around with a nice pipe like that?"

Toma Zho does not wait for a response. "This is a pipe that should belong to old, distinguished persons. The kids can have a drag on it, but it's not for the kids to have." Toma Zho's voice becomes barely audible. "What a pipe. . .what a pipe."

The mood becomes extremely relaxed. Toma Zho begins reminiscing. "This reminds me of those great dances we used to have up at Kangwa years ago, when my older brother and I used to go up there for dances. These dances would go on all day, and people would be lying all over the place. By nighttime I'd go to sleep. I'd go to sleep with one woman on my left side and one on my right. And when I lay down, I'd suddenly realize what kind of a spot I was in. 'What the hell, you mean there is a woman on either side of me?' And then what happened is that both would start after me, and each one wanted to have sex first, each one wanted to get sex first. And then I'd say, 'Oh, no! What a place this is. What a place we're in. Are these girls crazy? Are the girls of Kangwa crazy?' We used to do it, but now I'm too old for that sort of thing. I used to really like it. I used to get two, but sometimes I still get the urge to get three. Boy, was I an expert! Boy, was I a smart dancer in those days! We used to dance the whole night while the women sat and sang. I used to do sex. I used to get a lot of it, but today I am too old."

"Num or sex?" I wonder.

"Sex."

"Toma Zho, if a guy has a lot of num, is he also a big lover?"

Toma Zho continues: "The women used to love me. They were crazy about me, because I was a healer, because I was a dancer, because I was good at everything."

"Did the women really like the healers?"

"Yes," says Toma Zho, "the women really did like the healers. Whenever I see one who is just getting num, I say, 'Think of the sex the guy's going to get!' I remember all the sex I used to get as a healer. Yes, the women really liked the healers, but first and foremost, they liked me."

I take a few moments, considering how to phrase a question I have. "Toma Zho, I have heard it said that some persons 'grow up with num.' What do those words 'grow up with num' mean?"

Toma Zho looks slightly puzzled, as if the question is too complicated. "The words mean exactly what they say, that you grow up with num. You grow up. If you've got num, you've got it. There are some, like me, who are small and take num and num grows them up. Sometimes you grow up with num, sometimes num grows you up." There are others, like Kinachau, who grow up and then take num.

"Toma Zho, I've heard it said that healers can go to the place where the gods and spirits are?"

"Yes, I've been to their place."

His simple reply catches me by surprise. "During the dance, when you're in kia and you're pulling, do you go to other places?"

Again a simple, "Yes."

"What do you see?"

"I've been to the place up there," Toma Zho says pointing to the sky, "and all around."

"What did you see when you were up there?"

"The day I went up there, I didn't see any of our own people." Toma Zho pauses. "I can travel to Kangwa while I'm experiencing kia in the dance here at Xaixai, and I see how my daughter's doing there at Kangwa, and I see that she's doing fine. Then I return to Xaixai."

"When you dance," I ask, "how do you go traveling to other places?"

"My soul travels there."

"Where else does your soul go?"

"I don't have a person in other places to visit," says Toma Zho.

The sun has reached us again, and I am now the one without shade. Moving around the tree, we rearrange ourselves so the full brightness of the sun falls beyond us. As we settle into our new places, I check the tape recorder we are using to record our talk.

"Since I first saw one of those machines, I've asked myself, 'What are all these tricks the Europeans have?'" Toma

Zho looks carefully at the tape recorder as he speaks. He points his finger toward the machine, tracing its outline in the air. "It's a fantastic little gadget. You speak today, and tomorrow we'll be listening to it."

"It's fantastic," I agree.

Toma Zho nods as if responding to ideas still forming in his mind. He starts expressing his thoughts, at first as if talking to himself. "The beauty of this machine is that it copies so exactly what we do. You know, if you look at it, it's just a piece of metal. *That* is certainly not anything that's going to throw back your voices at you. But then, when that little box actually brings back to you exactly what you've just been saying, well, all I can think is, 'My god, the European is some magician.' There are times when I sit looking at it and I forget it's a box, and I think the people are right in there talking, and I imagine seeing the people in front of me. Can you imagine how a piece of iron like this and a box like that, can you *imagine* how they could bring your voices back, how they could collect your voices? This is quite out of my experience. This is quite out of my understanding. If you had a terrific night, then people will hear you just as you were, dancing and singing. But if you had a bad night, the machine will pick it up sure as hell, and those who listen to the machine will say, 'Here's a guy with a bad night.' When I try to imagine an explanation for this wonder, this machine of magic, I think, "Ah, it's very unlikely that the Europeans would tell me how it works."

I labor to explain and begin simply. "How do I explain? OK, what happens is, when you make sound, this little part," I point to the microphone, "picks up – "

Toma Zho interrupts, not impatiently but with eagerness. "Look," he says, "I know about that, I know about the part the voice goes in. It goes in here," he says, pointing to the microphone, "and then it goes up that line," and he points to the microphone wire, "and then it goes into that box," and he nods toward the tape recorder, "and the voice is collected there. But what I suspect is that this thing [the microphone] doesn't hear anything. It's not really hearing. This [the recorder] is the one that's got the real power in it. This [the microphone] is just a pickup, it's like an extension. The sound goes through and then *really* gets caught up in the main box."

All I can say is, "That's it."

Toma Zho smiles and pushes on. "Dick, you should be telling us about things like that. What makes it go? How do its insides work?"

I am at a loss. "Toma Zho, I wish I could explain it better, but it's pretty much of a mystery to me. I bought this recorder from another, and that person made it, and what I know about the recorder is that – "

Toma Zho interrupts again, trying persistently to get to the heart of the matter. "Look, you bought the machine, right? You know whom you bought it from. Did he tell you where the sound is collected? I mean, is this [microphone] an organ for picking up sounds? Do you happen to know the answers to these questions? Is it like an ear?"

"It is like an ear, yes."

"Now, does that mean that if this is like your ear, then the soul of the sound is carried up the line and is collected in the box?"

"Yeah. Yes, yes." I am relieved and happy.

"If you bring the box," he says, "and only the box, and put it here, you will pick up no sounds?" Excitedly, I confirm his understanding. Toma Zho then moves to a different perspective on the subject. "From the day of your birth, Dick, from the moment of your creation, did your elders and your ancestors tell you these things? Is this thing, this speech machine, something that was handed down to you by your ancestors?"

"Not really. This machine is somewhat new," I respond, and immediately realize the absurd complexity of that statement.

Toma Zho pauses briefly, takes a deep breath, and speaks. "You mean to tell me your ancestors, the greatest of your oldest ancestors, didn't give you that machine? They didn't give it up? It didn't come down to you, the children? Look, if your ancestors didn't know the explanation for this, then there's something really wrong. There's something *really* wrong, if you think about it clearly. Look, we guys have our num, and this machine is evidently part of your num. If we get a fantastically good thing from our ancestors, we don't say, 'Our ancestors didn't know anything about this.' So how can *you* say that, when you get this remarkable thing? How can you say that this isn't something great, given to you from your ancestors?"

I feel the impact of Toma Zho's words. I begin again. "The people who gave it to us are people who are somewhat older than ourselves, but not ancestors. They are the people who know about the machine."

"Look, this is just ridiculous," Toma Zho concludes, "this is *just ridiculous* that you say your ancestors didn't have a hand in this." Toma Zho develops his point further. "Around here we've already seen the truck, and we're used to that. We've seen its head opened up and the thing which makes it go taken apart. And that brings me back to what I was saying before, which is that you can't kid me that there isn't something wonderful and marvelous in this machine." Toma Zho speaks with conviction, pointing once again to the tape recorder. "If I ever could learn how to operate one of these, I'd seek one out for my own. Listen, you know what happened when we first saw one of these speech machines? We had a dance, and when it was over, we all went back to our villages. About nine o'clock the next morning Bau woke up and said, 'What's going on? Is there a dance starting up?' Someone else said, 'It's coming from the Europeans. The Europeans have started their own dance.' We went dashing over to the Europeans' campsite, but didn't see a single person. Nobody was singing. And then we saw this box, and we said, 'My god, do you think – is that little box making all that singing?'

"Gee, I'd love to have one of these. Then imagine what I'd do. You go out to visit your friends in another camp. You sit down with them. You exchange the news. You've got some tobacco to distribute, you give out the tobacco. Then you're sitting around, taking it easy. And you bring out this. And let's say people are feeling a bit sad or a bit tired or something like that. Then you just remember that you collected a dance from the previous week. And you just turn it on. Imagine what a wonderful effect it will have! How nice it will make people feel to have this nice singing going on. And they can just sit there and listen to it." Toma Zho looks again toward the tape recorder and reaches for the pipe and tobacco. He stuffs the pipe until the tobacco rises in a small mound from the bowl. After lighting it, he draws several long drags in rapid succession and passes the pipe along. He rubs his chest in pleasure and laughs warmly. Turning to me, his open smile and expectant look signal that we should continue our talk.

"Toma Zho, have you ever pulled sickness from someone without dancing first?"

"Yes," he says. "If a person is very sick, I will kia and do him, even without singing. I will pull sickness from him so that he may live."

"Who have you healed without dancing first?"

"I do it a lot," he says. "Koto is one example. That was many years before you came to Xaixai. It was the middle of the night, and Koto's son came to get me and said, 'Come, the old man, my father, is dying. Come and do him." Then I went and I entered kia and I pulled and pulled and pulled him, and the sun rose. Then I came back to our camp. I stayed there one night, and Koto lived."

"What was wrong with Koto?"

"Haven't you seen the way Koto breathes? He has pains in his side and can't breathe properly."

"Toma Zho, when you went to Koto's place, did you kia right away?"

"When I got there, I was just normal. Then when I saw him and saw how sick he was, I said to myself, 'Oh, god's killing this man.' And then I went into kia. I just sang and went into kia. I sang the songs the women have sung and given me, the same songs I sing along with the women during the dance. That night with Koto I sang the Giraffe num song. I am an owner of that."

"As you walked over to Koto's, were you getting yourself ready for kia?"

"I didn't sing as I went over to his place."

"Toma Zho, can you tell me about another time when you healed without dancing first?"

"I've done it lots of times. I don't count them." Toma Zho speaks calmly. "There was another man who was as good as dead, and I sang and I entered kia and pulled him and he lived. He had said, 'I have a chest and body ailment.' It wasn't a proper dance. We just started it for him, and the women backed me. I was the only healer there that night. I just acted on what I saw and said, 'What god gave me, I am going to do.' That man did not have to ask me to heal him."

"Toma Zho, does an ill person have to ask for the healer to heal him?"

"If you don't ask, you don't get it." He speaks in a direct manner.

"Would you ever just go over to an ill person in order to help him and maybe say, 'Come on, let's see what's the matter with you?' "

In a flash, Toma Zho's mood shifts, and he responds with humor. "You want me to say *what* to some guy who is ill – some guy that's probably a foreigner, maybe a northern Kung who has a different color, and is from a different area altogether? You expect me to go up and heal such a complete stranger? And anyway, if he isn't long for this world,then I can marry his wife!" Toma Zho's mood again changes, and his tone becomes serious. "It's important to be asked. There is nobody ill around here. If there was anybody ill, and if someone came over to me and told me about it, I'd go over and try."

"Do you ever pull with other healers?"

"What other healers?" Toma Zho gestures grandly. "You think there are other healers here at Xaixai?"

"At the dance, Toma Zho, do you pull with others?"

"I never pull with anyone else." Toma Zho rubs his face and appears deep in thought. Then he looks up. "Wait, sometimes Kinachau and I go into kia together and pull each other. And sometimes Kinachau pulls and I sit. Wi pulls me, and sometimes I pull him. But on a serious case, with a dying person, we don't pull together. I only pull alone on those cases. No, wait, there is someone I like to pull with, and that's Kamto. I think Kamto and I are equal. He's got num, that guy.

"There are times when I'm pulling with another healer and I say, 'He's not doing it right.' I say that because my partner starts pulling things out of a place in the sick person's body that has no sickness. I seek the sickness, and suppose I find it in the chest. Then I start pulling the sickness from the chest. But when I see my partner working over there on the sick person's head, I say, 'There's nothing wrong over there in his head!' In your own European num, if you know exactly what's wrong with a sick person, say a cut on one leg, and you fix it, then if another white man comes along and puts num on the sick person's *other* leg, you would say, 'What's that other guy doing? Doesn't he know the sickness has already been fixed on the one leg?' And so I would say to my partner in healing, 'OK, you try the head and see if you can remove the sickness.' If my partner doesn't remove the sickness, if he fails, then I try the chest. And when I pull the sickness out, I say, 'Ah, it was in the chest.' "

"Toma Zho, do you ever tell your partner to stop pulling?"

"No," Toma Zho replies. "I would say to my partner, 'Well, if you're sure it's the head, go on working.' "

"How do you prove to the other healer that you've pulled the sickness out of the chest, and he hasn't pulled it out of the head?"

"God sometimes denies the answer to one healer and gives it to the other. Whoever cures the sick one has not been denied."

The sun has reached us again. We move into an area of deep shade, behind the little grove of trees where we have been talking. Our talk begins to take on its ending.

"How is your wife?" I ask. Toma Zho's wife has a badly infected finger. We have been treating it twice a day, soaking it in hot water and applying an antibiotic salve.

"She's still a little ill in her hand."

"If a person is ill the way she is, isn't that the sort of thing you want to pull?"

"No, a thing like that infection is a thing that comes out itself. It just comes out. I had something like that on my own finger here. Such an infection just starts and then it comes out."

"Did you try to pull at all for your wife's infected finger?"

"No, I didn't – " He hesitates, and then smiles playfully. "I didn't pull it because I've seen that another healer has cured her, and so all I can say is, 'Thank you.' "

"Toma Zho, how does your num make you feel?"

"It makes me feel very good!" says Toma Zho with enthusiasm. "Look, I kia, and then I see a sick person and I look at the sick person and say, 'Oh, you are not well. Couldn't I do something for you and pull you and remove what's bothering you?' So I go to the sick person and pull and pull him. And the next day he sees me and says, 'Toma Zho, I feel terrific.' And when I hear him say that, my heart is glad. I feel very happy to have helped him. We seek num so we can help people properly. If someone is sick unto death, I say, 'Oh, no, this guy is going to die unless I can do something,' and so I pull him and pull him and pull him. If I save his life, he says to me, 'You've saved my life,' and he's very happy and loves me."

"Toma Zho, you once said, 'I want to dance so I can hxabe.' What did you mean by that?"

"I want to hxabe so I can feel myself again. When I hxabe, I feel my body and my flesh properly; I unwind and unfold myself, I open myself up in dance. I feel lousy when there is no dancing. The singing and num lets you hxabe yourself. I want to pull myself so that I can hxabe myself." Toma Zho enjoys talking about hxabe. "Num does it to you. If you have num, you can hxabe," he says.

"How about Debe?" Debe often danced with great enthusiasm but did not kia.

As if offering his approval, Toma Zho replies, "Debe's heart hxabe."

"Do you hxabe when you see a relative you haven't seen for a while?"

"Yes. When I see her face after a long absence, I would say my heart hxabe."

"What about when you kill a large animal?"

"Then my heart hxabe, it is happy. For that matter, my heart hxabe whenever there is a good meal."

"Do you ever hxabe after sex?"

Toma Zho's smile broadens. "When I have sex, my heart is sad."

We focus now on the exchange of goods that we have agreed upon when our talk began. "Toma Zho, what should I give you in exchange for that stick you are going to dance with and put num into?"

Toma Zho thinks briefly and looks me over. "Your pants."

I turn to Lee. "Do you think that's a fair exchange?"

"One pair of pants for one dancing stick is a good trade in Toma Zho's favor," Lee replies.

"It seems more than a fair trade for *me*, I say. "There is no num in my pants."

11 The Tradition of Sharing

TOMA ZHO is certainly a complex person. His humor provokes and stimulates. His probes challenge and excite. His silent unpredictability frustrates and attracts. But it is the particular way he relates to num that makes Toma Zho most memorable for me. His approach is individualistic, stressing his own special relationship to num. He says he got num directly from god, and he claims to be the strongest healer in the area. His emphasis is more on accumulating num than on sharing it. He often experiences kia without pulling sickness and is not especially willing to give num to students.

Toma Zho is not unique in these various aspects of his approach to num. His is one type of response to the cash economy whose influence is beginning to impact on the Kung. The explicitness of his struggle highlights the often inchoate and stressful dilemmas the Kung must increasingly face. The ways in which Toma Zho relates to num strike at the heart of the traditional approach to healing, which is "synergistic."

The term *synergy* describes a pattern, a particular way in which phenomena relate to each other, including how people relate to each other and other phenomena (Fuller, 1963; Benedict, 1970; Maslow, 1971). A synergistic pattern brings phenomena together, inter-relating them, creating a new and greater whole from the disparate parts. In that pattern phenomena exist in harmony with each other, maximizing each others' potential. Two phrases capture this quality: "The whole is greater than the sum of the parts," and "What is good for one is good for all."

The traditional approach to healing is synergistic in that num is freely shared throughout the community. As it heats up, num expands, bursting beyond the limits of any one person. As Wi, old in the ways of healing, puts it, "Num comes up in me and bursts me open like a ripe seed pod." Wi waves his arms about and flicks out his fingers as he de-

Page 196: After a night of dance

scribes the action of the seeds being expelled from their ripe pod. He also speaks of the sparks which leap out in every direction from a fire, especially when it is disturbed. Num moves throughout the participants of a dance in just such a manner, bursting beyond one healer, leaping out to others. "I burst open my num and give others some," says Wi.

Num is not in limited supply. Individuals need not compete for its healing power. The activation of num in one person stimulates the activation in others. When num boils in one healer, more num becomes available to all. Num can be infinitely divided without anything being subtracted. The total healing effect of num at a dance far exceeds the individual contributions toward activating that num. The healing energy released binds people together in harmonious, mutually reinforcing relationships. The profound alterations of kia are integrated into the behaviors of daily life, and the two realms of experience stimulate and benefit from each other. In working with num, the Kung are simultaneously dealing with ordinary life issues and participating in a spiritual discipline. The individual enhancement of kia is firmly lodged in a care-giving social context. Healing simultaneously affirms the individual's worth and creates cultural meaning. The result can be remarkable. Large numbers of persons regularly enhance their state of consciousness in a way that is not only harmonious with their society but also essential to its maintenance.

In his characteristically dramatic and controversial manner, Toma Zho is struggling with the approach of the cash economy, and what is especially relevant to him now, its attendant professionalization of the healing dance and the healers. Toma Zho's individualistic approach is intended to establish him as a professional. By emphasizing the power of his own num, he hopes to build a reputation for healing that will attract others to him and make them willing to "pay" for his services. The extended and mutually reciprocating context of the traditional approach would be undermined.

Synergy exists throughout Kung culture. It resides in the

collaborative use of the land and its resources. A group of men hunting or a group of women gathering bring in more food for each person than individual hunters and gatherers could. It also appears in the extensive sharing of material goods, made explicit in the way meat is distributed and in the exchange network called hxaro.

It may be that goods like land and food do not expand like num and are therefore intrinsically less easy to share. Complaints about stinginess in sharing food often punctuate the conversation and sometimes ring out with anger from one eating fire to another. Rarely does one hear any complaints about a healer withholding his healing or a camp refusing to support a dance. But the very nature of the Kung's physical environment – the unpredictability of rains, the absence of modern technology, the variable access to roots and game – seems to demand a synergistic adaptation if the Kung are to survive. The Kung healing dance gains additional power because the synergy that makes it work is also part of the culture's general mode of adaptation and maintenance. The network of mutually supportive relationships which maintains camp and intercamp life comes alive at the dance, providing a safe ground for the terrifying passage into kia. The movement of healing num from person to person throughout the dance reaffirms this network, at times recreating its fabric.

The key to synergy in the healing dance is the boiling num and how it is activated, received and applied. Although the Kung basically believe that num functions synergistically within the dance, there are also times and places at which this is not the case. For example, in the dance with Toma Zho, he resists the activation of num, avoiding kia until dawn, and then, with the abrupt ending of the dance, never gets to heal others. At that time synergy does not prevail because of the way Toma Zho has been relating to his num and the decision of the women to end the dance. If the dance had continued and Toma Zho had healed, his relationship to num as well as the healing dance would have become synergistic. There are also occasions when a less dominant healer relates nonsynergistically to num while others at the dance bring a synergistic quality to the dance as a whole.

The way in which num is activated seems to be the key to the healing power of the dance. When num is received and applied synergistically, its healing power is greatest. During healing, the Kung relate synergistically to num. Synergy at the healing dance is expressed in and released by this relationship of persons to num or energy. Num is the substance and medium of what might be called "synergistic consciousness" among the Kung.

At present, the forces in Kung culture and at the dance encourage this synergistic relationship between persons and num. Num, though given the substance and "reality" of a material – num is seen and held – is infinitely expandable when activated at the dance. Such an infinitely expandable phenomenon becomes very difficult, perhaps impossible, to treat nonsynergistically. That would be like trying to contain smoke in a cheesecloth bag. Perhaps if, in attempting to become a professional, one tries to accumulate or withhold num, one is no longer dealing with num but with some "containable" image of num.

The Kung education for healing is very much a process of learning to relate synergistically to num. The Kung try to experience boiling num in such a way that they can heal others. They are not meant to accumulate num, but to receive it in order to pass it on to others. As the num flows freely among participants at the dance, it prevents individuals from having exclusive access to healing powers or from using those powers for personal aggrandizement or manipulation of others.

Furthermore, the healers experience num in such a way that when they are benefiting themselves, they are benefiting others. Wi talks about wanting to be healed, for once healed, he then would heal others: "I need num and my heart seeks it. I'm really hot for it. I want the youngsters to look at my shoulder and I want to have a taste of their num. I would say to someone like Gau, 'Hey, this shoulder of mine is killing me. Let me see if you can do your stuff and pull something out of it.' If I get a good taste of the num, then I'll have kia and pull, and then I'll say, 'Oh, my children, today you've done me properly, for now I feel my-self again.' "

Finally, the Kung try to experience num in such a way that their kia harmonizes with everyday responsibilities. Healing is not supposed to interfere with the healers' contribution to the group's needs. Healers are Kung first and foremost; they hunt, gather, carry on an active social interchange, and kia. When the dance ends, kia should end. The day after the dance is usually relaxed, with little gathering or hunting and much socializing. But if food must be secured, the healers who experienced kia as well as the other participants must be prepared to gather or hunt, if not immediately, then following a brief rest. And everyone should be able to interact normally when the dance is over: it is felt that no healers should be so deeply into kia that they cannot converse if they have to. Setting up these boundaries on the experience of kia reflects the importance of meeting everyday responsibilities if the group is to survive. The Kung do not accumulate food and goods, so if too many persons were unable to assume normal responsibilities because they were still in kia, there would be an inadequate supply.

Several years ago, at Christmas 1964, there was a large dance. Richard Lee had a cow killed for the celebration, providing ample food for the participants. The dance lasted nearly three days, ending early in the morning of the third day. Tsaa, an old and experienced healer, had experienced kia and pulled often during the dance. But when it ended, he remained in kia.

Late in the final morning, several hours after the dance had ended, Tsaa went to Lee, asking for help in cooling down his num. Lee, the "European who had the cow killed," was viewed as a powerful figure and therefore a person one might turn to for such help. Tsaa told Lee that he wanted to end his kia, that it was not right for him still to be in kia because he could not carry on with his usual activities. He felt fearful and confused. Lee assured Tsaa that in time his num would cool down, and in general tried to calm him.

Tsaa left Lee after a while; evidently, by the early afternoon, he was out of kia.

During my fieldwork I speak with Tsaa about this experience. Time has softened the fear and confusion he felt that morning in 1964, but the prohibition against a kia which gets out of control and extends beyond the dance remains.

"Tsaa, could you tell me about that dance several Christmases ago when your num stayed up *after* the dance had ended?" I ask.

"I'm beyond the age when I could do that," he replies jokingly.

"Did you pull out sickness at that dance?"

"Yes," he says, "that was the time I pulled my wife. The num was still good then, but now it's all left me. I remember that morning well. My body was still shivering, the num was still up in me."

"How long did the num stay up?"

"If you do a lot of pulling the night before," Tsaa answers, "the num may still be shivering you until the next day, because your stomach and spine still have the num in it. It happens often that I've been pulling a lot and the num stays up. You dance all night and then when people break up and lie in the shade, you go to the shade also because your skin is hot. And then you drink a lot of water and pour it over yourself to cool off, so you make the num harmless, so that it doesn't stay up long."

"Why not keep the num up all day long?"

"No," he replies emphatically, "no, what you want to do is to make it harmless."

"What does a person look like whose num is still up the next day?"

"In that state, you're not fit for anything. No thoughts in your head. You can't speak properly to people as we're speaking now. So you should make the num harmless so you can talk to others." Tsaa speaks softly but intensely. "I've seen somebody whose num stayed up all day long. He just sat there and shivered during that day. That is bad. Num is fire and it hurts. If you stay up with it like that all day, it could kill you. Num is a fire given us by god. It is not like the sun which wouldn't kill you."

During kia, the healer may hxabe himself. *Hxabe* means to "unfold" or "unwind" or "untie" oneself, to "spread oneself apart," or to "feel oneself." It is a pleasurable feeling, considered one of the rewards of kia. Gau describes hxabe: "You dance and your body is hot, and then you pull and massage yourself, and then you hxabe yourself, you spread apart your flesh. You hxabe yourself when you dance and kia and pull. Hxabe feels good. It makes your heart sweet."

The pleasurable effects of hxabe often linger on into the day after a dance. Gau speaks of this outcome: "When I hxabe myself, I feel good again. Then when I walk across the pan, I want to see people, and I enjoy talking with them. When I meet with people, I can play and play with them." But hxabe is a very unobstrusive state in this period after the dance. The Kung go about their normal activities, only in a more open and relaxed manner, a special playfulness and warmth emanating from their presence.

Having the individual relate synergistically to num is the goal, but the task of maintaining that relationship is a continuing and dynamic process, with its successes and setbacks. A balance must be struck between the depth of the kia experienced and the ability to retain enough control of the kia so that it can be applied to healing. Education for kia is a process in which that balance is continually being struck, upset, and restruck. As dancers seek num, they often withdraw in fear from the boiling num. As healers seek to become expert, they may be unexpectedly overwhelmed by boiling num. As healers try to become professionals, they may try to overcontrol and overmanipulate num. During these transition points, it is more difficult for the individual to have a synergistic relationship to num. But most often these transition points are preludes to a new balance, to the re-establishment of synergy.

Sometimes older, experienced healers settle into a kind of balance, as if seeking kia experiences of only a certain intensity. But there will be dances during which, despite their expectations, despite their efforts to the contrary, the num boils quicker and hotter than they can handle. At least for that dance, the synergy must be re-established, maybe even created at a new balance point.

Then there are those few special healers whose num represents the standard of power. Wa Na is one example. It seems that she maintains an on-going synergistic relationship to num. To reach such a balance, the synergistic relationship with num must be recreated each time the num appears in increasingly intense and accessible forms.

Healing is still very much a family affair. The extended Kung family, a prototypically synergistic unit, is the context within which num is activated. Num moves along an exchange network whose unique pervasiveness and strength come from the special bondings of family. Parents teach their children to heal; children support their parents through the agonies of kia; sisters and brothers, husbands and wives, sing and dance to activate each other's num. Familial supports relieve healers of some of the solitary burdens of kia and move their healing num along well-established and extensive sharing routes.

One dance at Xaixai captures unforgettably the way a family intensifies the synergistic quality of boiling num. It is a small family-oriented dance at Chuko's little camp. Although toward the end, persons come from other camps, the family focus remains. Chuko, a strong healer, holds the dance to heal her son Dau, himself a healer, though still inexperienced. Dau has been complaining for several days of "tiredness" and "tired blood." He lies around a lot during the day. He does little except walk slowly around the camp or occasionally to the water-hole. He appears to have little energy; he seems "depressed." "I'm going to pull my son tonight," Chuko says.

After the dance has been under way for about an hour, Dau, who has been sitting impassively on the outskirts, begins to dance. Soon he is overwhelmed by num. He falls with a thud, confirming his entrance into kia.

Chuko leans over from her spot in the singing circle and begins to work on Dau, who is lying on the sand. She rubs his head vigorously, one hand cupped over each ear. Then she blows sharply into his ears. She takes a stick from the fire, glowing orange-hot at its tip, and lifting Dau's head, she passes the glowing hot tip under his head, back and forth, many times. Chuko then lies on top of her son, her stomach rubbing against his back. Their two bodies are in full contact, their sweat mingling. Chuko tries to rise up, staggers, and completely off-balance, falls back down on Dau. Her kia has already begun.

Chuko moves off to Dau's side, lying at right angles to him, rubbing her head all over his head. She then tries to turn Dau over onto his side. She begins to sing softly to her son, crawling across his back, almost rolling over him into the fire. Then she moves her head along his back, up and down his spine. Dau reaches for his mother and holds her supportively.

Mother and son fuse in kia, simultaneously healing each other and being healed. They emerge from their intense kia as a pair, stimulating and "awakening" each other. They start singing and struggle to get up together. They rise slowly, holding tightly to each other, swaying violently, trying to prevent each other's fall, but finally falling. Back down on the sand, they are still in each other's tight grasp. Chuko begins to heal her son, and he shouts the kowhedili.

As mother and child work with num, their healing power is intensified and radiates outward as each then heals others at the dance. Those at the dance speak of its especially strong num. The next day Dau walks about with his usual vigor, conversing with his usual outgoing smile. "Today I am well," he says. "The num has cured me." The processes of being healed and healing interact, stimulating and intensifying each other.

The movement of num synergistically throughout the camp is exemplified by the healing dance. The camp becomes a community healer. At the basis of this synergy is the num flowing freely among all participants. The healers only confirm or focus num's healing energy as they lay on their fluttering hands. Participating in the dance, the camp can experience a communal transformation. Individuals are healed, and the camp, as a unity greater than the sum of its members, is also healed and set right in its environment.

When num is activated at a dance, individual efforts are transformed into communal ones, and specific functions merge into common ones. Through an intricate and subtle process of kia management, the dance is orchestrated so that not too many persons experience kia at once, and help is available to those whose struggle with num is out of control. Singers, dancers, and others at the dance are in communication with each other, usually without speaking, keeping their eyes and ears open for the signs of impending kia, deciding implicitly with each other who will take responsibility for working on which healer. Through this communal effort, individual experiences of kia are regulated so that num becomes maximally available to the group.

Often, several persons work in intimate physical contact on someone in kia, especially if that person is experiencing an intense kia without sufficient control. These helpers' bodies may tremble and shake in rhythm with the distressed one's spasm-wracked body. Num can flow easily across individual boundaries, creating a healing unit more powerful than the strength of its component individuals. In these situations it becomes hard to distinguish the particular function of num, whether it is being put into someone to intensify kia, or is being cooled down so a person can gain control of kia, or is being used to pull sickness from someone. Likely all are occuring to some extent, and at times simultaneously.

This group management of kia is expressed in many other forms. Healers communicate with each other during their kia, sharing and confirming each other's perceptions and visions. This mutual reinforcement can strengthen each one's ability to heal. Wi speaks about how he dances with another experienced healer: "We do the giraffe dance together. We do num together. We usually see the same spirits, but there are times when only I can see a spirit, and I then point the spirit out to him. He can't see it at first. Then he sees it. There are other times when I say, 'Today I can't see the spirit. Tell me about it, so together we can cure this person's life.' "

The dance is an opportunity for people to exchange in many ways. People at a dance are in the same space for many hours, often in close physical contact: sitting closely around the talking fire, huddling under the blankets asleep, sitting side by side and knee over knee in the singing group, rubbing and holding and carrying a fallen healer. This kind of body contact is not unusual for the Kung, but the intensity and intimacy of the contact, and the fact that it occurs over an extended period, are unusual. News is exchanged, gossip enjoyed. When num is being received and distributed synergistically, many exchanges are facilitated. When the dance is a good one, persons are more inclined to open up the channels of communication.

In one large dance we put on at Xaixai, the activation of num releases a significant social exchange. The dance is attended by all the camps at Xaixai, despite the fact there is a major, ongoing argument between the two larger camps over a prospective divorce, the wife coming from one of the camps, the husband from the other. The dispute is still raging as the dance begins. People are just not in the mood to be together, let alone in the intimate context of the dance. The fact that the dance can be held is in part explained by the Kung's desire to respect our invitation to come, and their interest in eating the food we have promised to provide.

More than sixty persons gather in a open area near our camp. The dance begins listlessly, the singing flat and uninspired, the dancing perfunctory and fragmented. What is most unusual, the singers form themselves into two curved lines, neither more than a quarter-circle. These two lines wrap around opposite sides of the fire, and between the lines there is a clear open space, like an unclaimed land. Nothing is exchanged across that open space – no looks, conversation, or physical contact. Each quarter-circle is composed predominantly of women from one of the two camps involved in the dispute, and there is no cross-representation in the other camp's line.

As the men dance around the singers, the tension becomes more evident. Arguments are being carried on between the two lines of women, shouts about each other's "stinginess" or "bad manners." The shouting escalates, dominating the dance for a moment. Two older women, facing each other at opposite ends of the two lines, have brought the angry exchange to a climax. Then suddenly, as each feels some redress has been won, they agree to resolve their differences, at least for a time. Each of the women grandly rises from her spot at the end of her line and moves around the fire toward the other. They sit down next to each other. The other women follow their lead, merging to form one tight singing circle. The mood of the dance immediately lightens, and laughter is heard. The songs take on a new vitality and enthusiasm. Very soon the dance is ignited, and strong num becomes activated within several hours.

The Kung wish all persons to have access to num, either by being healers or by being related to healers. Practically speaking, both forms of access are equivalent. Moreover, the kinship links are so pervasive in the small Kung population clusters that it is rare for anyone not to have a close relative who is a healer. If by chance there is no close relative, the individual is not denied access to a healer, because some relationship will be emphasized, perhaps by drawing upon more distant kinship ties. Also, since boundaries between camps are permeable, kinship ties guarantee access to the num in some other camp if one's own camp cannot put on a dance. Num is available to those in need. It cannot be completely withheld because of personality differences, and it is not completely cut off because of a dispute between camps.

This fluid, need-determined use of num expresses the way num moves synergistically throughout the village. It also explains Koto's philosophical acceptance. After nearly eighty years without ever receiving num himself, he is still relaxed and confident about his continuing access to num. He does not feel he must "personally" possess num, and does not view himself as being deprived or inadequate because he is not a healer.

Some kind of balance seems to emerge in the number of healers in a camp. No one is a priori excluded from receiving num. But only about half the adult men and ten percent of the adult women become healers. A balance is sought between the healing needs of a camp, the number of dances held, and the number of healers who kia and heal at these dances. The camp trains enough persons to become healers, and those who are disinclined, or too fearful, do not have to receive num.

"Wild" and disruptive behaviors during kia, or experiencing kia without pulling sickness, are discouraged unless it is an aspect of a student's search for num or is part of an experienced healer's way. Those few whom sickness consistently defeats are discouraged from dancing altogether. The enormous effort involved in putting on a dance is meant to reap healing benefits for the camp.

Another aspect of this balance concerns those rare healers, such as Wa Na, who provide the strongest healing. She used to enter kia and heal on a daily basis, doing little else. Persons like Wa Na are essential to the Kung, but they are invariably not primary subsistence providers. If these exceptional healers were more numerous and were primary providers, adaptation patterns could be threatened. Large groups of older and younger persons are supported by the adult population's subsistence activities, and this division of labor assumes the full participation of adult healers.

The activation of num is an old and rich tradition, extolled in Kung myths. This tradition is also thoroughly integrated into the mainstream of contemporary Kung life. The general sharing which characterizes the basic patterns of adaptation and interaction provides a supportive foundation for healing. The fact that learning to be a healer is a regular aspect of socialization builds on that foundation. The public and routine nature of the healing dance keeps the workings of num open to all. The circumstance of healers being ordinary Kung first, and healers second, prevents the development of an exclusive, isolated class of num practitioners. The careful preparation for entry into kia and re-entry back into an ordinary state ensures a continuity in the individual's ability to meet the group's needs. Finally, the emphasis of the entire healing dance directs the dance toward meeting society's needs first and foremost. This does not limit the power of num. Rather, by focusing the healing impact of num on something beyond the individual's own personal needs, it increases num's power.

When the Kung, through their healers in kia, contact the spiritual realm, the entire healing process comes full circle. Num originally comes from the great god. The Kung use that num for healing and protection. When in kia, they often argue and battle with the spirits sent by the gods to carry away the sick. As num is activated, it recreates the relationship between humans and gods, between the human and spiritual dimensions. Protection is forthcoming from the gods. The sick one is saved, or the sick one is taken away. In all cases, an exchange occurs which can be understood as continuing the existence of the Kung hunting and gathering society. In these points of contact with the gods, in these courageous and outrageous struggles with the gods, the Kung seek to face uncertainty and conflict and to affirm the substance and dignity of their existence. They are, in a sense, seeking to re-establish a balance in their universe, but not out of guilt about undone acts. In kia, they are acknowledging, in yet one more time and one more place, the nature of their universe as a whole and their place in it. Through the medium of boiling num, that acknowledgment is made particularly eloquent and convincing.

12 Kau Dwa, a Strong Healer

TOWARD THE END of my stay in the Kalahari, we travel to Kangwa, looking for Kau Dwa, reputed to be a "very big" healer, perhaps the strongest aside from Wa Na, now legendary for the power of her num. These two have an exceptional relationship to num. Num pervades their lives, granting them impressive knowledge, distinguishing them from other experienced healers. Each also acts at times as a professional healer, receiving gifts as payment for services.

Kau Dwa is totally blind, but he can see in kia. Without assistance, he dances fervently, finding those he wishes to heal with uncanny accuracy, in contrast with his ordinary behavior, where he is led around and moves haltingly. Tsaa, the old healer from Xaixai, says of Kau Dwa: "He's blind, but he can see to heal. His num gives him the power to see. And his num is getting stronger as he gets older."

One of the younger healers also speaks of Kau Dwa's power: "Kau Dwa is a different type from the other healers. If a person is sick, he'll tell you exactly what's wrong with him. He'll say, 'This person is sick from such and such, or he's sick over here or there,' and then Kau Dwa will make that person live. But sometimes Kau Dwa will tell people, 'No! This person god has refused. God is going to take this person away.' Kau Dwa and Wa Na are alike. They are the same in that when they pull a person, that person rises and lives." Kau Dwa himself is not immodest: "Wa Na and I are equal."

When I meet Kau Dwa, I am meeting as much my image of him as the man himself. Unpretentiously, he proceeds to fulfill his reputation.

"Kau Dwa, how did you first get num?" I ask.

"When I was a tiny thing, still sucking at my mother's breast, I took num, I drank num," Kau Dwa says.

His wife, who comes by at that point, nods in agreement to his words and adds, "Kau Dwa was born with it."

"I was small and at the breast," he continues. "The num

Page 211: Kau Dwa

was just like today. It started when I was at the breast. I was about three or four years old. I would cry and cry and cry. My mother would sing to me, and I would cry and suck the breast and cry. I just sat in my mother's lap and danced. I was afraid of num. Num was hot and it hurt. People said, 'What's this youngster still at the breast doing?' I was little and taught myself. That's my story. Others are much older than me but started their num later than me." All this time Kau Dwa's wife has been signifying his story is true. Now she leaves, saying she has to attend to other matters.

"Kau Dwa, you are a person who has done num for a very long time. Do people come to you for advice?" I ask.

Kau Dwa laughs, enjoying his own laughter. "Maybe I'll wear your jacket," he offers.

"Kau Dwa, what happens when you kia?"

Kau Dwa is now talking directly to and about me. "When you kia, you fall, you die. I ask god for num and put it into you. I say to god, 'Here's my child, give me some more num so I may put it into him.' Even today I'm going to put it into you, and you'll dance, dance, dance. One of these days soon, when the women start singing, you'll start shivering. Let's dance tonight, let's dance tonight, and then pile on the truck and go to Kangwa and dance tomorrow night, and then I'm going to dance you again. I'll dance you tonight and dance you tomorrow night."

"Can a European like me learn to kia and heal?"

"I'm going to do both you and Lee, one over there and one over here, and the two of you will be trembling like leaves in the wind. It makes no difference if you're one of our people or not. When I pull you, I will feel num trembling in my body and then in your body, and then I'll say, 'Oh, today this fellow has drunk num.' "

"Are you putting num into your son?"

"My son's got it!" says Kau Dwa. "He pulls sickness from people, and when I'm dead, he'll have it. He asked for num and I gave it to him. I haven't been asked by anyone else, and I haven't given num. If ever I were asked, I'd give num. But I haven't been asked."

"How come a powerful healer like you hasn't taught more people?" I wonder.

"People are afraid of num. It's hot and painful. They wish it was cool but it's not. People are afraid of num because if they ask me for it and I give it to them, and then they eat meat and maize without my preparing it the right way for them, they'll die." Kau Dwa again turns his talk directly to me. "That's why I told you yesterday that if you want to eat meat and maize, then bring them to me and let me feed them to you. We'll cook together, and I'll eat a bite and then I'll give you some. I'll have a bit and then you'll have a bit. Then I'll say, 'OK, you've eaten this meat and maize with my preparation, and now even when I'm not around, at any other time or wherever you are, you'll be able to eat this stuff without any worry.' I gave some of this food, prepared by me, to Hotun too. I'm giving him num also. I fixed him up, and now he's entitled to eat it all the time. I've broken him in on all the different foods, and now I've left him. I'd have to do this will all the foods. You'll die if you disregard these things I do. You'll just die if you're drinking num and you don't go through these dietary routines with me."

"What else must a student do besides observing these dietary routines?" I ask.

"You must do the student's gebesi properly. You've got to fire arrows of num into the gebesi. You fire them in and fire them in until these arrows of num, which are a lot like long thorns, are sticking out of your gebesi, and your abdomen is like a pin cushion, with arrows sticking out in all directions from your gebesi." Kau Dwa leans closer to me, drawing me into his presence, with intimate intensity. He makes it clear he is also talking about *my* gebesi, and about rubbing *me*. "So you see why we rub you like that. It's because the arrows are popping out of your body and going out into space, and we're rubbing them back into your body. That's what we do with our sweat. We try to work the arrows around in the back. When we do that, your breath and soul return properly to your body. But if we don't do that, then you might die. You might die if we just left those things sticking out." Kau Dwa speaks on in an animated fashion, the rhythm of his talk accelerating. "There is another thing, a thing where the spirits are just hovering at the edges of the num dance, and they're firing these arrows of num at you, firing them at your belly. And then it's up to you to dodge. It's people like myself who can see these creatures and tell them, 'Get out! Get out of here! Beat it!' Those who can't see these creatures just get stuck by their arrows."

Softening his tone somewhat, Kau Dwa continues. "My father was the one who had num, and when he gave it to me, he lost it in himself. God said to him, 'Look, if you're going to give it to your son, it's your son who's going to carry this, and it will leave you completely and you'll die.' That's what god told him."

"God told your father he'd die?" I repeat as much as I ask.

"It's this death that I've been talking about, this very death that makes you fear num. Because if this num goes into you, you can die. An enormous projectile is in your body." Kau Dwa fingers his walking stick, marking off a section about fourteen inches long. "The projectile is embedded in your chest, and it kills you. You fall over dead and lie there until something or someone comes along and pulls it out of you and throws it away. And only then, when it is removed from your body, do you begin to shiver and start uttering shrieks, showing that you're alive again, that you live." Kau Dwa pauses briefly. When he speaks further, his tone remains serious. "It's the death that kills us all. It's the death that people fear, the death that kills our fathers and mothers."

"Do some people die and then live again when they heal?" I ponder.

Kau Dwa's words are elusive yet firm. "In death, you don't return to the living. You just die." Kau Dwa feels around near the edge of the fire, but his blindness prevents him from completing the task. "I've got no eyes, and it's hard for me to get coals from the fire. How can I find coals? I just fiddle around. Do you have matches for me to light my pipe?" With some of our matches he lights up and draws the smoke deeply into his lungs. Then he returns to my question, speaking with conviction. "Those who like num get it and own it. Those who don't like it, don't get it. Those who fear death, don't get num and live. The other people, those who grab num and take hold of it and dance it, are the ones who fall or die." Kau Dwa pauses a moment or two, but his tone barely changes. "What kills those who have num is when they don't get paid properly. When they don't get anything to wear, when they don't get anything to put around their necks, when they don't get anything to put on their heads."

Another pipeful of tobacco is lit up, and Kau Dwa, who draws hard and often on the pipe, becomes surrounded with a cloud of smoke. The talk ceases for several minutes while the enjoyment of smoking takes over. When Kau Dwa puts down the pipe, I ask him, "How did you lose your sight?"

"God," he says. "I was working hard at healing people, but people didn't pay me. I was working hard at putting things into their gebesi, but people didn't pay me or give me things. So god collected my eyes and took them away. God keeps my eyeballs in a little cloth bag. When he first collected them, he got a little cloth bag and plucked my eyeballs out and put them into the bag, and then he tied the eyeballs to his belt and went up to heaven. And now when I dance, on the nights that I dance and when the singing rises up, god comes down from heaven swinging the bag with the eyeballs above my head, and he lowers the eyeballs to my eye level, and as the singing gets strong, he puts the eyeballs into my sockets and they stay there and I heal. And when the women stop singing and separate out, he removes the eyeballs, puts them back in the cloth bag, and takes them up to heaven."

"Kau Dwa, when you're at a dance, how do you know where people are so you can heal them?"

"I can see them," he replies without any hesitation, then stops for a moment. "Right now, during the day, I don't see people. But at a dance, when people sing and clap, I see everybody. When the women sing, I can see everything, even if there's a snake crawling through the bush out in the dark. I say to everybody, 'There's a snake crawling through the bush. Watch out for it.' " Kau Dwa leans even more intently toward me. "That's the stuff I'm talking about putting into you, Dick, and I'm not kidding. I'm not playing around. That's the stuff I'm talking about putting into you, so that you too can see things when you dance." He smiles for several moments.

"What else do you see when you dance?" I ask.

"I see everything," he shoots back. "I can see hyenas, lions, and leopards. I can even see trucks and motor cars, even a truck coming from as far away as Chumkwe, as far away as that. My eyes start turning around in my head like the wheels of the truck spinning, and I say, 'There's a truck coming.' Even something as far as the other side of Maun!"

"And what do you do when you see these things?"

"I tell people about it," he says, as if this is obvious. "When I look out to the bush, I can see a lion making low growling sounds, far away. I can see his face very clearly, and I tell the others, 'Hey! Hey! There's a lion out there.' And the lion sees me, it sees me too. When it sees my face, it lowers it head to the ground."

"Suppose someone at the dance says, 'How can you see that far?' "

"I would say, 'That's what I see.' "

"What if people say, 'Bullshit?' "

"There are people who say that. Then later on they see the tracks of the animal and say, 'Kau Dwa was right.' All the people in this area had given me up. They said I'm no good. But they've seen me, and now they know I don't lie. Maybe they've given up on trying to outwit or dispute me. I don't lie, because what I see always turns out to be true." Kau Dwa's voice remains calm.

"Kau Dwa, what do people want from you?"

He is still considering the previous question. "When people come to me, I think, 'These are the people who said I've been telling lies.' " Then he responds to the question I have just asked. "They seek num."

"Does one go to a healer if one has problems in one's marriage?" I wonder.

"No, such a person does not come to me."

"If a man said to you, 'Kau Dwa, my children are hungry. I want to go hunting. Which direction should I go, north or east?' what would you tell him?"

"I would say, 'Don't go north, because it's far.' "

"How would you know to tell him that?"

"The spirits would tell me about the direction in which such a person should hunt."

"When you're just like you are now, that is, not experiencing kia, can you give such advice?"

"Yes," Kau Dwa replies with assurance. He then turns his focus back onto us, with renewed excitement. "Today, if I fix you guys, don't worry. It's all right to go wherever you want. It's OK. You can go in any direction you want. We healers help people, we help each other. That makes our heart glad. When I make a sick person well, my heart is glad. And then when that person gives me a nice shirt or jacket to put on, like this jacket here" – he fingers the Western-style jacket he is wearing, a payment for his curing – "I feel good about having a shirt on my back, it covers my body. And then, that person who gives me something like this jacket, god will shoot arrows into that person. One arrow, then another, and another and another. And then that person too will be able to kia. And I will be able to help by rubbing his gebesi."

The conversation stops for a moment. I take the opportunity to pursue a new subject. "Kau Dwa," I inquire, "what happens when you dream?"

"When you dream of spirits, they are the creatures that are trying to kill people. So you fight them and you kill them. It's just like picking up this club in my hand and bashing them over the head." Kau Dwa gestures vigorously with his right hand, as if he were beating something. "But you must kia first. You don't kill the spirits in the dream. You wake up first, kia, and then you can kill them. The spirits try to kill you. They try to kill you so that you're dead. And then you say to the spirits, 'No, you can't do that to me. Get out of here. Beat it. Don't come back. You're bringing bad words and I refuse. Get away from here.' So you take your club and beat them and kill them." Again

Kau Dwa's right arm moves fiercely through the air, up and down, many times.

Kau Dwa's strident, martial tone lingers only a moment before evaporating into his wide, open smile. "A sick person asks a healer to kia. And the healer pulls the sick one back from the hands of god and refuses to let god take him away. The healer puts the soul back into the sick one's body. But there are times when god is selfish and takes the sick person away. You might be sick some day, and I, a healer, might pull and pull and pull you. But in spite of this, god may be selfish and take you away, and you will just die."

"Kau Dwa, did you ever work on someone who died?"

"Yes, I pulled Xoma in vain. God was selfish with us and took him away. When Xoma died, his head was on my left thigh, his back was against my lap. I was pulling sickness from him when he died. I was pulling in vain when he died."

"How did that feel?"

"I didn't feel anything," says Kau Dwa. "My own first wife also died in my arms. Yes, my wife died and left me. God was selfish."

"Was it hard working on Xoma? Was it harder to pull him than when you pull and there is no serious sickness?"

"I won't pull a person who isn't sick," Kau Dwa states. "The one who isn't sick, isn't sick. There was a person who fell off a horse, and his ribs got shattered, and he was full of blood. He was very ill. His whole chest was full of blood. Another woman, her chest was killing her. I removed things. I removed – " Kau Dwa hesitates, then continues, "live coals. I removed live coals that were fired into her by god."

"Kau Dwa, how can you tell when the pulling is strong or weak? Do you pull stronger sometimes than other times?"

"I pull stronger every day. It's all strong. It's all the same," he replies. "My blind age-mates don't pull as strongly. God has told those guys to dance but they do not really dance, while I'm the only one who *really* dances."

"Do you pull with others?"

"I pull with others. Some I like very much to pull with.

But Nau and I don't get along and so we don't pull together."

"You don't get along with Nau?"

"Nau won't help me. I've called him before and said, 'Come and help me,' and he won't help me. Others will come when I call them, even though they are far away."

"What kinds of sicknesses have you cured recently?"

"Lately some people I've saved and some people have died." Kau Dwa becomes more intense. "But if I hadn't saved them, they all would have died." He speaks more dramatically, pointing all around. "All these people at Goshe I've saved. I saved two men, one a Herero, the other a Tswana. The Herero had a mysterious sickness. God told me to tell that Herero to stop digging a well at a certain place because god didn't want a well dug in that place. And so the Herero stopped digging that well, and he lived, and later he dug a well in another place."

After this recounting of cures, I take a new tack. "Kau Dwa, what do you think of European medicine?"

"It is like ours."

"Would you take it?"

"European medicine is just as good as our own num," he says. "Sure I would take European medicine. I would take it in the morning and be up in the evening. And for some things if I didn't take it, I might die."

"If you were sick, and there were both one of your own healers and a European healer here, whom would you choose?"

Kau Dwa thinks about this for a while. "If I were sick, and if the European healer were close by, I would go to him and drink his medicine. But if the European were far away and one of our own healers was close by, I'd go to our own and get healed." Kau Dwa's broad, sparkling smile speaks of his desire not to offend, but also of his easy acceptance of the pills and antibiotics we at times dispense.

Our talk nears its end. "Kau Dwa, have you ever pulled yourself? I don't mean pulling another one alone, but pulling sickness from yourself?"

"Yes," he replies with enthusiasm. "There are nights when

the women don't sing and I'm sitting by myself, and god comes to me and tells me to sing to myself. And I sing to myself, and then num comes up in me and I kia. I pull myself, and pull myself, and pull myself. And then I get up and pull others. That's when you fix yourself."

"Is pulling yourself the same as pulling others?"

"It's the same thing."

"How do you pull something out of yourself?"

"The very things we've been talking about," he says, "the sickness things. You remove them from your own flesh and make your flesh good again." Kau Dwa becomes reflective and seems to collect his thoughts for a while. "There are some nights when my wife and I are alone in our hut, and we sometimes begin to sing with each other. And then, after some of this singing, we may kia. We kia to make ourselves feel right, and we kia with each other. That may happen on a particular night."

Our talk has reached a new level of intimacy, and we all become quiet. Then, picking up from cues in Kau Dwa's expression, I move to another question. "Kau Dwa, do you ever kia without pulling?"

"At times I've experienced kia," he replies, "and not pulled, and I say, 'There, I'm not doing any pulling.' "

"Is it good to kia without pulling, or bad?"

"It's good," says Kau Dwa. This perplexes me slightly. Then Kau Dwa's message becomes clearer. "If you save a person's life, he should give you lots of things. If he doesn't give you things, then in the future you'll just leave him alone and let him die if he's sick." Kau Dwa's smile peers from the edges of his theatrical frown.

We go on naturally from there and make the exchange we have agreed upon for his time and help. I take off my shirt and hand it to Kau Dwa. He gladly puts it on. Then grasping both my hands in his and pumping them enthusiastically, he says, "Now, this was what I call a good talk."

13 Wa Na, a Healer among Healers

"SHE'S JUST GOT IT. She's just got the num and she'll die with it," says Kau Dwa of Wa Na. Coming from Kau Dwa, himself one of the most powerful healers in Dobe, this statement firmly establishes Wa Na's stature. Others speak of Wa Na with similar respect, some with awe. Even among the strongest healers, Wa Na is looked upon as a standard of strength. As Tsaa, wise in the ways of num, puts it: "She's fantastic. She's terrible with num."

Now in her mid-eighties, Wa Na remains the dominant force in her village of Goshe. Until 1964 she was an active dancer. For a period of months in 1964, she danced and healed every afternoon (Lee, personal communication). A group of five or six women would sing and clap for her, putting on the dance just so that her num could be activated. They were her regular supporters and followers, valuing this special relationship with Wa Na and the intimacy with her num that it entailed.

Wa Na does not attend all the dances at Goshe now. When she does, she dances only occasionally, and then only a few turns. Yet her num is still regarded as uniquely powerful. For many years persons have been coming to her for healing, and the non-Kung who come to be healed compensate her. Wa Na remains a professional in this sense, though she no longer has the physical strength to heal as many persons as she once did. Her num is no less powerful, just less available.

Wa Na's political significance at Goshe is also great. She is acknowledged as the "owner" of the Goshe water-hole, her father having come to it first among the Kung. With her extensive kinship ties, her social significance is just as central as her political position. Wa Na is someone quite special. Her great age, her political centrality, her extensive kinship ties, and her uniquely powerful num are all signs of importance, enhancing each other. I enthusiastically agree with Richard Lee's suggestion that we make a trip to Goshe.

Page 222: Wa Na

We arrive late in the afternoon. A dance begins in the evening, continuing into the morning. Kau Dwa and several others from his village have come with us. Kau Dwa enters the dance just after dawn, emerging from the shadows of a nearby hut with bouncing, rhythmic steps. As he approaches the dance circle, his steps become dance steps, and by the time he enters the dance groove he is dancing passionately. Soon he is in kia with his characteristic fervor, pulling everyone at the dance with great expansive gestures, an ecstatic joy rippling over his face and through his body.

The dance reaches a quieter period. Kau Dwa's pulling has become more intimate, as he works thoroughly and intensively on a few persons. I happen to look around the dance area. Two old women are sitting on the periphery of the dance circle. One is full-bodied, the other somewhat thin. They both sit very still, almost impassive, their knees drawn up close to their chests, a blanket wrapped around their shoulders, each holding on to a tall walking stick. They are like ancient but proud statues.

The full-bodied one is studying the dance. Then she methodically and laboriously raises herself up with the walking stick. Approaching the dance, she begins to move about, slowly, gracefully, with great dignity. She is dancing, but all she shows with her body is the suggestion of a dance step, the mere fragment of a dance gesture. Her presence, though, is unmistakable. This old, almost heavy body is floating along the sand's fragile surface. After no more than two minutes, she is again sitting down, still and silent. Her dance has emerged from a statue and returned to a statue in one continuous rhythm. That is my first contact with Wa Na.

Later that day we are sitting under the shade of a tree. Lee and I have agreed that we would try to talk with Wa Na that afternoon. As it happened, Wa Na has just come by and is sitting, half in the shade, half in the sun, about ten yards away. Wa Na often looks off into space, her head tilting upward, sometimes resting on the open palm of her hand. Several times she bursts into laughter, her mouth wide open, her toothless gums showing, her face wrinkled up in a shudder of joy, her blind eyes squeezed tight. Her laugh suffuses her whole body. It seems as solid as her sitting, and it punctuates that sitting in unexpected, dramatic outbursts. Wa Na is not always in conversation with other people when laughter overtakes her. Some might call this evidence of senility. But after more than fifty years of powerful kia and pulling, these inner conversations could as much be the expression of an enhanced state of consciousness as of the deteriorated state of senility.

Unfortunately, we have to leave Goshe before a talk with Wa Na can be arranged, although I believe that I met her. Because I would like her to talk in this book, I ask Richard Lee if I can include parts of an interview he had with Wa Na in December 1964, almost four years before. He generously agrees. These, then, are excerpts of Wa Na's talk.

"I'm afraid to begin my story because my healing work has some very deep mixtures. There are Goba things, and European things, and our people's things. I don't know whether to tell others about the details of my num. If I do, how will I heal myself tomorrow? These things I'm talking about are very difficult things and different ways of living. Just as a European has his own way of living, a Goba has his own way of living, and we people have a very different way of living. And with all these kinds of people, I fear to say anything about our num, because if I do, I may find myself in an argument with the spirits. And that is why I want someone to pay for my story. Because if I get into a dispute with the spirits, I will know that at least I got something for telling the story, because my things are serious. Our num, and our healing, are very difficult and serious things. Sometimes you see healers with different ways of healing. Some are big healers, and some are small healers. Myself, I am a big healer, because I have been able to do things right ever since I was given the num.

"You are told not to eat certain types of food, for if you eat them, they will make your num weak. Or if you roast your meat in the fire made by another healer who is stronger than you, your num will also become weak. There are lots of different things that must be kept in order if one's num is to remain powerful. Europeans have their own ways of keeping their 'num' powerful. We have our ways also.

"Today I am an old person. Today I am very old. Sometimes I can speak well; sometimes I forget what I am speaking about.

"Today most people come to me and I heal them, although I am a woman. They know and are convinced that I am a good healer. For example, a Herero woman was ill. Then I cured her. A second person I cured was a Tswana man. Some of our men healers had tried to cure him and they failed. When I came to that Tswana's hut, that's when I right away found out that he had been witched by the parents of his first wife. And the num that I used on him was mixed with the bone of one of his cattle. The third person I cured was his wife, who gave me a dress, which I then gave to one of my daughters."

Lee interrupts Wa Na's long soliloquy. "I have heard that you are a strong healer, but these words you have been speaking, are they the words about num that you are afraid to utter?"

"The things I'm telling you about eating food and having num are the things I was afraid to tell you," Wa Na responds. "It is telling you about those things that might make me less a healer.

"The powerful healer at my mother's village was Koshe. He was one of those who gave me num. The respectful way of addressing Koshe was Hwa Na. I called him Hwa Na because, if I was far away and called him that, he would hear his name called and would turn himself into a lion and go around looking for the one who had called him. The term Hwa Na is applied to all the big healers. This is the name that makes them turn into lions."

"Can you utter the name Hwa Na in normal conversation?" Lee inquires.

"The name Hwa Na is a term of respect," she responds. "It may be used publicly in addressing a great healer. The great healers were my husband, and two other men, both of whom gave me num. All are now dead. None were killed by god. All were killed by people. These great healers went hunting as lions, searching for people to kill. Then someone would shoot an arrow or throw a spear into these healers who were prowling around as lions. When these great healers tried to change back into their own human skins, they usually died. When a healer changes into a lion, only other healers can still see him. To ordinary people, he is invisible."

"When this healer in the form of a lion searches for victims to kill," Lee asks, "does he kill anyone or only other healers?"

"Those lions that people hunt, which then turn around and kill a person, are not proper lions of god. They are our healers prowling around as lions. There is the case of a man from Xaixai who was bitten by a lion. He was bitten by one of our healers prowling as a lion, who came from west of Xaixai. I don't know who from the west is playing the game of changing into a lion. All I know is that one of us bit him."

It is now late afternoon. Just before the talk ends, Wa Na says: "I don't want to be called Hwa Na. I am just a healer."

Two days later, Richard Lee again speaks with Wa Na about num. They meet in the late afternoon. Lee asks her about the great healers. At first she says she will not talk about num, but then she begins. "There are women healers all over, in Chumkwe, in Xaixai, and elsewhere. The women are stronger healers than the men. There are some women who have eaten properly. Those become good healers. In my case, I was created in a different way, according to my num. When I start healing, I first see the thing that is going to kill a person. Then I heal that."

"What is that thing you heal?" Lee wonders.

"My kowhedili tells me about it," she replies.

"Are the spirits always involved in killing people?"

"It is god who kills," Wa Na says. "God is the one who creates and kills. Even if you are in difficulties, if he wants to take you out of them, he can. If he wants to kill you, he can."

"Who else kills people?" Lee continues.

"Everyone kills. Both we people and Goba people kill. Everyone kills and was given the power to kill by god. So I say that god kills."

"Do the spirits kill?"

"Yes," she replies. "I cured a Tswana child who was suffering from the spell cast by the shadow of a bird. I cured that child by taking everything out of him." Wa Na changes her position, so as to look more directly at Lee and alters her tone to a mock-scolding seriousness. "What's wrong with Lee? Doesn't he know a healer like me is his mother? Why does he ask me such hard questions?" Wa Na's laughter, which has been lurking behind her words, now breaks out into the open. "God gave us different things, different food and dances, but how could god put such difficult questions into the world?" Her face wrinkles up, her head tilts back, and her shoulders shake as her whole body expresses the laughter that now fills her. "Lee, you are my child. You came from very far away from Goshe. When one comes from so far away and has many things, we call him a healer. But now I am surprised at these questions you ask. How can one healer ask such questions of another?"

"Wa Na, your remarks flatter me. What do *you* want to talk about now?" Lee offers.

With little hesitation, Wa Na picks her own topic and again touches on num, but again touches on it "in her own way." "We people are known by the Tswana head man who lives near us. He knows our num works because in some cases he calls for one of us to do the healing. He is the man who has proved that we can heal, because he has seen our num work. Also the other Europeans who were around this Dobe area saw the healing work.

"Now if you want to see how strong we healers are, you can prove our strength only when there is one of our people sick to death. Then you call one of our healers to come and heal the sick person. And then you will see how we take things out of people. I am surprised that you, Lee, who came long ago and have asked many questions, don't know anything about our num or the way we heal.

"And now I am finished with our talk," Wa Na concludes. She asks for the gifts Lee has promised her in exchange for the talk. The gifts are given.

14 Psychological and Spiritual Growth

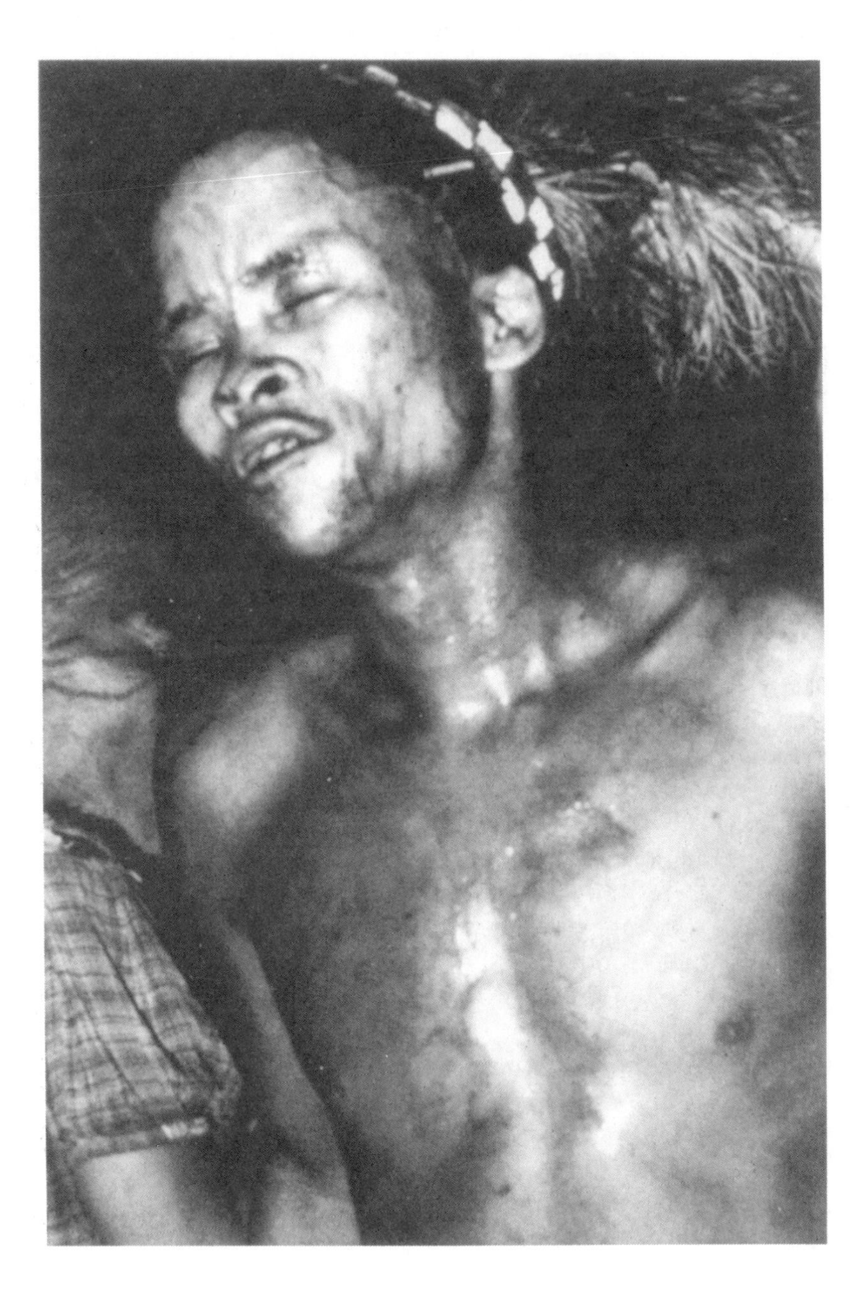

NUM HAS ENTERED into the lives of Kau Dwa and Wa Na in an especially pervasive way, affecting their everyday behavior and their inner lives, enhancing their knowledge and understanding. Their relationship to num seems different from other experienced healers. They are less reliant on a formal dance to activate their num, and they heal themselves more easily. They kia more frequently, and their experience of kia often seems deeper, more profound: travels to god's home and the transformation of healers into lions are more a part of their experience. Their healing efforts are more often directed to serious situations and more often result in dramatic cures. Such healers, of whom there are only a few, represent the standard of healing power. They are healers *ama ama*, the "real ones," the "biggest."

Healers in general, and the experienced ones in particular, are themselves somewhat different from those who do not heal. Although in their ordinary, everyday behavior these healers are indistinguishable from people who do not kia, they have distinctive psychological attributes. These attributes, intensified by increased contact with kia, are harmonious with the state of consciousness represented by kia-healing.

These attributes and the phenomenon of healing power raise numerous questions, many still unanswered. For example, how do these distinguishing psychological attributes of healers come about? Do they represent predispositions to engage in healing, or are they the result of accumulated healing activities? How do the few most powerful healers, the healers ama ama, emerge from the larger group of experienced healers? How does their distinctive life-style exist within the egalitarian structure of Kung living and healing? Finally, these distinctive psychological attributes and the phenomenon of healing power raise a more general question of the healer's spiritual growth within Kung culture.

Page 229: Experiencing kia

What is the meaning of Toma Zho's phrase – "sometimes you grow up with num . . . sometimes num grows you up"? Those who do not kia provide an important perspective on these questions, for they are in no way viewed as inadequate in their functioning or stunted in their development.

The dance itself raises another important question. Some transformation of consciousness occurs in almost everybody at the dance; being at the dance is tantamount to participating. The actual experience of kia is in this sense only the most intense expression of a generally enhanced state. What function do these temporary, dance-limited states have in the lives of those who do not kia?

In terms of their basic social, economic, and political functioning, healers are generally no different from those who do not heal. Richard Lee (personal communication) gathered data that support this conclusion. He asked Kung men, healers and nonhealers alike, a series of questions, such as: how many animals they have hunted and killed; whether they own hunting dogs or a hunting gun; who they have done hxaro with; what their kinship relation is to key figures in the Dobe area; where they live, and with what relatives; how often and how far they have traveled; how many languages they speak; whether they own or manage goats, donkeys, or cattle; whether they plant any crops, such as melons, maize, or tobacco, and how successfully; whether they have lived with blacks; and whether they have worked for blacks, for whites, or in the mines of South Africa. The answers suggest that healers and nonhealers are generally indistinguishable over a broad range of areas, including social, economic, and political functioning which has implications for the future. For example, the ownership of domestic animals, planting experience, and work experiences for blacks and whites are behaviors that are likely to become more relevant as the Kung are increasingly challenged by the culture of their pastoral neighbors.

As far as their basic everyday adaptation, the healers are like everyone else. There is no priestly caste or shamanistic tradition or even strong headman structure among the Kung. In their egalitarian manner, the Kung accord the healer no special role or privileges of an enduring nature.

Healing, however, is not a thankless job, unnoticed and unrewarded. Education for kia and kia itself are filled with physical and emotional supports of a special kind. A young person's first deep drink of num is usually celebrated by those at the dance, who express their joy at having another entrant into num, even while they express their concern over the young person's struggle with that num. The immediate family may even express a bit of pride. But such special supports and recognitions are tied into the activation of num during the dance. They do not adhere to the healers as they go about their ordinary day.

Healers definitely "get something in return" for their healing efforts. The emphasis is on a generalized reciprocity, not a quid pro quo. Although there is talk about withholding healing from those who do not "pay" for it, when the dance is under way and the num is boiling, all usually participate in the healing without hesitation.

When persons are cured of a particular ailment, they usually give some gift to the healer responsible. For minor ailments – a coughing spell or a fever – the gifts are usually small, maybe a kerchief or a necklace. Such gifts rarely accumulate in the hands of healers, or even of their family; they are dispersed throughout the Kung community along the hxaro network. For major ailments – a bad leopard mauling or a sickness that brings one "close to death" – the gift is usually substantial. If the patient is another Kung, the gift might be a blanket or two, or even a goat, if that is available. A Herero or Tswana patient may give a cow as "payment" for such a dramatic cure. Here again, despite their substance, such gifts rarely accumulate with particular healers or their family. The hxaro network, driven by the Kung's egalitarian principles, disperses even these large rewards. The appearance of a cow in a Kung camp is the occasion for a general feast, not the building of a kraal. And no Kung store extra blankets when another in their camp feels the early morning cold through an old, worn blanket.

Such gifts are not the only thanks healers receive. Those

who are healed, and especially those who are cured, feel deep gratitude for the effort and pain the healer must experience in that healing effort. Their gifts are really expressions of this gratitude. Even the Herero who makes a "payment" for his cure does so with gratitude. This appreciation goes beyond the relief a sick person feels upon being cured. It is a gratitude which acknowledges that Kung healers heal the Herero more because they want to and the Herero needs it than because it is a "job" the healers are expected to do. These feelings of appreciation are only one part of the reciprocating relationship established between healers and the community they serve. Healers themselves feel good about healing others, about doing what they have been trained to do.

To find out about the psychological attributes of healers, I gather data on a group of thirty-two Kung. The group includes sixteen healers – of whom eight are over the age of forty and experienced in num, and eight are between twenty and forty and inexperienced – and sixteen nonhealers, matched with the healers by age. I focus on three areas – personality traits, self-image, and fantasy life – which I think will be relevant to the functioning of Kung healers and researchable in the Kung context. The research effort is exploratory, intending to be suggestive and not comprehensive. To gather data on personality traits, I use a rating scale in which I ask persons to make judgments about another's personality. To gather data on self-image, I use a version of the Draw-a-Person test in which I ask persons to draw a picture of themselves. That self-portrait is considered an example of their self-images. To gather data on fantasy life, I use a test modeled after the Thematic Apperception Test (TAT), in which I show persons an unfamiliar and ambiguous picture and ask them to tell a story about the picture. The story is considered an expression of their fantasy life.

This effort is neither simple nor direct. Any attempt to gather cross-cultural data on psychological variables is beset with obstacles (Triandis and Berry, 1980). The Kung do different things and conceptualize them differently from

Westerners. They also conceptualize and describe differently the things they do that Westerners recognize as familiar. This is characteristic of any cross-cultural situation. Several of the personality traits I thought would be most relevant to healing cannot be translated into Kung. These conceptualizations of traits are not relevant to the Kung experience. The Kung simply do not think about each other in these terms. My list of "usuable" traits is based on the dual criteria of meaning and cross-cultural relevance.

In the Draw-a-Person test, I find that when I ask the Kung to draw a picture of themselves, they respond in either of two ways: they either draw a self-portrait or sign their name. And since the Kung are without a written language, that signature is usually a scribble or squiggly line, which can easily be taken as part of a nonrepresentational portrait of oneself. I realize that a signature can be a way of "drawing" oneself, and I have to make sure I am collecting self-portraits.

The TAT-type test reveals that most of the Kung are as interested in the back of the picture they are shown as in the picture itself, as fascinated with the *process* of capturing a multidimensional world on a two-dimensional surface as with what is captured. Some Kung also find it difficult to distinguish between telling a story about a picture they have never seen before and what they call "lying." I try to give each person time and room to tell a story, but I respect their unwillingness to do so as more than mere psychological resistance.

The effort with these research instruments is also exploratory. Throughout I try to stay close to what in the West is called common sense, and also to what might be called Kung sense. The actual instruments are developed in the field and are adaptations of standard procedures. Each instrument is conceived and presented in terms of simple and common human activities so as to increase its cross-cultural validity: the ratings on traits are conceived and presented in terms of offering one's opinions or judgments of another; the Draw-a-Person test in terms of the activity of drawing; and the TAT test in terms of the activity of storytelling. In interpreting the results, I try to stress only what seems obvious and observable, at least from a Western standpoint. In this I eschew the numerous, and in some cases highly elaborated, Western theories of interpretation that accompany these instruments.

The study reveals that in three areas healers, especially experienced ones, manifest different psychological attributes from Kung who do not heal, differences that seem to make healers more harmonious with kia. Also experienced healers display these distinctive attributes more than inexperienced ones. First, healers, as compared to nonhealers, seem more predisposed to kia by dint of their personality traits. Healers are judged, for example, as being more emotionally labile. They are said to be more *xga ku tsiu*; that is, their "heart rises" more, they are more "expressive" or "passionate." This trait certainly is in harmony with kia and its profound emotional quality. During the dance, the healer's emotions must be readily available and capable of quickly changing their intensity and content. The movement from intense fear into the total release of kowhedili is only one instance of this need for emotional lability.

Second, healers, as compared to nonhealers, seem predisposed to kia by dint of their distinctive self-image. Their body self-image, for example, is determined more by their own inner states than by external anatomical criteria. Healing is an extremely physical experience, expressing itself in and through the body. Healers speak about what kia does to their bodies. Yet in describing themselves and their bodies during kia, healers emphasize the central importance of fluid psychological processes and transitions that break out of the body's ordinary anatomical boundaries. The healers' drawings of themselves when *not* in kia suggest a similar self-image. In sharp contrast to the nonhealers' drawings, the healers' violate the ordinary rules of anatomy: as body lines become fluid, body parts become separated.

This contrast shows up in Toma Zho's self-portrait, compared to the self-portrait of someone of Toma Zho's age who has never experienced kia (drawings a–b), as well as in the old healer Wi's self-portrait, compared to the self-portrait of someone of Wi's age who has never entered kia (drawings c–d). In the experienced healer Kinachau's drawing of himself (drawing e), the spirals, which he says are his body, dominated by the long spiral, which he says is his spinal cord, are reminiscent of the descriptions of rapidly boiling and rising num.

Third, healers seem predisposed to kia by dint of their fantasy lives. For example, they have easier access to a rich fantasy life. Since fantasy life and kia are both altered states of consciousness, experiences with one state may affect the other. Kia demands from the healer an openness to the unfamiliar and a primarily intuitive and emotional response, rather than a logical or rational one. Only then can the healer accept the pain and mystery of boiling num. In an analogous fashion, healers, when not in kia, respond to the strange TAT-like pictures in an emotional, intuitive way, willingly, at times eagerly, telling stories which express elaborate fantasies. Those who have never experienced kia respond to the intrinisically ambiguous, and at times illogical, pictures in a more logical, rational way, which is doomed to frustration. They tell stories only with hestitation, and then usually brief ones. Some avoid telling any stories. Very little of their fantasy life emerges. This is not to say that kia is merely another fantasy experience. But it seems that healers must emphasize their fantasy-related capacities in order to enter the extraordinary reality of kia.

Each of the three differences between healers and nonhealers in their psychological attributes is statistically significant (.05 level), and each of the three attributes in healers is significantly intercorrelated (.05 level). Together the data provide the beginning strokes in a psychological portrait of the healer. As compared to those who do not kia, the healer has a more inner-directed functioning, more of an ability to deal with unfamiliar situations, a more intuitive and emotional way of responding, and more access to the altered state of fantasy. Such attributes help prepare one to accept boiling num and are harmonious with the ac-

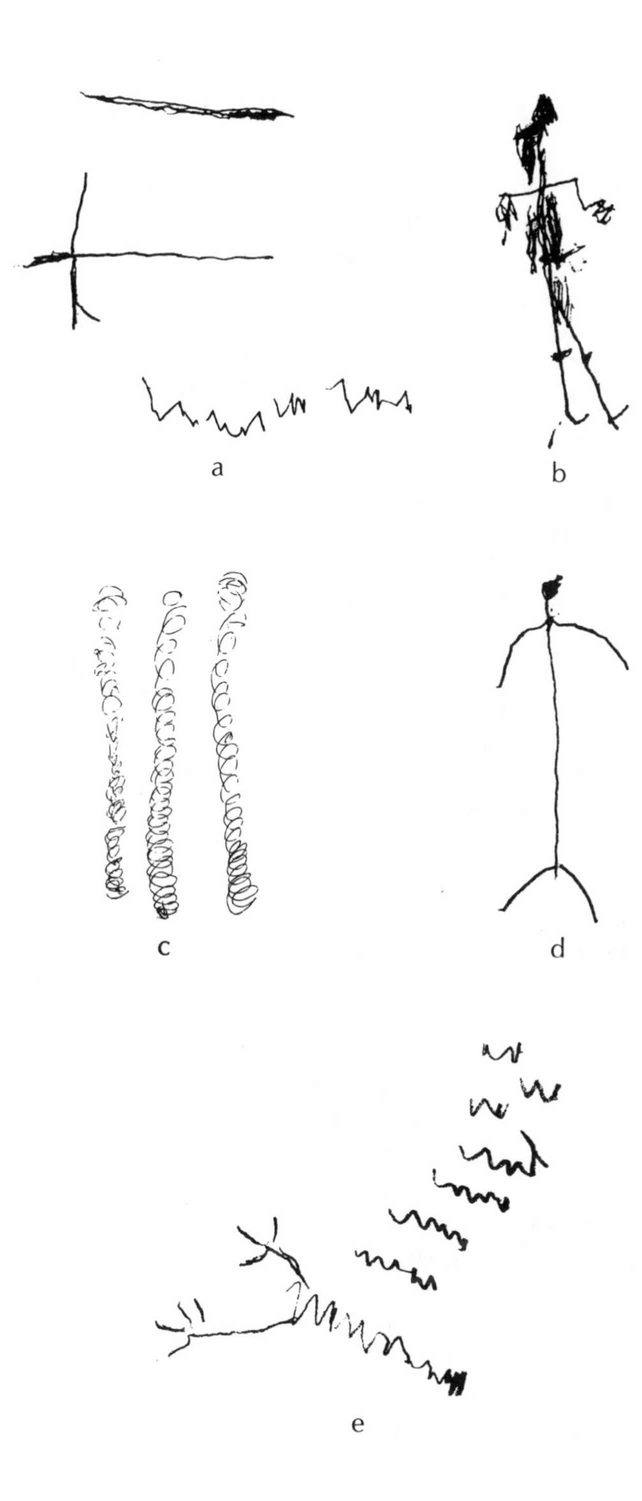
a
b
c
d
e

tual experience of kia. Inexperienced healers display these attributes, but experienced healers display them more dramatically. Therefore these attributes seem to represent both a factor in the healers' predisposition toward kia and a result of their accumulated experience with kia.

There are as yet no data on the relative importance of these psychological attributes in the healers' predisposition to or subsequent experience with kia, nor on the actual onset of these attributes. It is highly unlikely they are either completely innate or completely learned. It would be interesting to know when they do make their appearance, and in what form. Do Kung children already have a psychological disposition toward or against an experience like kia? How much do the first contacts with num, even before it boils up in a person and well before kia, determine or release these attributes?

The family situation is known to make a difference in whether or not one receives num. Lee (personal communication) has shown that if the father has num, the son is more likely to receive num himself. Whether or not the father teaches the son, there are also instances of a family tradition for healing. Certain families identify themselves as "healing families," others as "families without num." Toma Zho, with his oldest son already an established healer, two of his other sons actively seeking num, his two wives very strong singers, and his sister a strong singer and healer, is at the head of a healing family. Koto, who, like his wife, their four sons, and their grandchildren, has never tasted num, considers his to be a family without num, despite the facts that Kinachau is his nephew, that one of his daughters-in-law is a strong singer, and that his youngest grandson has just begun the active phase of his search for num.

But there is not even a suggestion of any division of society based on such distinctions. Rather, the situation is flexible. If Koto's grandson were to receive num, the identification of his family as "being without num" would be weakened if not abandoned. And more important, no family is isolated from num.

The few most powerful healers, like Wa Na and Kau

Dwa, stand out even among the experienced healers. Whereas healers generally evidence changes in their personality, self-image, and fantasy life, the few most powerful healers evidence changes in their whole life-style. For most healers, their distinctive psychological characteristics are expressed within a standard Kung life-style; but for these few, in a special life-style. This special life-style, though still appropriate to Kung culture, is governed by an intense and dedicated pursuit of num, which takes the person deeply into what in the West is called "spiritual growth."

The Kung call an experienced healer a *geiha* or one who is "completely learned" in regard to num. But they reserve the term *geiha ama ama*, or the "real one," for a few distinctively powerful healers among those who are completely learned. The "power" is a healing power or healing knowledge, not, for example, a power over others. The power is in the num which resides within the healer. An ama ama is said to have "big" num, num that is "very strong" and "very powerful." Ama ama refers to an absolute level of power, not to the most powerful healer in a particular camp or at a particular water-hole. There is not an ama ama in every camp, sometimes not even one among the several camps around a water-hole.

The Kung are clear about who is or is not an ama ama and how much power healers have in relation to each other. Moreover, the healers' own judgment about their power generally agrees with the judgment of others about them, even though healers who are members of one's immediate family are consistently judged as having more powerful num than healers not so closely related, and even though the strength of num seems to fluctuate. Healers have "off-nights," and there are periods in a healer's life when the num is stronger or weaker. There is also an almost whimsical fluctuation from day to day, sometimes even within a day. One afternoon, Kinachau says: "I used to have num, but now I no longer do. Now I just sit." That night he experiences kia and heals at a dance, at times with a rare intensity. The next day he simply says, "My num returned to me."

Although the Kung have little difficulty talking about power and making its dimensions or criteria explicit, their egalitarianism makes them reluctant to acknowledge fixed hierarchies and loath to create them. It keeps their focus on a differential valuation of the healers' *power* which does not entail a differential accumulation of prestige or possessions. Their judgments on the power among healers are made in response to rating scales I administer. I never hear the Kung use any systematic or fixed ranking of healers. Caution is their byword. Tsaa puts it this way when I ask him if there is any ama ama at Xaixai: "Oh, there is no ama ama here at Xaixai. You have Toma Zho who's alone at his camp, then Kinachau at his camp, and here you have Wi. But to say who the real geiha is would be hard. Now in the old days . . . I don't see a real geiha today. If I had to pick a geiha, I would say Toma Zho, Kinachau and Wi, but there's not much num here at Xaixai." And Wa Na's tales of the healers who became lions, the lion healers, evoke a picture of awesome power; but such healers, she says, no longer live.

It may always have been the Kung way to locate healers of the greatest strength, like these lion healers, in the past. This could be another instance of Kung modesty. Whether or not the num of today is in fact less powerful than it once was – or may become – it is the most powerful healing force to which the Kung presently have access.

There are several signs or criteria of power in healers. A first criterion is the healers' ability to receive num in a special way and to gain special knowledge from their activation of num. Receiving num at an early age, directly from god, in a very intense form, or in a form immediately available for healing – each of these special ways of receiving num, singly or in combination, can be a sign of power. Profound kia experiences, and in particular extensive contact with the gods during kia, can yield special knowledge about num, which reveals aspects of the culture's fundamental mysteries. Ordinary and even experienced healers do not usually talk about the lion healers of old, or the death and rebirth of kia, or the detailed geography and functioning of god's village, as each of these topics is based upon a special knowledge of num.

A second criterion of power is the adeptness with which a person controls the rapidly boiling num. Powerful healers can enter kia quickly. As Kau Dwa puts it, on one occasion he started to kia when he first heard the singing from his hut, and as he walked toward the dance, his kia increased, and as he stepped into the dance circle, he was ready to heal. Even as their kia deepens, their control remains and, in that, becomes more impressive. Whenever there is an acute or severe illness, these powerful healers can be counted on to heal strongly. They are also able to heal regularly and persistently, as in Wa Na's regular afternoon dances.

The effectiveness and drama of one's curing ability is a third criterion of power. The most powerful healers are invariably called in on the most difficult cases, and they are often called in to help other healers. They might work with these other healers or take over the case. This idea of "who calls on whom for help" is one of the most decisive criteria used by the Kung in judging a healer's degree of power. The fact that the powerful healers take on all cases distinguishes them from ordinary healers, who seem more selective and at times choose not to work on a sick person. I say "choose not" because they put it in terms of their incapacity to deal with a particular illness rather than their unwillingness. The most dramatic cures, where persons recover from severe injuries or are "brought back to life" by the healer's intervention, always seem to be attributed, at least primarily, to a powerful healer. And one of the standard ways in which these powerful healers describe their work is to describe one or more of their dramatic cures. The drama is enhanced not only by the severity of the illness and the closeness to death, but also by the large reward the recovered patient gives in gratitude.

Taking on all cases, regardless of their severity, means that the powerful healers work on dying persons, some of whom eventually die, at times in the arms of the healer. When someone dies while being worked on by a powerful healer, it is said that the healer did everything possible but that the sick one's time had come. In saving certain patients from death, healers demonstrate their power.

A fourth criterion of power in healers is the charismatic influence that they exert at the healing dances. Special dances are sometimes held just to release the num of a particularly powerful healer. Wa Na's afternoon dances and healings are made possible by a group of women who regularly gather to sing for her. A powerful healer can dominate the rhythm and atmosphere of the traditional dance. As such healers work toward activating their num, the other dancers may begin to orient their movements around them, and the singers may sing the songs these healers find most pleasing and stimulating.

Having a separate identity as a healer is a fifth criterion of power. Healing activities dominate the lives of the most powerful healers. Although woven into the fabric of Kung life, the powerful healers see themselves primarily as healers, and are seen so by others. Wa Na and Kau Dwa do not hunt and gather. Yet their existence, which is filled with strong healing, is more than justified; it is respected and, especially with Wa Na, revered. Certainly Kau Dwa's blindness and Wa Na's advanced age alone could justify their lack of subsistence effort; yet there are other Kung with similar disabilities who still gather. Tsaa, who is old enough to stop gathering, is fiercely independent in his gathering. And Tsaa has strong num. With Kau Dwa and Wa Na, priorities and values have shifted; with them, their healing power better explains their existence.

These five criteria of power are dynamic and interrelated. They signify a level of power, while they continually interact with the healers' ongoing work with num. A dramatic cure, for example, is said to be an indication of the healers' power. Such a cure also enhances the healers' power, or at least their reputation of power. That reputation is, moreover, one of the reasons healers can cure others, which further enhances their power and reputation.

An example of this interaction is Toma Zho's story about his reception of num from god. That story, which is questioned by another Kung at Xaixai, may have been invented by Toma Zho, designed to build up his reputation as a healer. But this is not necessarily evidence of his diminished power. As healers become more powerful, they may create stories about that power, which in turn enhance that power. Stories as metaphors to express the strength of num are accepted by the Kung and not viewed as "lies." At several times and in different ways, I ask certain healers, "Did you receive num directly from god because your num was so powerful, or did your receiving num from god begin the development of your num's power?" The answer to both questions is invariably "yes."

An experienced healer, the geiha, exhibits one or more of the signs of power. When all the signs have intensified and combined, one finds the geiha ama ama, like Wa Na and Kau Dwa. Wa Na is considered the most powerful healer in the Dobe area, and Kau Dwa is seen as probably the next most powerful In their persons, power takes on additional meaning.

The lives of Wa Na and Kau Dwa are soaked with num; they are continually thinking about num, and their num is activated in many situations outside the standard healing dance. They are personally affected, or perhaps transformed, by the num which boils so often and so fiercely within them. It is in a large part because of her num that Wa Na is held in awe; it is in a large part because of his num that Kau Dwa is so respected. But they themselves are personally awesome and stimulate respect. The power of their num and the charisma of their personalities seem to have fused. And yet the emphasis remains on the power of their num, not the power of their personality.

Kinachau and Toma Zho provide a contrasting perspective on this phenomenon of power. Kinachau is one of the most powerful healers at Xaixai, but he is not considered an ama ama. His reputation is largely local, his power confined mostly to Xaixai. He does not seek to develop the signs of power. He does not, for example, see himself solely, or even primarily, as a healer. He is still a talented hunter, and he goes about his daily maintenance tasks with verve. He has few stories about his dramatic cures or about the specialness of his num. Nor does he travel around taking on cases. Although his num is more powerful than most, it does not pervade his life. In his long association with num, Kinachau as a person still seems largely unaffected.

Toma Zho, too, is considered one of the most powerful healers at Xaixai, though few would call him an ama ama. But Toma Zho is trying to become more powerful, trying to change as a person by working with num. He sees himself primarily, if not solely, as a healer. He is convinced that he is a very good healer, perhaps as good as Kau Dwa. He has many stories, both about his dramatic cures and about how he had received num directly from god as a young boy. And he certainly stands out as a person. He is charismatic. Yet it is not clear how much that charisma reflects real power, and how much it reflects merely the kind of personality needed to launch a professional career, where power may not have to be exceptional.

Kia healing is at its roots a spiritual phenomenon. Num is from the gods. The healing act involves a bargaining with the gods and their messengers over the fate of the sick one and the general course of sickness and well-being. The healing approach deals with what the Kung believe to be the most powerful force in their universe. The activation of num and the contact with num over time effect certain changes. For example, participants at the healing dance experience to varying degrees, a temporary transformation of consciousness. Other effects are more enduring. For example, healers generally have distinctive psychological characteristics, and the most powerful healers have in addition a distinctive life-style. The career of healers, and their development of "power," suggest patterns to the unfolding of these more enduring effects. These patterns could be considered instances of what in the West is called "psychosocial development" or "growth." Given their tie with num, they could also be called instances of "spiritual growth." These enduring changes in Kung consciousness and life-style are similar to what has been called "spiritual consciousness" or "growth" in other cultures (e.g. Eliade, 1960,

1967; Katz, 1976). The connection between such changes and individual or societal enhancement has also been described and documented (e.g. Eliade, 1960; Guenon, 1962; Katz, 1973; Smith, 1969).

But a caution must be emphasized. The Kung are not interested in making a separate issue out of what Westerners might call spiritual growth. They are not interested in abstracting that growth out of its everyday context. Toma Zho is being realistic, not evasive, when he resists my attempts at logical clarification and stays simply with his words: "Sometimes you grow up with num, sometimes num grows you up." The permutations of that statement are endless, and are probably meant to be. Num can "grow you up," but you must also "grow up" in order to use it. Sometimes you are "born to drink num"; sometimes you "wake up later to num." Sometimes you merely "grow old" with your num; sometimes your num gives you knowledge. The Kung talk explicitly about aspects of this growth, such as the development of "power," but only hint at tying them together into an overall pattern. The constant danger for the Westerner is to isolate and dramatize as "spiritual growth" that which for the Kung is merely a way of living.

These patterns of growth have certain distinctive Kung characteristics. They are always firmly rooted in everyday life. Though the gods are an expression of the greatest power imaginable, they are also connected with everyday affairs. Though a visit with the great god may be reserved for the most experienced healers, the existence of that god is no less real for other Kung. Furthermore, these patterns of growth are finely tuned to the needs of Kung culture. The emphasis is on releasing num's healing power to the group. Kau Dwa says: "The boiling num is painful and the work of healing is difficult. But that is what we have learned to do, and that is what we want to do. We drink num because we want to heal others of their sickness." This simple statement sums up a lifetime of intense communication with the spirit world.

Healers are more involved in their own inner processes, more open to the unfamiliar both within and outside of them. Yet while they are more open to their inner processes, they are also able to control them. Within the healer a balance is struck between this psychology, so congenial to transcendence, and the need for daily maintenance activities. Neither side of functioning is sacrificed.

The few most powerful healers strike the same kind of balance and also stress the balance between themselves and their larger groups. These healers, the ama ama, not only have a psychology congenial to transcendence, but also live a life that expresses spiritual qualities. Again, their development is rooted in the everyday existence of the culture. The group supports only a few such individuals. The group is especially protected by the strong healing of these few and inspired by their contacts with the gods. But the group cannot afford to have too many adults not hunting and gathering. The economics of consciousness are irrefutable.

The patterns of growth for healers emphasize the activation of num of increasing strength, not the accumulation of individual or personal benefits from working with num. The healer is a receptacle of, or a vehicle for, num. It is the num that is respected and held in awe. During healing, one's personality is not exaggerated. Neither is one's personality submerged, as it would be if kia were a possession state, where the healer is taken over by a spiritual entity. Many healers bring an idiosyncratic characteristic to their dancing and healing, little "trademarks" which add interest and excitement to their efforts. When dancing, Kinachau often holds his arms, bent at the elbow, up in the air, like a large bird circling in to land. Dau usually dances with his head forward, his trunk almost perpendicular to the ground as he leans heavily on his dance stick. When she sings, even when she heals, Chuko has a faraway look, as if concentrating on her own thoughts. Kau Dwa heals with unusual abandon, an ecstatic smile often dominating his expression. But these idiosyncracies, though appreciated by the people, are merely touches. Traditionally, when healers say they are the "strongest," they are emphasizing the power of the Kung num, not the power of their personal num, certainly not of their personal power. In the most fundamental sense, healers approach num impersonally; they do not activate it for their own needs or use it in their own style.

The relationship, though impersonal, is not superficial. In fact, the superficial aspects of personality are precisely what are not intensified in healing. What dominates during healing is a more essential aspect of the healer. Certain experienced healers verbalize this. They speak of healing as providing an essential self-definition or self-affirmation. During healing, they "unfold" themselves. "When I dance," says Wi, "I am myself." Tsaa states it this way: "I don't know myself today because I have no num, I no longer have num." And when Megan Biesele wants to stop a healer in kia from going into the fire, she is told by another Kung: "Let her be. We must each do what we do."

There are instances where the healers' personality merges with their num and seems enhanced by it. But here, too, the healers must be relating essentially to num if the num is to remain strong. Wa Na is charismatic, and healing enhances her charisma. She is distinctive, but she relates to her num impersonally. Her num is still activated by and for her people, given freely to them. She stands out as an individual without exaggerating the superficial and idiosyncratic aspects of her personality. Despite the respect in which she is held, young healers do not speak of wanting to be like her, nor do they try to imitate her. There is no competition to achieve her level of power, no envy about her kind of num. As one experienced healer puts it, "Wa Na does her num, and I do mine."

The healer's growth is neither a specialized process nor a reason for special privileges. Learning to heal is an aspect of normal socialization. The healer's growth can be best understood as the normal development of a potential rather than as an instance of specialized change or the cultivation of a special talent.

The dynamic which releases the healers' growth is clear.

The Kung speak of the death and rebirth in kia. They speak of plumbing their culture's mysteries in their contacts with the gods and their travels to god's home. They describe the effects of this journey to and with the spirits in terms of their increased healing power. This dynamic is the hallmark of what has been considered the path of spiritual development (e.g. Eliade, 1960). In this sense, the healing dance can be seen as a spiritual technique, and working with one's boiling num as a spiritual discipline. This seems an especially relevant perspective on the character and functioning of the few most powerful healers, such as Wa Na. But such powerful healers are not the classic "gurus." They may give advice, as do other healers. But the Kung do not go to such a geiha ama ama, sit at her feet in awe, and reverently ask for answers.

The Kung do not elaborate on how such a dynamic might unfold. For example, when I ask the Kung if a particular student is likely to become a healer, they will often talk only about the student's present relation to num or refrain from making any judgment, as in saying, "I have not seen him dance recently." Post-hoc explanations for the "drinking of num" are common, and sometimes students quite unexpectedly receive num. But prognoses about future healing ability are consistently given only for those few who most actively pursue or run away from boiling num.

A central basis for such prognoses seems to be the judgment about whether the student is accepting or rejecting num, is overcoming or being overcome by his fear. This Kung judgment is consonant with the data on the distinctive psychological attributes of the healer. Those data suggest that healers both are predisposed toward kia and become more open to its influence over time. All who seek num must meet their fear of death during kia. Perhaps the healers' distinctive psychological attributes help them cross that barrier of fear, from which those who do not kia fall back. Perhaps these attributes help healers direct the fiercely boiling num into healing efforts, while those who kia but do not heal remained overwhelmed by their num. How the few most powerful healers, the ama ama, emerge from among the experienced healers is even less clear. Experienced healers differ in their degree of power. Such differences, if intensified, point toward the emergence of an ama ama. Age and concurrent experience with num are factors that might explain this emergence. Certain experienced healers lose their power as they grow older; others keep their power; while still others – a few potential ama ama – increase their power with age.

15 The Challenge of Change

THE TRADITION of healing in the Giraffe dance is like a mighty tree, sustained and nourished by the Kung hunting-gathering life-style, offering its fruits of protection and enhancement to individuals and the culture as a whole. But changes are occurring that threaten the very existence of the healing tradition. As with all viable cultures, the Kung have probably always been in transition. The very resiliency of their culture is one of its more remarkable features. But radical changes are now impinging upon them with accelerating speed and growing intensity. Their hunting-gathering life-style is being eroded, as they are thrust, with enormous dislocation and suffering and at great disadvantage, into an economy dominated by the pastoralism of their black neighbors, who themselves are under great stress in struggling to adapt to the increasing impact of a capitalistic economy (Biesele and Lee, unpublished; Lee, 1979). Treated as an inferior minority by their black and white neighbors, the Kung are entering this new economy at the lowest possible social, economic, and political level. It is an open question whether the Giraffe dance as a healing model can be expected to continue under the gradually pervading life patterns of what Lee characterizes as "dependent peripheral capitalism" (1978, p. 7).

The establishment of some degree of sedentism as opposed to an earlier nomadism lies at the base of most of the recent changes. In moving toward sedentism, the Kung are giving up much of the freedom and self-sufficiency of their hunting-gathering life. One fundamental change is in the patterns of land usage. The Kung's water sources are being preempted by cattle, which are also causing ecological changes, destroying the plant food and game the Kung have relied upon. Whereas the Kung once moved freely over familiar areas of land, making a living from and sharing known resources, they are increasingly becoming sedentary serfs and squatters around the settlements of

Page 250: Kau Dwa healing a pregnant Herero

Tswana and Herero pastoralists. Kung families attach themselves to a particular Tswana or Herero family and, in exchange for working their cattle, receive food and a place to build their shelters. Only occasionally do they gather; rarely do they hunt. The quid-pro-quo exchange of services for money, or its equivalent, begins to dominate economic exchanges. The old sharing weakens.

These changes in the use of land and in the access to land strike at the heart of the Kung gathering and hunting life-style. Private ownership of resources, accumulation of property, cultivation of a piece of land, differential wealth – all these signs and mainsprings of capitalism, increasingly evident among the neighboring pastoralists, threaten to overwhelm the Kung's present-oriented use of land, emphasis on sharing, and egalitarianism.

One characteristic of the more sedentary life-style now adopted by some Kung is the emergence of hierarchical differences between the sexes. In the hunting-gathering context, relationships between men and women, though at times challenging and always dynamic, have generally been egalitarian. In the more sedentary setting, relationships are becoming more formalized, static, and male-dominated, at least in the public spheres of behavior.

Draper (1975) points out that the ranking of persons according to prestige and wealth has begun in the more sedentary villages, and that men, more than women, are defined as owners of important capital items such as domestic animals. In the political and economic realm, men are more likely to speak for their group, and the official position of headman is being encouraged. The neighboring pastoralist peoples expect to speak to one person, specifically to the "man of the house," rather than to a group on issues of importance. Women have begun to display more deferential behavior in relation to men. For example, whereas in the bush women do not hesitate to interrupt or walk through a group of men in conversation, in the more sedentary setting women more often walk around or avoid such a male group. Other factors contribute to this loss of prestige for women in the sedentary context, including a greater rigidity in task specialization by sex, concomitant changes in child socialization, the decrease in mobility for women as compared with men, and a diminution in women's contribution to the economy.

As the capitalistic principles of exchange begin to dominate Kung life, the principles by which num is exchanged come under attack. And as the healing tradition is threatened, essential values in Kung hunting-gathering life are further undermined. The cycle continues. As one of the deepest facets of hunting-gathering life, healing may become one of the most sensitive barometers of the degree and destructiveness of culture change among the Kung.

At times healing is singled out for attack because it has the visible and circumscribed form of the healing dance. Christian missionaries have carried the message of the capitalistic culture to the Kung within the language framework of their Christian religion. These missionaries make a strong and persistent effort to "root out" the Kung's "superstitions" and "magical" practices. The Kung are "bushmen," "savages" to be "civilized." The classic ethnocentric pattern of considering unfamiliar religious behavior as "un-Christian" and "pagan" and therefore bereft of any value is repeated once more. The intrinsic strengths of the Kung spiritual approach are totally ignored. The influence of such missionary work is shown by a newspaper report, entitled "New Era Dawns for Chumkwe Bushmen," describing recent events in a Kung settlement in Namibia which has close kinship ties to the Dobe area:

> An amazing development which could bring about a completely new era for South West Africa's Bushmen population has caught Chumkwe by storm. A full-scale revival . . . is now in process. It is fast changing the life of a community considered to be amongst the most primitive societies in Africa . . .
>
> Bushmen are praying. They pray out loud in the grass shanties in the mornings. They are praying in the veld. They are flooding to religious services and giving witness to their fellow clan members . . . The whole Bushmanland revival was triggered in the middle of last month when two clan leaders, both named Bo, an-

nounced that they want to be "cleansed" of their sinful existence and follow "The Way."

The Secretary for the Mission action of the Dutch Reformed Church, said yesterday: "it has been a slow ripening process of the seeds sown over these past twelve years. And now it is harvest time. We are extremely thankful."

With the religious revival the Bushmen are fast changing primitive habits. This change, along with that already achieved by ordinary social guidance, is bringing to a close an era in the almost Stone Age culture of the Bushmen, in an isolated society, riddled with petty crime and crimes of passion and bogged down in unsanitary and unhygenic conditions brought about by a nomadic existence and superstition . . .

The first Bo was converted to the Christian religion, at a church meeting. After the teachings were explained and demonstrated repeatedly, Bo announced that he wanted to confess and "break from a dirty life." And then the first Christian prayer in Bushmen language came out, stammered at first and then chanted over and over: "Please God, help me." Others followed soon afterwards and have been attending meetings regularly since . . .

This development makes it necessary to consider the instruction of Bushmen Evangelists and the establishment of a Bushman church . . . "Chumkwe will never be the same after this," the secretary commented (*Windhoek Advertiser*, June 1972).

Two recent phenomena shed further light on this issue of culture change and the Kung approach to healing. One phenomenon is the increasing professionalization of Kung healers; the other is the "creation" of a new kia dance, called Trees. The Kung view both phenomena ambivalently. Some see them as destructive of the "traditional" approach to healing; others see them as an innovative trend in healing which recognizes the current realities of acculturation and incorporates them into a "Kung thing."

The word *traditional*, used to describe the healing approach I studied in the relatively unacculturated areas of Dobe in the late 1960s, is merely a relative term, meant to distinguish the healing approach found in a primarily hunting-gathering setting from the healing approach of more sedentary Kung. It is hard to imagine one "original" setting for the healing, just as it is very difficult to specify any one individual or event as the beginning of a healing dance. The context for healing among the Kung seems to have continually changed and is still changing. The emergence of the Trees dance and professionalism among healers is recent evidence of that flux. The "traditional" healing of the Dobe area during the 1960s is itself considered by some of the more powerful healers to be a dilution of its "earlier" form.

In a similar vein, the relationship of environment and the means of production to egalitarianism suggests that there is no "natural" egalitarian baseline for *all* San societies, but only for San society under very specific economic conditions such as happened to prevail for the Dobe Kung into the late 1960s. The Eastern Kalahari Gana, for example, do not live under the same economic constraints as do the Kung (Cashdan, 1980). The addition of some food production and storage among the Gana, resulting from the beginning adoption of agriculture and husbandry, supports the existence of greater wealth disparities and a differential distribution of political influence. As compared to the Trees dance, the Giraffe, in its support of the egalitarian situation of the Dobe Kung, can be said to epitomize relationships in the traditional hunting-gathering situation.

In contrast to a healing system where healers are professionals, the traditional hunting-gathering context for receiving and distributing num defines healers as part of a larger network of generalized reciprocity. Among the subsistence and other functions they fulfill, they provide healing for their community, simply because they are one of the community who has "drunk num." Their healing efforts are acknowledged and appreciated, but they are not rewarded with any explicit, on-the-spot compensation. Certainly there is no need for professionals who are paid on a quid-pro-quo basis for healing services rendered.

The professionalization of healing could come about in several ways. Here is one possible scenario. On the Herero cattle-posts, some Kung have extensive contact with the Hereros, working as cattle-boys and sometimes attaching themselves in a serflike relationship to Herero families. The Hereros respect and seek out the healing power of Kung num. These new and increased demands for healing from non-Kung put a strain on the traditional exchange network. To have a healing dance requires great expenditure of time and effort. In terms of healing within the Kung camp, such an expenditure is worthwhile. The camp takes from itself and gives to itself. But the Hereros are not part of that camp exchange network, so something new must come into the camp from the Hereros in order to make the Kung healing effort worthwhile. The Kung take what the Herero pastoralists are accustomed to giving for something they value, an explicit quid-pro-quo payment, at present usually in the form of goods.

The arrangement of explicit payments, or "fees for services," has further consequences. As is its character, "payment," begins to exert influence, even control, on persons. The Kung are now beginning to use payment as a criterion for the strength of one's num: "Yes, yes, she's good at num. She gets paid to pull, doesn't she?" There is also the implicit "threat" that, if one is not "paid," one will no longer heal.

At this point whether one actually gets paid is only part of the issue. That one's healing is worth being paid for is a status which some healers seek. Some healers want such recognition even from members of their own villages. In addition to the generalized exchanges coming from camp relationships, they want an extra acknowledgment of the value of their healing or a symbolic recognition of the strength of their num. In some instances, they even say that members of the camp, especially those with whom relations are strained, should pay for their healing.

But professionalism in the traditional Kung approach to healing is still mainly an attitude rather than an actual system. Instead of demanding and receiving payment, most healers who talk about payments do so as a way of venting disappointment at other people's stinginess, of exerting pressure, or of expressing their own hope for a more plentiful future. Here is Bau, one of the strong healers at Xaixai, on the subject of payment: "You mean I should heal my people here at Xaixai? They don't pay me. I have healed them before and saved them, but they don't pay me. Now I only heal my children and my husband." Yet Bau goes regularly to the dances at Xaixai, where she is a vigorous and spirited singer and an active dancer. She consistently pulls sickness from others as she experiences kia in the singing circle.

Kinachau could be called a "family" or "camp-oriented healer." This is in no way a pejorative term, nor is his an inferior position. His num is regarded as powerful. But his healing efforts are focused on his own camp and extend mainly to the other Xaixai camps. Kinachau realizes that some of his colleagues talk about and even demand payment for the healing he still gives in exchange for familial supports. But he is not interested in that form of exchange at this time.

Whereas Kinachau, as a camp-oriented healer, represents the traditional pattern, Toma Zho represents a traditional healer in transition. Like Kinachau, he is greatly respected as a healer among the Xaixai camps. Yet he wants to practice healing beyond the Xaixai area, to establish a reputation as a healer that will take him to other camps and will bring persons from other camps to him for healing. He wants to be paid on a quid-pro-quo basis.

When Toma Zho talks about his wishes for the future, he refers mostly to two healers whom he respects and would like to emulate. One is Kau Dwa, a geiha ama ama or exceptional healer, who on occasion is paid to heal but still heals primarily within the camp context. The other is Kumsa, a consummate dancer-entertainer and powerful healer, who often is paid just to dance as well as to heal. Kumsa performs almost exclusively for compensation and for persons outside his family or camp. Kau Dwa and Kumsa represent for Toma Zho the two paths he might pursue in his quest for professional status. They represent two forms in which professionalism is affecting the Kung healing dance.

There is no linear or logical development from Kinachau to Toma Zho to either Kau Dwa or Kumsa. That is why Toma Zho is struggling so to determine the direction of his future. There is no one clear path he is supposed to follow. How persons like Toma Zho will bridge the camp and professional emphases, how their emerging professionalism will relate to prior family obligations, is important to watch.

Kau Dwa is one of the most powerful healers in the entire Dobe area. His village is located outside of Kangwa. The only store in the Dobe area is in Kangwa, and the first school in the Dobe area, a secondary school, opened there in 1973. The sugar available at the store has lead to active beer-making and considerable drinking; the cloth and pots at the store have become desired objects. The store, in short, has introduced commercialism into a somewhat bewildered and certainly unprepared Kung culture. When the school opened, only Herero and Tswana children in the Kangwa area enrolled, though it was also meant to accommodate about a dozen Kung children. As Kung children do enroll, the impact on Kung life is bound to be enormous. Having young Kung learn to read and write is only one facet of the school's impact. Having families of school children live next to the school so that their children can attend, in essence establishing a sedentary life-style, is another impact.

Although Kangwa is a center of change and potential cultural ferment, Kau Dwa's camp on the outskirts of "town" still functions in many ways like a traditional Kung camp. Although the camp remains at the permanent Kangwa water-hole most of the year, hunting and gathering is still the primary form of subsistence, and the Kung there share in the traditional way in securing and distributing resources.

Just as Kau Dwa's camp life retains the basic characteristics of a hunting-gathering society, so does his approach to num. He dances and heals primarily in the traditional manner, like Kinachau. He dances in order to heal, and whatever entertainment such dances provide – and such dances are very great entertainment – is subsidiary to the healing process.

But Kau Dwa also is very different from Kinachau. He has another aspect to his healing, a professional aspect, supported by his strong familial base. Kau Dwa has a reputation for strong num that is known far beyond Kangwa, throughout much of the Dobe area. Kung from other camps, as well as Hereros and Tswana in the area, come to his camp to be healed. Kau Dwa travels to other Kung camps to cure Kung and non-Kung alike. In many cases, Kau Dwa is paid for the healing services he renders. Sometimes he is paid when he works on a Kung to whom he is not closely related. Invariably he is paid when he works on a non-Kung. But the goods which constitute his payment do not accumulate with him or his family. In keeping with the traditional Kung emphasis on egalitarianism and sharing, these goods are dispersed throughout the community through the hxaro network.

At the healings for which Kau Dwa is given payment, which may be called "professionalized" dances, he devotes particular attention to the "patient" paying for the cure. The dance is, in a fundamental sense, held for that patient. The patient's desire for a cure and his promise of payment are what initiate the dance. Although Kau Dwa heals everyone at the dance, he returns again and again to the patient, working on him sometimes for several minutes at a time. Although the dance sometimes begins to function for the singers and other dancers like a traditional dance, the focus periodically returns to the patient, who is in effect the patron. In the traditional dance, if someone needs special care, the healer may return continually to him, giving him extensive healing. The "professionalized" dance can be seen as a development of this kind of focused healing.

Members of Kau Dwa's camp usually accompany him to these professionalized dances, singing for him and dancing with him. They, in a sense, put on the dance for him. But they are not a professional dance troupe, like the one that supports Kumsa's dancing efforts. Persons from Kau Dwa's camp do not accompany him consistently, and more important, they do not see themselves as his supporting troupe. The request for a professionalized dance represents for them an opportunity to visit relatives in a neighboring camp.

In the dances at his own camp, Kau Dwa is a dominating figure. Like Kinachau, Kau Dwa is the most powerful healer in his camp, and the camp holds dances primarily to activate his num. When Kau Dwa is being paid for his healing, he is even more dominant. He orchestrates the pace and direction of the dance more completely. He knows he has a job to do, namely curing the patient, and he tries to ensure that the singers keep his num activated when he needs its healing power. Kau Dwa's healing power remains intact during his professional cures. His kia seems as profound and his pulling as strong as when he works at home. His professional healings do not intrude upon his traditional healings; in fact, they are an outgrowth of and are fueled by his traditional work with num.

Kumsa presents a quite different picture (Guenther, 1975, 1976). He too is considered a powerful healer. He is also considered an exciting and entertaining dancer, and it is for his dancing, as much as for his healing, that he is paid. Kumsa's life-style is also quite different. A Kung, he lives among the highly acculturated Ghanzi area San, a population that consists primarily of two other San groups, the Nharo and the Gwi.

About three years ago, Kumsa left Xaixai for the Ghanzi farm area. At Xaixai he had been one of the stronger healers, in the traditional, camp-oriented style. He knew that in the Ghanzi area there were many who would be willing, even eager, to pay for his healing efforts. Gau describes the move: "Kumsa went down to Ghanzi in the first place because for years in his own place, here at Xaixai, he danced, and people came from far and wide to watch him, and never paid him anything. So he said, 'Why dance here at Xaixai and not get paid when I can go to Ghanzi and get paid?' Today he gets donkeys and goats at Ghanzi; he gets paid."

The Ghanzi area is dominated by large ranches owned by white Afrikaaners. The Ghanzi San, including the Kung, have lost their lands, that is, their rights to hunt and gather freely on the land. Though they still do a little hunting and gathering to supplement their diet, they are basically squatters on the ranches, economically dependent on the Afrikaaner farmers for work and subsistence. Their work as farm laborers is poorly paid and unreliable. They occupy the lowest place on the economic ladder, and they live in the most squalid conditions.

It can be truly said that the Ghanzi San are a dispossessed and oppressed people plagued by alcoholism, disease, and hunger. This has produced much social tension and conflict between the San and other groups in the area. At the same time, perhaps in response to this oppression and tension, a cultural revitalization process is underway among the San, especially in the healing dance.

The role of the healer has become more clearly defined and specialized. Kumsa has assumed this role and enhanced it. As the healing and religious specialist among the Ghanzi San, he has become both a symbol and a source of revitalization. There are other healers in Ghanzi, but their num is not valued so highly. Kumsa is more than a healer. His presence engenders great respect, and his activities assume political importance among the San, even to some extent among the neighboring black groups.

There are many superficial similarities between Kumsa's dances and the traditional healing dance. In structure, for example, Kumsa's dance usually lasts from dusk to dawn, and it includes a dance fire, a singing circle, and a dance circle. But in many essential ways, Kumsa's dance is different. Kumsa dances when there is illness, and during a dance he devotes most of his healing efforts to the patient. He is paid for such healing. People also pay just to watch Kumsa dance. His dancing is sometimes compensated for its own sake, even when there is no healing and little if any kia. As Gau puts it, "Kumsa is more famous for his dancing than his healing." The fact that Kumsa can heal in his dance makes any dance, whether there is healing or not, more exciting and significant.

Whether it is for dancing alone, or for dancing and healing, Kumsa invariably is paid. His clients are primarily blacks. Although black medicines are available, Kung healing is often the treatment of choice. Kumsa's dances are usually held at one of the San villages located on the large Afrikaaner farms. He has a regular troupe of performers who put on dances with and for him. The dances serve as an effective means of bringing goods into Kumsa's group, which now looks toward Kumsa's dancing as a primary means of support, whereas before, as hunter-gatherers, they were self-sufficient as a group and self-reliant as individuals.

Instead of being a conduit for num, passing it freely on to others in teaching and healing, Kumsa tries to accumulate num. He emphasizes his particular num, and emphasizes himself as its source. In the dances put on by his troupe of performers he is the star performer. In this group there is a retinue of women who sing for him, and a number of men who are apprentices to him, seeking to learn how to dance from him and assisting at the dance. The retinue of singers and apprentices provides some of the support that healers get in the traditional dance. But there is a major difference. Kumsa is essentially a solo performer. The singers and apprentices are economically indebted to him. They travel with him, putting on dances with and for him. In return, they share in the payments he receives. It is not a cold business relationship. Kumas has family relationships with some of the members of the dance troupe, and the atmosphere between him and the troupe is informal and friendly. But the deep extensive reciprocities that bind together the typical Kung camp are absent.

Kumsa was experienced in kia and pulled sickness from the people before he left Xaixai, where his num was considered strong. In Ghanzi, he still experiences kia and pulls at dances. Persons still speak of his strong num, but in the same breath they speak of his heavy drinking, implying that this has undermined the power of his num. Also, there is a suggestion that, more than traditional healers, Kumsa offers healing even though his num is not strongly activated. Whereas the traditional healer may feel a generalized pressure to help the people, Kumsa feels a more specific pressure to cure a particular patient, to heal *on demand.*

No one questions the excitement and skill of Kumsa's dancing. The num which may be connected to that dancing lends it a special, if often only potential, significance. What is in some question is the actual healing power of Kumsa's num. A diminution of healing power could undermine his cultural importance and political influence. Yet as of now, the Ghanzi San still turn to him for healing and protection.

Toma Zho is trying to become a professional, but what kind is not clear to him. The models of both Kau Dwa and Kumsa still intrigue him. For now, he is merely trying to build up the power of his num, and the belief of others in its power. He regards his num as special, and himself as a special carrier of num. His ordinary conversation is interlaced with references to num and his healing powers. He loves to dance and goes to all the dances. To an unusual degree, his thoughts and actions revolve around num, kia, and healing. He tries to key his rising num to the rising of the sun. This demands an extra effort from the singers and dancers, not always possible, as they struggle to continue the exhausting dance into the day's heat.

Toma Zho's evaluation of the unique power of his num is not agreed to by all. When comparing himself with others, he invariably places himself at the top of the list, devaluing others in the process. He emphasizes that other healers call upon him to help them heal, and that he alone "carries" the camp. When offered with Toma Zho's seriousness, such exaggerated self-commendations are not typical for Kung; the devaluations of others are even less so. Toma Zho's story of how he got num as a youngster, directly from god, further establishes the special power of his num.

Once at a dance, in an action antithetical to the Kung approach to num, Toma Zho flaunts the power of his num (Lee, personal communication). In the middle of a section of intense singing, while he is dancing with several other men, he stops, turns, and points his finger at a dancer across the dance fire. The dancer falls over immediately. Through this pointing action, Toma Zho has caused his own num to become dangerous. It has become what the Kung call a "fight" or a "death thing." Those at the dance are shocked. Toma Zho does the same thing to the same person several minutes later, with the same outcome.

Another way in which Toma Zho is trying to build up his reputation is by accumulating num. Traditionally, num, once activated, flows freely among those at the dance. Toma Zho tries to withhold num. At a dance, he may experience kia only briefly, with little or no healing. He says that he does not want to deal with serious illnesses, as if to say he does not want to waste his num on "hopeless" cases. He apparently does not want his healing efforts to be associated with a person who might die, lest it damage his reputation.

Toma Zho also withholds num as a teacher. Unlike the traditional Kung teacher, who at least tries to give num to most of those who ask, Toma Zho is selective. He wants to give num to someone who has the potential to become a strong healer. It could be that he believes his reputation will be enhanced if his students display strong healing power. Toma Zho is reluctant to part with his num. He believes that if he gives his num indiscriminately to others, he will deplete his own supply. This idea that the person who teaches others becomes weaker in his own num is not unique with Toma Zho. But when expressed by others, the idea has a different meaning. Others say that after a healer has taught many persons and has himself grown old, then his num becomes weak *as the num in his students* becomes strong. The total amount is not decreased; in fact, it usually increases. Also, other healers feel more positive about giving their healing power to others and giving up the power in themselves. They have little of Toma Zho's guarding of his own healing powers.

In his efforts to become professional, Toma Zho is relating to his num nonsynergistically. The question remains whether his nonsynergistic phase is a prelude to another nonsynergistic phase as a professional, sometimes displayed by Kumsa, or a prelude to a synergistic phase as a professional, in the manner of Kau Dwa. And there is always the possibility that Toma Zho will reassume the synergistic functioning of the total camp-oriented healer.

The dilemma facing Toma Zho is only one drama in the general struggle of the Kung in their movement toward sedentism. His struggle to clarify his relationship to num exists within a pragmatic framework. He sometimes expresses his confusions and hopes in a simple yet revealing form: "If I don't get paid, why should I heal?"

Another aspect of this process of culture change is the introduction at Xaixai of the Trees, a new dance form for the activation of kia. The healing dance has undoubtedly changed over time. In fact, for healing to remain alive, its form must be flexible enough to meet changing conditions. With the acculturation pressures now becoming so intense, there may be a special impetus for the creation of new forms. The "new" dance at Xaixai raises some interesting questions about the preservation of healing.

The Trees dance is said to have been "created" by Tikay, though it may be more accurate to say that the dance is being brought together by him, as it draws on several continuing dance traditions. It has elements from the dances of neighboring pastoralists, as well as from the Sunday dances performed by black groups working in the Johannesburg mines, where Tikay, a man in his late thirties, has spent some time (Lee, personal communication). But these elements are fused into a unique dance by Tikay, who claims that he "thought up the dance up all by himself." Athough this statement is an exaggeration, it captures the general Kung understanding about the Trees dance. It is Tikay's dance.

The Trees was first performed at Xaixai in 1967 (Lee, personal communication). The dance usually begins at dusk and may continue into the early morning. At times it may begin in the afternoon, with an emphasis on rehearsing the parts and sequences, and continue into the night and early morning, evolving gradually from rehearsal into uninterrupted dance. The dance does not seem to occur at any particular interval or in response to any special needs in the group for healing or protection. It occurs when Tikay wants to dance it and when he can convince his troupe of women to put it on. During my fieldwork it was held once or twice a month, and most of the people in the camps around the Xaixai water-hole attended.

The Trees dance is performed within an enclosed structure that looks something like a cattle corral with a chute at one end. The structure is about twenty feet long, about six feet wide at its narrowest end, and up to fifteen feet at its widest. It is surrounded by a simple fence of branches about six feet high, lashed together. There is a gate at the narrow "cattle chute" end, through which Tikay and his dance troupe enter and exit. The dance enclosure is a permanent feature in the middle of the village, and all the dance paraphernalia stays inside the enclosure even when it rains. The walls are repaired when necessary, and they are taken down when the camp moves.

The dance is dominated by one person, Tikay. He is the creator, organizer, and leader. Tikay is enigmatic and unpredictable. Phlegmatic, quiet, sometimes sullen, he has an active mind that expresses itself in sharp, penetrating questions and a personal spark that bursts into often mocking laughter. He is not a central figure in camp life, but his creativity is respected, and he is well liked. Tikay comes completely alive in his dance. His appearance is transformed by an overpowering handsomeness. A charismatic light burns from his ordinarily withdrawn features.

A group of about fifteen women act as the chorus for Tikay's solo behavior, singing, clapping, and dancing in response to his singing and dancing. The troupe was conceived specifically for the dance and forms solely in order to put on a dance. Most of the women in Tikay's own camp are members. The group includes women of varying ages, the youngest in her mid-teens, the oldest in her early sixties. This group is ordered about by Tikay, "herded," he says, "like cattle," into and out of the cattle chute. A major symbolism of the dance is trees. The women moving along in tightly formed lines inside and outside the enclosure, passing by the surrounding huts, represent the trees of Xaixai. Their dance steps usually consist of a short, rhythmic shuffle; their posture remains erect. Tikay lines up the fourteen women according to height, in two rows inside the enclosure, the tallest at the front, the shortest at the rear. He often leads them out of the enclosure himself, dancing and singing at the head of the two lines, going around the outside of the enclosure before coming back in.

When Tikay sings, his words come so rapidly that they seem a wail. He sings in Fanagalong, a language he learned while working the mines in Johannesburg. In his songs, he tells stories about life in the mines and at Xaixai. The tales are intricate elaborations of everyday events. He sings as much as he can in as few breaths as possible, clinging to the last breath to squeeze out a few final indistinguishable sounds. The stories continue through a number of these short bursts of song. At the end of each song burst, the tension breaks as he takes a deep breath and gives a hoarse, nasal order to the troupe: "Ya ga da." At this signal, the members of the troupe begin to sing and clap in response.

The leader-chorus pattern prevails through most of the dance. At the start, more time is spent on getting the troupe to move in the right way and at the right time. Tikay rearranges them if they are out of order by size. He pushes them out of the enclosure when they forget to leave at the correct point in his singing.

As the dance continues, there is less and less need for verbal and explicit directions. The troupe becomes attuned to the dance, moving easily into the correct positions at the correct times. The idea of "correct" positions and times is put forth less rigidly. The entire dance grows more organic and spontaneous. It is then that Tikay's mood becomes more focused and intense, his dancing more strenuous and exciting. Sweating profusely, grimacing painfully, and shouting joyously, he sometimes falls into kia, writhing on the ground like a snake.

During these more intense periods, Tikay often dances with his eyes closed, expelling his song sounds with violent breaths, dancing an intricate pattern in place, punctuated by stomping, jarring steps. Or the women sit in a circle within the enclosure, while Tikay lies on his back in the center of their circle, churning in the sand. He sits up, lies down, then stands up. At each change in position, he starts a song, his eyes closed, his head turning from side to side or resting on his chest. Then he shudders and falls to the ground. Crawling on his belly away from the women's circle, he burrows into the sand, finally coming to an uneasy rest, sand piled up in front of his head.

Tikay is the director telling his troupe what to do, bossing them around, dragging them forward or backward so that they are in the correct order and place, exhorting them to follow his song bursts with singing and clapping that can sustain the intense mood he has created. The dance is both a rehearsal for the event and the event itself. Because the dance is new, Tikay must spend some time teaching the troupe what to do. At the same time, he is also developing the form of his own singing and dancing, and sections of the dance continue for periods of up to an hour without his having to destroy the atmosphere by making major changes in how the troupe is performing. Then the singing and dancing build in intensity, and Tikay experiences kia. During these periods he at times orders members of the troupe to go to a different place, but without breaking the atmosphere that supports kia.

Sometimes the leader-chorus pattern of the Trees dance gives way to a form of the Giraffe dance. The troupe stands in a tight circle. Tikay dances in the center. The women sing the Giraffe song, accompanied by its characteristic clapping. Tikay continues dancing in the style he has developed in the Trees. He dances out of the circle and lies down on his back. He pushes himself around the circle, still lying on his back, his feet stomping fiercely on the sand, thrusting his body in spurts, head first, through the sand. He goes around the circle of singers, then re-enters the circle and sits upright. Sometimes he coughs violently, trying to vomit, his eyes closed, his face without expression.

At other times the dance shifts into a drone pattern, in which a monotonic beat is constantly repeated with the women's singing and clapping. At these points, Tikay goes even deeper into himself, his eyes becoming blank and rolling up in their sockets. Dancing with tremendous intensity, though practically on the same spot, he appears physically exhausted. The droning beat becomes louder and more insistent. Tikay drips with sweat and begins to grimace. Experiencing kia, he swoons and is caught by two of the women, who lower him gently to the ground. He lies there for perhaps five minutes, several women sitting next to him, laying a hand on his back or head, sometimes rubbing his back. The singing stops except for a few soft voices.

Tikay and his troupe of women are the main participants. Others who come to the dance sit outside the enclosure and act mostly as an audience. They are not uninvolved in the dance, joining at times in the singing, shouting in glee at funny parts, giving advice to the troupe and Tikay on how they should do the dance, breaking everyone up with raucous jokes. The young men are keenly interested in Tikay's position in the dance. They seem both jealous and appreciative of his role and eager to take part in it. They sit around commenting on Tikay's herding behavior, occasionally imitating his shouted commands, and sometimes trying a few of his elaborate steps near the edges of the enclosure. Nevertheless the Trees does not have the open access to various levels of participation characteristic of the Giraffe.

Tikay's two brothers-in-law, Gau and Naesi, support him through the entire dance. They keep the ground in the enclosure clear of onlookers and, if so moved, dance briefly with Tikay, introducing a counterpoint to his dancing. They sing along with the women and help them keep Tikay from hurting himself with the fire.

Tsama, a playful fifteen-year-old, has a special place in Tikay's dance. He is the factotum, to whom Tikay has taught fragments of the Fanagalong language. Tikay issues his crisp orders to the troupe, and then Tsama translates these orders to the crowd watching the dance. Tsama also helps Tikay carry out the commands he has just shouted. Tikay calls for Tsama by yelling out: "Boss-boy! Boss-boy!" Tsama responds quickly, brandishing a whip to herd the women, while smiling sheepishly at those watching the dance. Some from the crowd yell back at Tsama: "Boss-boy! Boss-boy!" The young men also express great interest in Tsama's position in the dance. They too would like to be a boss-boy. They joke about Tsama's herding behavior, tease his authoritative gestures, and sometimes imitate his dance steps.

Tsama has learned some of the exquisite steps Tikay weaves into his dance. Sometimes they dance together, a beautifully attuned pair. In one pattern, one behind the other, they kick high into the air as they step forward. Then they do the same high-kicking step side by side. Each pattern may last for a minute. It is initiated by a string of Fanagalong commands to the troupe, and Tikay's song, as the two dance through the gate and into the enclosure, moving into the women's circle. Each pattern is terminated by Tikay, who breaks off suddenly and walks or runs out of the circle of women. Then he initiates a new pattern.

The atmosphere in the Trees dance explicitly emphasizes cross-sexual interaction within a highly structured framework. The boundaries between male and female are sharp and firm. The male-female relationship is distinctly hierarchical as compared to the egalitarian relationship in the Giraffe. In general, there is much more physical separation between the sexes in the Trees. There is also a strong female-to-female relationship which develops among the members of the dance troupe, not unlike that among the women in the singing circle of the Giraffe.

The num in the Trees dance seems similar to the num in the Giraffe, but Tikay says it is different: "God gave the healers who dance the Giraffe that type of num, and they kia in that. But I'm the only one who dances my type of num and who enters kia in my dance. Have you ever seen me put another person into kia in my dance?" Tikay's distinguishing of the two nums is perhaps meant more to establish his own dance and to explain his own relationship to the Trees and the Giraffe than to describe the fundamental differences. For example, he describes his experience of kia during the Trees: "I kia when I dance the Trees. God gave Trees to me and told me to kia in it. When the num throws me down, I am experiencing kia. One section of the dance where the women keep repeating their singing and clapping is called 'the dance of the kite.' I kia during that section, but not at every dance. I hold my arms like the wings of the kite, very loosely. The way the kite acts is this: it flaps its wings loosely and then soars way up, higher and higher, and at the end it swoops down and dives on its prey. When I kia in my dance, my thoughts are nothing. My body shivers. There's a stick in the base of my spine keeping my spine rigid. My gebesi rise up and float out. The num rushes into my spleen. My breathing is short. My heart thumps. I feel bad. And then I ask, 'What's happening to me today?' Sometimes people become completely different when I see them while I'm in kia. Sometimes people are just like bushes, not like people but like things. Other times when you're dancing around, you see the dancers crisscross in front of your eyes. When you see people as bushes, you may pick up your club and want to hit them, or scoop up sand and throw it at them, because they're not people, they're just things. And that's when people have to restrain you."

The way Tikay describes his experience of num and kia is similar to how these experiences are described in the Giraffe by other Kung. And though he says otherwise, his behavior makes clear that he still seeks num in the Giraffe, and he does not exclude the possibility that one can have num in both dances: "I almost experienced kia in the Giraffe, but god has refused me. No, I'm not going to kia there. I don't know why I still dance Giraffe. I'm not seeking Giraffe num, because it is a different type from the num in my dance. God gave others the Giraffe dance and gave me the Trees dance. But I could have num in both dances."

Only Tikay, however, has received the num of the Trees dance, and only he has experienced kia in that dance. His behavior in kia is idiosyncratic, though still in some ways characteristic of those just learning to kia in the Giraffe. As with those newcomers, Tikay is almost "wild." Both in his preparation for kia and in kia itself, his behavior is expressive and dramatic. He focuses all the attention of the troupe and audience on himself. The dominance of his role and the centrality of his presence are in clear contrast to the troupe with its stylized, regimented movements.

Tikay's behavior also contrasts sharply with the requirements of the Giraffe. There, the small body movements of most of those working toward or even experiencing kia and the flexible size and form of the dance circles allow room for many at the dance, so that no one is denied active participation for lack of space. Personal expressivity is contained for a group purpose. Tikay's large, exaggerated gestures put him at "center stage" and, given the space restrictions of the dance enclosure, leave room for only a limited number of people who will support his particular dancing efforts. No one person in the Giraffe consistently demands as much room and attention as Tikay during his dance.

There is presently a definite difference between healing in the Trees and the Giraffe. Tikay describes how his dance troupe alone is now protected from sickness, though eventually the two animal sources of his dance, the kite and the puff adder, will give him power to pull sickness from the people: "Some day I will pull during my dance. I won't take sickness out with my num. I'm just going to pull, but the sickness will be pulled out by my spirits. The spirits will look down on the people and spare them from sickness. Consider the women who now sing at my dance. Not one of them is sick. The kite says, 'These people are singing my song, so I will not send down sickness to spoil their hearts.' Then one time when the women weren't singing my dance, the kite sent down scorpions to cover the ground. The scorpions didn't bite people but just sent the message that the kite was waiting for his dance to be done, so the women sang it to me. And then just a few weeks ago, while I was sleeping in my camp, the kite said, 'What's this that you don't sing Tikay's song?' Then a puff adder slid under the children's blankets. In the morning, the children awoke to find this snake and the snake slithered away, and the children screamed, 'Kill it! Kill it!' They said, 'You do it! You do it!' So I killed it. I beat it over the head and flipped it out to the bush. But later in the afternoon, when I sought the body of the snake, it was gone, and we saw fresh snake tracks out to the bush. It was the kite that had brought the puff adder to life after I had killed it. The kite saved the snake because they are fond of each other. One of my first dances was the puff adder. Now I dance the puff adder and the kite so the two creatures are combined. I've been dancing the kite for so long that, when the time comes for me to pull sickness, the kites will say, 'He's the one who dances our dance. Let's give him num so that he can pull.' "

Tikay is unclear about the eventual significance of healing in the Trees or even about how much healing may be evoked. As of now, there is no laying on of hands or individual healing effort in the Trees as there is in the Giraffe. The protective healing veil that Tikay speaks of, available to the dance troupe, is in sharp contrast to the generalized healing energy available to all through the Giraffe. Healing is generally less emphasized in the Trees than in the Giraffe.

Education in the Trees dance is limited to Tikay, his troupe, and to some extent, Tikay's assistant, Tsama. Tikay's reception of num and search for kia are the central educational experience in that dance. The troupe allows Tikay to unfold and recreate his original vision of the dance and to keep creating elements of the dance as he goes along.

Tikay educates the troupe like a choreographer, telling them more about dance steps and sequences than about kia. His relationship to his assistant is very similar, because as Tikay says: "I want somebody who can learn the dance completely. That person will dance, and I'll just sit by and do nothing." Most of the women in fact already know how to work with someone in kia, having gained that experience as singers in the Giraffe.

Tikay teases other men about whether they too can do this dance or even kia in it. So far they have not. He is not teaching others in the sense of leading them toward kia, the central education experience in the Giraffe. He says of his two brother-in-law assistants: "Those two don't dance it much because they fear it. If they danced it any more, the spirits would shoot arrows at them and make them sick. The reason I do my dance alone is that if others did it, everyone would be dancing his own way, and the people would just chatter, chatter, chatter."

Yet the educational role that the troupe plays in regard to Tikay is similar to the educational process in the Giraffe. In their support of Tikay while guiding him toward kia, the troupe performs a function which occurs in and is central to the Giraffe. In the Giraffe, however, that function is performed by a variety of people, and no one is excluded. Whether the dance troupe can ever guide Tikay's kia toward a healing that is available to the entire community remains to be seen.

The Trees dance seems at present more peripheral to Kung hunting-gathering culture than the Giraffe. It is not an event that occurs regularly or around which the culture organizes itself, as is the Giraffe. Also, the Trees is a very localized phenomenon and expresses less the spontaneity of the entire group. The Giraffe occurs wherever Kung people live, but the Trees occurs only where Tikay and his troupe live, and only when they are willing to dance. Only one dance enclosure has been built, in the center of Tikay's camp. It is primarily in that enclosure that the Trees occurs.

The Trees has fundamental differences from the Giraffe, which by and large are attributable to the blacks' influence. The use of a dominant leader and a responding chorus is characteristic of Herero and other black dancing. The precision formations, marching lines, and stern discipline are elements of the black dancing of the Johannesburg mines culture. The similarities of the Trees to the Giraffe, however, connect Tikay's dance with the mainstream of Kung life.

The kia experience that is at the heart of both the Trees and the Giraffe, is fundamentally similar in both. That may be evidence that the Trees is evolving toward the characteristics of the Giraffe. There is a strong sense that num resides in the Trees, and the fact that Tikay differentiates it from the num in the Giraffe is less important than the fact that it is num.

In recent years, the Trees has tended to assume the characteristics of the Giraffe. This movement marks the development of the Trees not only over time, but even within a particular performance. The dance has become less clear in its separation of the sexes, less hierarchical in the relation between the leader and the troupe, less rigid in its distinction between performers and audience. It has become less a theatrical performance and more a vehicle for the experience of kia. As it becomes less filled with stage directions, more room emerges for kia. The singing and clapping in the Trees comes more and more to share the kia-evoking quality of the Giraffe.

As a particular Trees dance moves into its middle and later stages, the atmosphere changes. It still involves a leader and his troupe, as opposed to a circle of women with men dancing around it, but the influence of the Giraffe becomes strong. Tikay gives fewer stage directions; the troupe clap and sing more according to their own understanding; the singing and clapping become more like the Giraffe in sound and rhythm; the periods of dancing are more extended; and the dancing becomes more intensive. As the Trees unfolds through the late evening and early morning, the leader experiences kia more often and more profoundly.

This movement of the Trees toward the Giraffe goes beyond the fact that as the troupe learns the dance better, they need fewer instructions and there is less of a need for a leader-dominated hierarchical performance. It is also a sign of the enveloping influence of the num that is increasingly activated at the dance. The existence of num in the Trees helps explain the great interest of the Xaixai Kung in that dance. They are excited by it. As Tsau says: "I like Tikay's dance a lot. He does something for my heart."

Many Kung are on the edge of a more active involvement. Tikay is a respected member at Xaixai, fully integrated into his camp. He has little trouble getting others to perform in his dance. His creativity is admired. His moody personality is accepted and even piques curiosity. He could become, through his dance, a charismatic force.

Tikay's relationship with the Trees dance will probably determine the future form and substance of that dance. Two aspects in Tikay's career will have a bearing. One is the developing nature and availability of his healing in the Trees. The second is his relationship with the Giraffe. The two dance forms are not in competition, according to Tikay and others. Tikay admits the possibility of having num in both dances. He is an enthusiastic dancer in the Giraffe, working hard toward kia, though he has yet to experience it there. His search for num is for now focused more on his own dance.

If Tikay ever gets num in the Giraffe, and in particular if he develops a powerful num in both dances, the collaboration between the two dances will probably increase. But Tikay is still young in num, and as of now the distinctions between the dances are emphasized.

The elements in the Trees dance that conflict with at least the form of the Giraffe express the values and assumptions of the pastoral, capitalistic culture being forced upon the hunting-gathering Kung. Whereas the Giraffe emphasizes an egalitarian, though different, contribution of the sexes to the activation of num, the Trees is nonegalitarian. Whereas in the Giraffe there is an overlapping of roles, in the Trees there is a strict separation between what men and women do. Whereas the Giraffe emphasizes the exchange within a loosely formed circle, there is a rigid, linear patterning in the Trees. Whereas the Giraffe is primarily an experience involving all who attend, the Trees has a strong performance quality with active participation limited to a small, rather constant group. And most important, whereas the purpose of the Giraffe is to release a healing energy freely shared throughout the community, the healing power of the num in the Trees is less emphasized and more limited in its availability.

The relationship of the Trees dance to Kung sex roles in traditional and changed contexts raises more questions about the effects of economic change and sedentism on sexual and political egalitarianism. Can the changes that accompany sedentism account for the adoption and development of the Trees, a dance whose symbolic structure appears to challenge the balanced human relations epitomized in the Giraffe?

It is tempting to pinpoint this incipient sedentism as a watershed between the traditional dance form and the Trees dance. Some of the changes accompanying sedentism do seem to be reflected in the Trees. Because sedentism implies a major shift in the pattern of work, it also implies major shifts in sex roles and the socialization of both male and female children. For instance, the number of female maintenance tasks increases with the increased need for storage and storage-oriented food processing; work roles and tools become sex-typed; female mobility is reduced and female importance diminishes; and children's play groups tend to become single-sex (Draper, 1975; Draper and Cashdan, 1974; Hitchcock, 1978). The sedentary way of life seems to involve not only a measure of property accumulation and storage but some division of fixed resources among members of the community (Woodburn, 1980).

The devaluation of women, the property accumulation emphasis, and a new male ease with power-wielding are reflected in the Trees dance, where women are herded like cattle. From an original circular dance form, within and around which all the men and women of the community can participate as equals, the dance changes to an open oval shape, which can be symbolically dominated by a leader. The Trees dance can be viewed as an ironic semi-satire upon the invading culture – the world of wage-work, with its cash-nexus model for human relations, its new concepts of ownership, including ownership of the labor commodity, and its production orientation, mechanization, and division of labor that reduces women to objects such as cattle. The Trees is focused and animated, not as is the Giraffe by concerted group action, but by an individual innovator whose precise, mechanical style mocks and reveals the relative "inhumanity" of the incoming values.

The Trees can be seen as a commentary on the cash economy culture for the benefit of an incipient stressed and oppressed subculture, the Fourth-World San. The appearance and support of the Trees dance may be part of a constellation of related social changes, all of which may be connected to introduced economic realities and to sedentism, the dance itself being a possible strategy for coping with new social alignments. In a larger perspective, new kia dance forms can be viewed as emerging sub-themes of the culture, suggesting the potential adaptive and expressive vitality of these dances.

But healing is potentially at the core of the Trees, as it presently is at the core of the Giraffe. A concern for healing, potentially involving more and more people in an approximation of the whole-community aspects of the Giraffe, is unmistakable among Tikay and the other Kung who support the Trees. Although the black influence on the Trees is clear, its incorporation into Kung life is gradually changing the dance in Kung directions. How num is activated and applied in the dance will probably determine its future as a dance form and its relationship to the Giraffe. In microcosm, the evolution of a dance like the Trees can express the tensions and resolutions between the Kung hunting-gathering culture and the enveloping pastoral culture.

The issue is no longer *whether* hunting-gathering can survive, but *how* the Kung will move into another style of cultural and ecological adaptation. Can the essential values of that hunting-gathering life-style, can the heart of the healing tradition, thrive in the ostensibly antithetical capitalistic culture overtaking the Kung? A return to some "original" condition seems impossible. A romantic clinging to the past seems suicidal.

There is a whole literature on the functioning and historical development of spiritual traditions in a variety of cultures (e.g. Guenon, 1962). Although most of the data come from post-hunting and gathering cultures, they remain suggestive for the Kung. Spiritual traditions, and the knowledge they contain, fluctuate historically in both influence and accessibility. Periodically, a strict dualism emerges in a culture whereby such traditions are overwhelmed by an antispiritual materialism and are driven underground, where they are kept alive by a connection to their spiritual roots and a cultivation of their spiritual knowledge. As that materialistic emphasis becomes exaggerated, until in a sense it becomes "over-ripe," it gives way again to a more spiritual emphasis. Spiritual traditions become more influential and accessible, and more integrated into ordinary life. The spiritual knowledge is preserved as its message or "story" is retold to the new generation. The form in which that knowledge is conveyed is usually different in order to communicate to the new times, but the essential connection with the spiritual source must continue if the knowledge is to be valid. Whereas Kung healing is now a public and routine event, culture change could easily precipitate a period in which it would be forced underground. But whatever its form, effectiveness would continue to depend on its connection with num.

The influence of culture change could transform the traditional approach to healing into a viable force in the new sedentary, capitalistic environment. How recognizable this "new" form of healing might be to the Kung of today is questionable. The way in which such a transformation might come about, regardless of how the form of the healing or the dance changes, is more certain. Kinachau spoke of the necessary principle to guide such a transformation: "We people have num. We know we have that. It is our thing." Num, the healing energy from the gods, is the "Kung thing." If this spiritual source and ground of healing is kept alive, the possibility of an effective transformation remains.

16 A Final Meeting with Kinachau

DURING THE LAST WEEKS I am in the Kalahari, many things have to be done; fewer things can just happen. It is a typical effort to "finish up" my affairs, the kind of effort that sometimes closes off experiencing. I sense that trade-off and am not satisfied to let things proceed in their usual way. At a recent dance, I became more open to kia than I have ever been. I felt num coming up in me. The possibility of kia is real to me. So, while I am finishing up my research, I also want to intensify my understanding of kia. I want to experience num more fully.

But I am in a spot. There is no talk of a dance, and time is running out. Meanwhile, a possibility crosses my mind, one other thing I might try at the next dance, if and when it occurs. Earlier some Kung spoke of a root called *gaise noru noru*, which they say has mind-altering properties and is sometimes used at a dance as an aid in the teaching of kia. Yet these properties are in question, for others specifically say the root has no mind-altering properties and no relationship to kia. Still others say that, though once used as an aid to entering kia, the root is no longer used that way, no longer used for anything. An opportunity to gather some of the roots at last becomes available. Despite these mixed reports, I decide to collect some and to ask Kinachau if he will both prepare them for me, which he earlier offered to do, and then take some with me at a dance or be with me when I take some.

I look upon the gaise noru noru not merely as a possible stimulant for kia but, more importantly, as a representation of kia itself. Kinachau has the same thing in mind. His discussion about taking gaise noru noru goes far beyond the root. He deals with the very heart of Kung education for healing and the challenge for a Westerner – and for the Kung – to engage in that process.

My talk with Kinachau turns out to be my final approach to learning about num, since no other dance materializes

Page 280: Kinachau studying the root

before I leave the field. The care and understanding I first sensed in him has been clearly established over the several months of our developing relationship. I come to him with my still unanswered questions about healing. And I come with a pocketful of what I think is gaise noru noru.

Sitting in the light shade of a tree outside his camp, we begin to talk. "I'm leaving soon, Kinachau," I say, "and there are more things that I want to ask you before I leave."

Kinachau settles more deeply into the sand and looks at me with an openness and acceptance. "OK, you ask me what you want to know, and I'll tell you."

"Kinachau, you once said that a daylight dance can be bad, that the heat of the sun and the heat of num together can be bad. Could you speak more of that?"

"I remember one dance that had gone on into the day. I almost entered kia, but I was really afraid of the sun. I was really afraid of dying from the sun, so I sat down and stopped. By the last hour of the day, when it was cooler, I entered kia. Those who could have gone into kia at that dance but didn't were those who were made weak by the sun."

"Do the healing dances often occur during the day?"

"In mid-winter we dance at night," he says, "and sometimes we then go on to dance in the daytime. We start in the night and then go on to the day. But in the hot season we dance at night and then quit, because we're really afraid of the heat." Kinachau sits back, reflective.

"Do students kia on their own, or do you help them to kia?" I ask.

"No, the students *themselves* experience kia," Kinachau states firmly. "Others do not cause them to kia. All others can do is to put num in, put it in, put it in." Kinachau repeats that phrase intensely and rapidly, until reaching the end of his breath, when he stops and breathes deeply. Then in a more balanced tone he concludes, "The students themselves experience kia with num."

"Are there some who kia but don't pull sickness?"

Kinachau responds quickly. "Sure! Dau is like that. He experiences kia all over the place. Time after time he is in kia. You don't see him pull. I've never seen him pull. But what he does do is bother and pester the life out of people and throw himself around." Kinachau pauses a moment and then adds with finality, "But I've never seen him pull!"

This is very surprising, because I have seen Dau many times do what I thought was pulling, including the laying on of hands and the curing shriek, the kowhedili. I do not know quite how to respond to Kinachau's statements. "But I've seen Dau at dances do kowhedili," I say, and then imitate the shriek as best I could.

"I've never seen Dau do kowhedili," replies Kinachau. "I've never seen him do that. All I've seen him do is run around and trip over people and run all over the place, and act crazy. I've never seen him put his hands on anybody."

"How can we disagree like this when I've seen Dau pull everybody in the place, and you say you've not seen him pull?"

"Listen," says Kinachau, "I know everybody who pulls around here. I know who pulls, the old and the young, the men and the women, the children and the grownups, but I've not seen Dau do it." There is no anger in Kinachau's voice, only conviction. It is clear I have not fully appreciated that there is pulling and there is pulling.

We each shift position slightly, getting comfortable again in our sand-seats. I feel the gaise noru noru – or what I assume to be the gaise noru noru – bulging in one pocket of my shorts. I decide that now, with much daylight still left to the afternoon, is a good time to ask about it.

"Kinachau, you were talking the other day about gaise noru noru. When did you give it to people?"

"Well," observes Kinachau, "in the old days, when we used to give gaise noru noru to them, we used to do it in April. After the rains were over, we'd drink it. People of the older generation drank gaise noru noru and used it."

"How did they use gaise noru noru?" I ask.

"They wanted to do num with it," he says.

"And when did they take it?"

"In the night," he replies, then pauses a moment. "As a big dance was going on, they would feed it to others at the dance."

Though I sense Kinachau himself has been involved in the preparation and administration of gaise noru noru, I continue phrasing my questions in terms of the "older generation," as that seems to be Kinachau's wish. "And did they ever give gaise noru noru to the younger dancers," I ask, "those who were just starting, who hadn't reached kia yet?"

"Those who hadn't experienced kia yet were given it," he says. "Everybody at the dance, every man at the dance, drank it, except those who didn't intend to dance. Anybody who danced would take it. The thing is that those who hadn't reached kia yet would drink more than those who had already reached kia. We elders who had experienced kia long ago would just drink a little of the preparation."

"Who gave out the gaise noru noru?" I ask.

"The experienced healers."

"We used it very rarely. We'd use it at one dance and then we might go through a year or more without trying it again. But in the meantime, we'd be doing all our gebesi work, we'd be doing our teaching. We'd be pressing our students' gebesi, and rubbing sweat, and doing all our rubbing work."

"How did you decide which dance to use it at?"

"God told one of us to do it. God told one of us to start it off."

"Were the dances at which you used gaise noru noru different from the other dances where you didn't use it?"

"The dances were the same type, all the same type."

I persist. "Were the dances stronger as a result of using gaise noru noru?"

"The dancing was stronger," Kinach acknowledges, then appears to withdraw the emphasis from gaise noru noru itself. "But the dancing was stronger only after a good deal of work from the fall until April. Only after we had given num through the winter – working on the students and working on them, with them stopping and starting, stopping and sitting down, standing up and trying num again, and we putting more num in – only after this long winter did we get results with gaise noru noru."

"Did more persons kia during those dances when you drank gaise noru noru?"

"No, we didn't have any more kia then than at other times."

"Did persons pull sickness more?"

"No, we didn't pull more."

"Then why did you use it?"

"Because gaise noru noru is just for teaching. It is a teaching thing, and people were still learning," he says.

"A teaching thing?"

"I say gaise noru noru was a thing of teaching. It taught people, but it was also *people* who taught people." Kinachau rests on this statement, confirming the place of gaise noru noru in the larger context of educating for kia.

"Now take a guy like Tuka," I say. "He dances and dances but doesn't seem to be able to kia. Would you use gaise noru noru with him?"

"If we fed it to Tuka, and Toma Zho and I worked on Tuka, and worked on him and worked on him, then maybe, months later, he would kia."

"Have you ever tried that with Tuka?"

"We've never done it with Tuka." Kinachau's face becomes sad and perplexed. "Tuka's is a very difficult case. I've done him and done him and done him, and I've never seen anything."

I have begun to think more concretely about Kinachau preparing gaise noru noru for me. "Kinachau," I ask, "whom would you give gaise noru noru to?"

Immediately he understands my unasked question and states his position plainly. "I'm not going to give gaise noru noru to anyone. I don't know anything about it. I've finished with it, and I'm not going to do anything about it.

We back off a bit and start to consider gaise noru noru from other viewpoints. "When you used to give it at the dances," I go on, stressing the "used to," "you said you'd give a little bit to the big healers, and a lot more to those whom you were teaching to kia. How could you tell what was a 'little' and what was a 'lot?' "

"A lot would be a full, big cup," he says, pointing to a sixteen-ounce cup a few yards away near his hut.

"And a little amount?"

"Like the bottom of such a cup."

"And did the women and children get gaise noru noru too?"

"The women drank it. The children didn't drink it."

We are back together again, able to speak about gaise noru noru, both of us now recognizing that certain limits will be drawn. "What happens when you take gaise noru noru?" I ask.

"You start to feel something moving around in your stomach, in your chest, and in your back, a pulsating feeling in your back like a jabbing. And then you say, 'What's doing this? Oh, it must be the gaise noru noru.' You feel your front spine starting to pulsate with your heartbeat and starting to tremble."

"Is it like when num comes into you, or different?"

"It's the same thing. What I've been describing to you of the gaise noru noru is the same sort of thing real num does to you."

"Did it ever happen that you might be sitting around the fire in the evening, without any dance, and someone would say, 'Why don't we take some of that gaise noru noru tonight?' "

"What!" Surprised by the question, Kinachau's reply is sudden. He reflects for a moment, his face confused, and then relaxes. His next words are more measured. "No, we don't to that. In the beginning we drank it. But for a long time now we've been using our own bodies, because we've been taking the num out of our own bodies and putting it into the young men. As you see us now, and what we are doing with our sweat, we are taking sweat from our own bodies and putting it on and in the men. So we no longer use that gaise noru noru num."

"Did you ever take gaise noru noru other than at dances?"

"In the beginning, in the very beginning, in the old days, when we used to do the Gemsbok dance, which was before the coming of today's dance, the Giraffe, it was in those old days that we used to use gaise noru noru. But for a long time now we've been using our own body insides, and we've been doing people from that. We do them and do them and do them, and then they take num up themselves." After a pause, he continues. "We always took gaise noru noru at a dance. We never took it just sitting around the fire in the evening. Even when we did it at the dance, we didn't do it at every dance. We might do it once in a great while."

"Suppose there was a real bad sickness in the camp, and you decided to have a dance. Would you take gaise noru noru to make your num stronger?" I ask.

"No, I wouldn't use it. I don't have any need for it any more," Kinachau replies.

"When you used to use gaise noru noru, and when there was a sickness, did it help your num get stronger?"

"No," he replies, "you see, it wasn't that way with me. When I was just starting out, I drank gaise noru noru, one cupful. After that I was doing num and doing num, but I used to run around and act wild. Another year they gave me another cup, and another cup, and I finally learned to control num and do num properly. From that day I haven't drunk gaise noru noru again."

"Did gaise noru noru help you get num?"

"Yes, it helped."

"Why did people use gaise noru noru in the old days?"

"Because it's a thing that god created to give to our people to help us."

"If gaise noru noru was given to you by god, why don't you use it today?"

"At Chumkwe they've all drunk it. And over there today you don't see a young man lacking in num. Every one of them is a healer, every last one of them is filled with num at Chumkwe. Whereas here at Xaixai, you know, you see so many of our young men don't have num."

"Why don't you use gaise noru noru any more?" I persist.

"Why? Why? Why?" Kinachau asks slowly, pensively. "We've left it, we've just given it up."

"Why give up a thing that god gave to help you?" I say softly.

"We've just given it up," he replies once more.

"Do you know of others, maybe in other camps, or other places that use gaise noru noru?"

"I don't know of anyone or anything."

With that, a curtain is drawn, but Kinachau has not closed the subject entirely. He looks at me, ready to continue our talk. I still think that perhaps he will agree to demonstrate how gaise noru noru is prepared. "Kinachau," I say, "let me see if I understand you. Here's this gaise noru noru we've been talking about, which seems to help you to kia, and kia brings you the num which saves lives." Kinachau nods in agreement, smiling with his characteristic patience. "Well," I continue, "what I can't understand is why you seem to say gaise noru noru is no good, and why you don't take it any more, and why you've left it. If it's such a good thing, isn't it a help to everybody?"

"Well, no," Kinachau reflects thoughtfully. "It's not that gaise noru noru is no good. It's not that. It's just that gaise noru noru was something that was a custom of our elders, and it was they who gave it to us. And we of this generation, of our age, are people who don't know how to prepare it. Gaise noru noru is not a thing you can just drink." Kinachau looks me straight in the eyes. "Gaise noru noru has got to be given to you by an elder, who holds the cup in his hand while you drink out of the cup." He emphasizes the last phrases, speaking them slowly and carefully, but in a protective tone.

"Have you prepared it?" I ask.

"No, I've never cooked it."

"Is there anyone here at Xaixai who has prepared it?"

"No," he says somewhat sadly, "the people who cooked it are dead. I think that Tsaa still does gaise noru noru, I think that he knows how to do it. But since I was given gaise noru noru to drink by those elders in the old days, I haven't done it myself." Kinachau seems caught up in a reverie and for some moments is silent before he speaks further. "I'm thinking of another person who gave gaise noru noru to me, an old man, who is now dead. I remember a time when we were all young, when we young men were out at Chore, and this old man cooked up a batch and gave it to us, and we all danced. Then later on he carried us and carried us and carried us."

"How was the gaise noru noru prepared at that dance?"

"I didn't see," Kinachau replies. "They prepared it over there, away from us, and we just waited over here. And then when it was prepared, they gave it to us."

"How come the elders didn't teach the young people how to prepare it?"

"I don't know how to cook it." Kinachau stops again and then repeats softly, "They didn't teach us, they didn't teach us."

"Kinachau, remember when we first talked, you said you would show me how to prepare gaise noru noru?"

"Yes, I remember saying that. And what I meant was that I know the gaise noru noru plant, I can recognize it. And what I wanted to do was to go out and collect some of it, dig it up, and show you what it looks like. But I don't know how to prepare it, and I wasn't able to prepare it. But I did say I could show you what it looked like."

"Is there any gaise noru noru close by here at Xaixai?"

"No," he says, "even I've been out looking around for it since that day we first talked, and I haven't seen any."

I want to show him the roots we have collected outside the Dobe camp. If they are in fact gaise noru noru, we will then have a sample in hand, and perhaps we could talk further about preparation. "Before we left for Dobe," I say, "we spoke with you and said that we would try to get gaise noru noru roots and bring them back. And at Dobe we were able to get some, I think, and I'd like to show the roots to you to see if we've got the right thing."

I bring several of the roots out of my pocket and hold them in my palm, offering them for Kinachau's study. There is no intent to embarrass him. He understands that. Kinachau looks at the roots with surprise and immediately says, "This is the stuff." He takes several in his hand and turns them over once or twice. "It's all gaise noru noru; it all fits. That's the stuff all right. Maybe the rains are better around the Dobe water-hole than we had down here at Xaixai. There's rock around Dobe and that may be the reason why gaise noru noru has come up first at Dobe. But around here at Xaixai, it's heavy sand and we haven't had any yet."

He hands the roots back to me quickly, as if not wanting to hold them any longer than he has to. "How much would this amount of gaise noru noru make?" I point to the five roots I have put in the sand.

"You could feed a lot of people out of that," he replies.

"How many of the big cups?"

"A lot of cups." He studies the gaise noru noru roots more closely though they remain in the sand. "You could feed a lot of people out of this. You could fill a big pot." He studies the roots again and seems absorbed in his own thoughts.

Suddenly, Kinachau is engulfed in gales of ecstatic laughter that wrinkle his face in joy. He tries to speak several times, and each time a new gale breaks over him. Very soon we are all in an uncontrolled, uproarious state. I am completely overcome with laughter, though I have no idea of what is so funny.

Finally, with tears streaming from his eyes, Kinachau speaks, halting continually for still another laugh. "You know," he says, almost squealing, "you know, you really ought to get somebody to cook these roots for you, somebody who knows how to do it really ought to cook this for you so you could drink it."

"Yeah," I say enthusiastically, "that's the idea!"

"Why?" he asks, his eyes still wet. "Do you mean you're seeking num?"

"Yes, I'm seeking num."

Kinachau is again overwhelmed with laughter, his whole body trembling. And I am not far behind, and sometimes ahead. After gaining some control, he speaks. "You mean a big man like you, Dick, who is a healer in his own place, hasn't got num already? You mean you have got to seek it?" The sentence is hardly out before another wave shakes Kinachau. He tries to continue, between bursts of laughter from each of us. "Dick, you've been kidding us all along. Do you really mean to say we could add any num to the num you already have?" For a moment there is relative calm. "Listen, let's forget about this whole business. It's ridiculous. Gaise noru noru will turn your mouth rotten." Then another torrent of laughter. "Forget about it. Don't be ridiculous. Come on, you can't be serious. You can't possibly be serious. What kind of ideas do you have in mind here that you're going to take this stuff? You can't be serious. There are some men around here who have danced year after year after year and never touched gaise noru noru, and you really think you can come along and eat it and that's it?" Kinachau's laughter becomes more intense, inviting me to join in. "You just can't come along and put the stuff in the pot, thinking that makes a healer out of you."

Kinachau has finished and is wiping the tears from his eyes with his hands when Koto starts walking toward us from the shade of his hut. Koto, who with his wife adopted me as their grandson upon my arrival at Xaixai, has a real concern for my well-being, wanting my stay in the Kalahari to be as comfortable as possible. Now he sits down slightly to the side of our little circle, at right angles to the line of conversation, and leans forward, trying to pick up the words.

"Kinachau," I ask, "suppose I had someone prepare gaise noru noru and I drank it. What would happen to me?"

Koto sits up straight and speaks abruptly to Kinachau. "Are you saying that Dick, my grandson, has been drinking this gaise noru noru for a long time?" Koto's voice expresses both alarm and care.

"No," replies Kinachau reassuringly. "Dick, your grandson, has never drunk it. He wants me to give it to him. He wants to prepare it and drink it today." Kinachau glances back down at the roots lying on the sand. "This is definitely the stuff," he says softly. Then he turns to me. "If another big experienced healer gave gaise noru noru to you, if he prepared it for you and gave it to you, I wouldn't see anything wrong with that, if somebody knew how to do it." Turning to Koto, Kinachau continues. "I wanted to show gaise noru noru to Dick, but I went over to the Xaixai flats and I couldn't see it. I went up on the dunes and I couldn't see any. So I couldn't show it to him. But somebody at Dobe camp has dug these roots for him, and now he can see gaise noru noru properly and see what it looks like."

"But what would happen to me if I took it?" I ask again.

Koto remains uneasy. "My grandson Dick must have had gaise noru noru long ago," he says, voicing an inner concern.

"No," replies Kinachau, again in a reassuring tone, "what happened was that some time ago Dick came to me and asked me about gaise noru noru. And I said, 'Yeah, this is stuff that is taken for kia.' And I told him a little about it." Kinachau pauses, then laughter returns to overwhelm us all. "And now Dick turns up with gaise noru noru and he wants to drink it today. And so I told your grandson Dick that if he had a really good healer, someone who really knew what to do with gaise noru noru, someone who could really present the stuff to him, then that would be all right."

"Who could I get to prepare it?" I ask hopefully as I look at Kinachau.

"Someone else could prepare it, but not me, not me," he says, and the door finally closes.

"Is there anyone else here at Xaixai who could prepare it?"

Kinachau mumbles something that sounds like Toma Zho. Then as if to himself, still facing down at the sand at his feet, he speaks. "I've got something on my mind to talk about. In the old days when we took gaise noru noru –" Kinachau stops for a moment, looks up at me, and then, keeping strong eye contact, continues. "In the old days, the people who were *very* experienced gave gaise noru noru to us, and yet we didn't do num the day gaise noru noru was given to us. We didn't do num. We were carried and carried and helped and helped. And after that, only in another year, would we do our num. That's exactly what I've been trying to tell you. This gaise noru noru will not do anything for you. If you drink this stuff, you won't start to kia right away. You have to be carried, you have to be worked on, you have to dance year after year. Maybe two summers would pass before you got it. This gaise noru noru is powerful. Yeah, this stuff is powerful, but the num of healing, the num that boils in our stomachs, is *really* powerful.

"The reason I say this gaise noru noru is powerful is because you just didn't take it. You had to be washed, and you had to be fed certain foods. Certains foods were prohibited to you, and meat that was hunted, the blood of it, was rubbed on you. Then you were washed again with something else. All that is associated with this gaise noru noru. And that's why I say it was powerful. When you really get down to it, we had so much that went with gaise noru noru that really makes it difficult. We had to kill a gemsbok, and certain parts of it would be cooked in a special pot that we wouldn't cook other things in. And then that cooked material would be rubbed all over the bodies of those of us who had drunk this stuff. And then we would repeat doing all that. And in between there would be lots of gebesi work, where we'd be dancing and putting num in the gebesi. And after that something else would be rubbed on our heads. And after all of this we would be washed with something else. All this was part of what we had to do, part of the work that went with this gaise noru noru we've been talking about. So that's why I say it's powerful, and it's not a simple matter." Kinachau pauses and breathes deeply. "This gaise noru noru is a tough job. This is tough work this business," he says softly, his voice trailing off.

We sit silently for a long time, ending our talk. As we are getting ready to rise, I turn once more to Kinachau. "Why did you laugh so when I said I was seeking num?" I feel no hurt, only a desire to know.

Kinachau looks at me, his smile warming me as he speaks. "I laughed at the idea that this gaise noru noru, this thing that was so difficult for us, and so bad and so awful, that someone like you, whom I thought already had num, could be seeking it, and seeking it on his own and by his own choice. Don't do it. Don't take it." he adds with deep concern. "We people prepare it, but we know it's tough, and it's difficult. We people prepare it and control it."

17 "Tell Our Story to Your People"

I CAME TO KINACHAU in that final meeting with many questions about kia-healing. I also came with a pocketful of roots I had been told was gaise noru noru. Kinachau, as always, was helpful. He responded to my questions. He responded to the roots I took from my pocket. And he made it clear that healing, even in the matter of these roots, which might on occasion be used to aid kia, is a difficult, serious business. It must be taken in the Kung way, in the context of the Kung approach to healing. And that requires time and preparation. I wonder whether it also requires being a Kung. Kinachau may have believed that, but he did not have to go that far. "There is not enough time, not enough preparation for me in this difficult business," he was saying, and that said it all. Kinachau was not somber, merely firm. And he saw the humor of the situation: a well-meaning European who wanted to come closer to kia before he left. Kinachau laughed at that and with that, because he cared for my well-being.

That kind of meeting with Kinachau bears directly on the charge the Kung gave me: "Tell our story to your people." It was a charge, and with that a responsibility; an invitation, and with that a challenge. This book is, in part, my response.

But the Kung story of healing and the telling of that story go far beyond any book. Healing is the application of spiritual knowledge to everyday life, and that gives it a definite potential for enhancing individual, social, and cultural growth. But while the story seems eminently worth telling, the telling is not easy. For the history of spiritual knowledge is an incessant struggle to tell its story in a way that is clear and accurate. Often the telling fails, the stories get distorted, and the spiritual knowledge goes underground, where it becomes "lost" for generations. Then, if the telling of the story becomes purified, spiritual knowledge can reappear; it can again become accessible.

Page 295: Young girls singing

I believe the Kung story of healing revolves around the phenomenon of num and their use of it. The Kung see num as the key ingredient in the healing process. As Kinachau puts it, "It is num which makes our healing work." Because of the central importance of num, the Kung story deals with a healing power released by the community which expands as it is activated, and which is accessible throughout the community. The story describes a model of community self-healing in which a spiritual healing power comes to the people through a transformation of consciousness, and is shared with the people through an egalitarian social structure. The Kung story is not an idealized one. In their desire to drink num, the Kung are searching for relief from individual and group tensions and conflicts, as well as for enhancement. Learning to become a healer is a painful struggle, as is the healing itself. The joy and release experienced at the dance are within this context of struggle and pain. The healing dance is a way to deal with transitions, and the uncertainties as well as opportunities they release, whether a person seeks to transit from sickness to health or from a known state of consciousness to an unknown one.

Most important, the Kung story is not a "success story" in the conventional Western sense. The patient is not always cured. In fact, establishing a more general sense of balance throughout the community takes precedence over any specific cure. Since the balance is dynamic, it needs continual attention; it is not always achieved. This balance is what allows the camp to stay together, helping maintain the reciprocating network which is so important to hunting-gathering life. The establishment of that dynamic balance is symbolized in the specifics of the healing process. The healer goes as deeply into kia as possible as long as kia can be applied to healing; depth is balanced with control. Boiling num must be regulated until it is in the proper balance to be used for healing. When num is boiling, when it is potent for healing, it is seen as "hot," "heavy," "a lot." When it is weak, it is seen as "cold," "light," and "little." For example, as num boils, it is said to "heat up" or "rise up"; if it boils too rapidly, one must "cool" or "calm" or "bring down" the num. The well-being of the patient is an experience of coolness which comes from a balancing of hot and cold phenomena.

This Kung story of community healing is one that prevailed in the Dobe area in the late 1960s. It is a story of the traditional approach to healing among Kung hunter-gatherers. But it is a story in transition. Forces springing from a cash economy were already impacting the Kung in 1968 – an influence that has accelerated in more recent years. The new emphases on individualism, private property, and quid-pro-quo exchanges have begun to threaten the nature of num. It is not just that Kinachau and Toma Zho approach num differently. It is that they are struggling differently to make sense of the new money culture which has begun to offer alternatives in their lives, one aspect of which deals with healing. Exposure to the quid-pro-quo economy, for example, forces the community, especially healers, to re-examine the way healing is valued and compensated.

The Kung story of healing can remain available to them, despite these vast threats to their hunting-gathering culture. Although clearly it will not be easy, the Kung stress that a successful transition of their healing into their changed life circumstances will depend upon adhering to the *principle* of num as it functions in the traditional context.

The question is whether this Kung story can become available to the West, which is already so thoroughly capitalistic that in some areas it is moving toward a post-capitalistic economy. I want to guard against assuming the role of the alienated Westerner yearning for some romantic return to wholeness. Yet I also do not believe in a future which discards all the past as "primitive." What I value is reliance on essential principles which in the past as well as the future can guide human behavior. The functioning of num among the Kung illustrates one of these principles. Though the Kung story of healing is neither ideal nor the answer to the challenge of community healing, it offers lessons worth studying.

The activation of num creates a synergistic system in which to give more healing to the people means that not less but still more healing is available. This principle of an expansively accessible healing power has great relevance to studies of culture, consciousness, and community healing. It has particular relevance to the community mental health movement in the industrialized West, a system that closely parallels the Kung healing system. There is no lack of models to guide the development of community mental health programs, including ones that stress group process (e.g. Rogers, 1979), organizational development (e.g. Bennis *et al.*, 1976), social action (e.g. Case and Taylor, 1979), ecology (e.g. Barker, 1968; Moos, 1973; Lehman *et al.*, 1978), and systems theory (e.g. Von Bertalanffy, 1968; Gray *et al.*, 1969; Churchman, 1979). But as presently applied, these Western models do not go beyond the concept of a community with limited resources for which people must compete, so that healing remains a scarce, nonexpanding resource.

The Kung healing system helps distribute resources fairly throughout the community, emphasizes prevention more than treatment, and makes extensive use of community support networks. These elements represent the central goals of Western community mental health programs, yet they are usually unrealized (Caplan, 1964; Rappaport, 1978). Num expands within an environment where food is at times scarce. This ability increases the relevance of the Kung model to community mental health programs in the West, which are often directed to populations caught in a web of limited resources. Finally, the Kung reliance on community-based healing resources speaks directly to the increasingly poignant need for low-cost health programs throughout the world. Reliance on costly, high technology Western medical interventions must become selective, targeted to certain diseases.

But there are serious obstacles to achieving the communication necessary for the Kung story of healing to become available to the West. Hunting-gathering and industrial life-styles are incredibly different; it is probably beyond the ability of either the Kung or Westerners to conceive fully of the other's life-style. The problem goes beyond personal biases dependent on a particular family or educational background. It has to do with the fact that different cultural histories impart different qualities to consciousness and world views. Once having learned to read, once having lived with electricity, once having owned private property, Westerners find their consciousness affected in a way that separates them from the Kung.

Also, a book as a mode of communication has inherent limitations in telling the Kung story of healing. That story deals with experiences, like kia, which are uniquely beyond words. That story also deals with knowledge transmitted through a personal experiential contact within an oral tradition. Sounds themselves are used to express kia; certain sounds are in fact aspects of kia. Books are not suited to such a use of "language."

Yet while the Kung say num and healing are their things, they also say num and healing are "human things." That lays the groundwork for communication between them and us.

Although the Kung model of healing seems to address the essential needs of community healing in the West, its application to the West would not be simple. The process of educating healers maintains and confirms the nature of the healing system. Comparing the education of healers among the Kung and in the West points out some of the radical differences between cultures which make application so problematic.

The traditional education of Kung healers can be called "education as transformation" (Katz, 1981). The concept of transformation is alien to mainstream approaches to education and individual development in the industrialized West. Although the term *transformation* has been used among Western psychologists and educators to describe both a process and an outcome, it generally connotes changes that remain within the intra- and interpersonal spheres of a person's life. Change limited to this personal level does not address transformations described by Kung healers, with the accompanying permeability of the self's boundaries to the transpersonal and the resulting restructuring of the sense of self. But insofar as human illness and healing involve universal psychological processes, the question must be seriously considered whether the education of Kung healers includes essential characteristics absent from the Western approach.

Several general principles characterize the education of Kung healers, one of which is the healer's experiences of transformation. Becoming a healer depends on an initial transformation of consciousness, a new experience of reality in which the boundaries of self become more permeable to an intensified contact with a transpersonal or spiritual realm. At this juncture, prospective healers experience a sense of connectedness which joins a transpersonal or spiritual healing power, themselves, and their community. But gaining access to the healing power is not enough; healers must then learn to apply that power to healing within the community. This application occurs as the experience of transformation is continually enacted and reaffirmed in the healers. Thus transformation both initiates the intensive phase of becoming a healer and characterizes the healer's subsequent development.

In these transformations the emphasis is on the psychological process of transition rather than on the nature of barriers crossed or stages reached. Healers move continually between their fear of the transforming experience and their desire to heal others, their search for increased healing power and the difficulty of working with it. The emphasis on transition establishes flexible boundaries between career phases and psychological states. The healer's career focuses upon one recurring developmental issue, which may or may not be resolved at increasing levels of difficulty, namely, to die to oneself to accept boiling num, or to transcend fear and pain, even of one's death.

A second principle is that the experience of transformation, which makes healing possible, does not remove healers from the context of daily living nor diminish their everyday responsibilities. Kung healers are as hard-working in ordinary subsistence activities as nonhealers, and they contribute fully to their communities. The service orientation of the healing work is a third principle. Although healers themselves must become engaged in a difficult educational process, they do so as their community's emissary. The healers' commitment is to channel healing to the community rather than to accumulate power for personal use. Healers struggle for a sense of connectedness joining self, community, and the spiritual domain, and their commitment to community service guides their healing practice and their lives.

A fourth principle is that transformation sets in motion an inner development which is not manifested or rewarded by changes in external status. A fifth principle is the emphasis on heart as a critical context for healing and healing technology. It is qualities of heart, such as courage, that open the healers to the healing potential and keep them in the healing work. And a final principle is that the education of healers stresses the proper performance of the healing ritual rather than discrete outcomes. The cure of a patient assumes importance only in the larger context of the community's healing ritual. Proper performance demands that the healer serve as a focal point of intensity, embodying dedication to healing and reaffirming the community's self-healing capacity.

The structure of industrialized Western societies, characterized by specialization and professionalization, prevents an exact comparison between Western healers and those of the Kung. But the community psychiatrist offers a reasonable parallel. Community psychiatrists are health professionals in the West who assume medical, social, and psychological responsibilities; they are often called "priests of the new science" or "scientists of the new religion." The implications of Kung healer education or "education as transformation" are relevant not just to the community psychiatrist but to community mental health workers in general. In spite of the fact that community psychiatry has relatively few workers in the community mental health field and comprises a small specialty within psychiatry, community psychiatrists are exemplary community health workers because their discipline shapes the education and practice of other mental health workers, such as clinical psychologists and social workers. And although other factors are common to all forms of healing, such as a rationale or myth which explains the cause of the distress and a method of relieving it (e.g. Frank, 1971), the role of transformation is stressed here because of the lack of attention paid to this process in the education of community psychiatrists, which creates problems that interfere with their effective functioning. Also, Kung healers and community psychiatrists both express the dominant values of and respond to the needs in their respective cultures. Each group is educated in a culturally appropriate way.

In the West, medical school still dominates the education of the community psychiatrist. The psychiatric component of that education stresses a psychoanalytic orientation as well as a biomedical approach. There is a practicum component, including a residency, usually in a community mental health center. Among medical and psychiatric peers, community psychiatrists are often the ones struggling most actively to respond to the needs of their communities.

In comparison to education as transformation, the education of community psychiatrists, however, does not emphasize a new experience of reality. The psychiatrist learns a new set of values and attitudes, a change that does not require the restructuring of self as experienced by Kung healers. Community psychiatrists learn a "scientific" approach to behavior and human problem solving which stresses their own mastery over a body of concepts and techniques that are the result of their colleagues' collected wisdom. Unlike their Kung counterparts, they do not draw upon transpersonal knowledge, and they are more dependent on what they can conceptualize and control.

The education of community psychiatrists often separates them from the responsibilities of everyday life in the community. As rare and valued specialists, they are protected and isolated. They literally are "hard to reach." The highly differentiated and individualistic nature of Western society makes a sense of unity between self and community difficult. Rather than serving as community emissaries, community psychiatrists often act on the basis of professional commitments. They pursue individual careers, often at odds with what traditionally oriented Kung healers would see as their role. The development of empathy, a skill stressed in the psychiatrist's training, is necessary because of a preexisting gap between healer and client. In fact, the community psychiatrist is at times taught to treat the disease or problem, rather than the person, in order to maintain distance from the patient.

In sharp contrast to the Kung healers, the career growth experienced by the community psychiatrist is expressed by increased status. Achieving status is in fact a major contribution to this growth. Those seeking psychiatric help often judge competence on the basis of the psychiatrist's status, and attention is not focused upon erasing status differences between "doctor" and "patient." More than their Kung counterparts, psychiatrists are prey to expectations that may exceed their actual competence.

Community psychiatrists are expected to become individual respositories of healing. They are both respected and feared for their personal knowledge. Instead of being continuously available to serve the people, this knowledge serves different masters, including personal advancement. This is in marked contrast to the fact that among the Kung healing power and knowledge are neither meant to be personally owned or even controlled by the healer.

At times, the education of the community psychiatrist has been described as a journey, but the journey is rarely a guiding metaphor. Compared to the Kung healer's career, the psychiatrist's course follows a logical and linear progression, with clear markers of progress, such as grades, and discrete boundaries of transition, such as becoming a resident or staff psychiatrist. There is more emphasis on sociological transitions, such as career changes, than on the fluctuations in healing knowledge or power that characterize education as transformation. Regulating healing knowledge or power is less of a focus in the education of the community psychiatrist. Whereas transition states are of value in themselves in the transformation model, such periods are seen by community psychiatrists more as delays or sidetracks in the central business of career development.

The "heart" is often seen as a hindrance in the community psychiatrist's education rather than as the foundation of knowledge. This is partly a consequence of a narrow Western definition of heart, which reduces it at times to an "antiscientific" emotionalism. Intellectual skills are stressed, emotions, such as courage, are often dismissed as old-fashioned and sentimental. For Kung healers, technology follows in the wake of these latter qualities of character. For community psychiatrists, however, technical knowledge is the main ingredient of education, the measure of educational success, and the sign of competence. It is offered to students with few preconditions that they be prepared to use it properly by dint of character.

A recent movement in the Western medical community has begun to address some of the very principles proposed in the approach of education as transformation. Internal medicine and community mental health, for example, have taken steps toward stressing the role of caring in health delivery. But even though the importance of education as transformation is beginning to be realized, it plays, at most, a minor role in the education of community psychiatrists.

Kung society differs from the industrial West in basic ecological and sociocultural dimensions, although the necessity of describing the Kung material in English can create an illusion of familiarity with this culture in the Western reader. The degree to which particular aspects of education as transformation are embedded in the patterns of economic and social adaptation characteristic of Kung life remains an open question. Particulars may be culture-specific, but some general aspects of education as transformation seem applicable across cultures. Two important examples are the healers' relationship to a source of healing power beyond the self, and their service orientation to the community.

The community psychiatrist is sorely in need of a community healing ritual. Compared to the Kung healers, community psychiatrists are placed in a vulnerable position. They are personally expected to produce specific cures without any community support, a situation doomed to failure and sure to promote antagonism between healer and community. Education as transformation suggests ways to reconceptualize the issue of healing so that it entails mutual support between healer and community.

Another way in which education as transformation can effect changes in the community mental health system is by supporting multiple healing paradigms, such as a Western-oriented "medical model" *and* various non-Western approaches to healing. Research suggests not only that people in distress are able to utilize multiple and "conflicting" healing paradigms, but also that this is an effective strategy (Katz and Rolde, 1981). Rather than focusing only on improving the education of the community psychiatrist, one could support, alongside the Western healing system, the development of other healing systems that already use education as transformation in the training of their healers. Data on the usage of multiple healing paradigms in Fiji suggest ways to increase the likelihood this usage strategy will provide better care: healers from each system recognize the different assumptions of each system and respect the work of each other; they recognize the limitations and strengths of each system, especially their own; and they are knowledgeable about making referrals between systems and willing to do so (Katz, 1976–1978).

Education as transformation respects both aspects of the dialectic necessary to individual and community health (Rappaport, 1978; Turner, 1969). It supports experiences that are ordered by the structures of daily life, as well as those that occur in transitions between and beyond those structures. Education as transformation gives added weight to the experience of transition itself, emphasizing the intrinsic value of psychological movement. The experience of the transpersonal is intensified during these transitions but not restricted to them. Insights and power received during the transitions are activated only as they are applied within the structure of everyday life. Education as transformation emphasizes the intermingling and the continuum between everyday life and the transpersonal, eschewing any dualism.

The education of the community psychiatrist does not effectively maintain this necessary dialectic. It emphasizes a definition of reality which is based more on structures than on transitions, and which is confined more to an existence within the person and his or her social environment than beyond the person. Community psychiatrists learn what their culture teaches, but what they learn is inadequate to their tasks. Educated to emphasize the personal accumulation of healing power, they are ill prepared to meet the overriding need in community mental health for a wide distribution of healing resources and a pervasive collaboration between helper and community. They would be better trained to meet that need if their education stressed a broader definition of reality, which would allow for transformation and for a source of healing beyond the person.

The economic and political power that accompanies Western ways of education usually leads to their domination over an approach based on transformation. If misunderstood, an approach based on education as transformation can also encourage such attitudes as passivity and submission to the healer, which might impede access to resources in a modernizing context. But such attitudes are not intrinsic to the model, which stresses the collaborative and communal nature of healing. In fact, one could argue for the particular necessity of education as transformation in the industrialized context, not just for the community mental health worker but for all helpers and teachers charged with responsibility for the maintenance and growth of their respective communities.

Rappaport (1978) suggests that rituals in which we experience a transpersonal bonding are essential for the survival of the human species. He claims that only through participating in such rituals can we overcome our separateness as individuals and know the reality of the transpersonal which enables us to accomplish the communal tasks so essential to the survival of the human community. The present individualism and consequent fragmentation of these communal efforts in industrialized society are well documented (Berger, Berger, and Kellner, 1973). By connecting healing power, healer, and community, education as transformation stresses transpersonal bonding.

The Kung have much to teach us in the West. Their approach need not be applied in any literal way. Their story for us relates not so much to their particular dance or song forms, which are meant for the context in which they arise. Rather, it relates to the Kung community's journey together with num, in joy and determination, to relieve tension and conflict, to contact the spiritual dimension and release healing energy for all. If we can begin to understand the life of that journey, then the Kung teaching can begin. Our application of the Kung approach needs to be a subtle process, something like the cooking of a soup. Into the pot go many ingredients, and as the pot simmers, sometimes for days, the ingredients blend and merge. What comes out is not like what went in. By taking in the Kung approach to healing and letting it simmer for a while, we can change our understanding. Then perhaps we can approach our own issues of healing and growth with more insight and perspective.

The Kung story of healing offers a fundamental, perhaps necessary, resource for healing in and of the human community. Their approach to healing, through the magnifying vehicle of enhanced consciousness, introduces enormous potential for culture maintenance and change. That story can be seen as an open secret. Much depends on the quality of the telling, much also on the quality of the listening. To the extent that the story is told accurately, it is open to all. But unless someone really hears that story and knows how to make use of it in life, it will remain a secret. Kinachau's words have broad implications. The telling and listening, like the dancing, must be done with an "open heart."

Orthography
Glossary
Bibliography
Index

Orthography

The Kung have no written language. In committing their language to written form, I have followed the practice of Lee and DeVore (1976), except for the case of characteristic Kung language sounds not easily reproduced by the English speaker, such as click sounds, glottal stops, and nasalization. The publisher insisted that symbols for these sounds be omitted to render the book less costly to produce and less difficult to read, thereby making it more accessible. I intend no disrespect for the Kung language by the removal of these symbols. The sounds of Kung differ from English in complex ways which cannot be conveyed fully. Even the use of the English alphabet to create a written form of Kung is only an approximation. The version of the language used in this book fulfills the essence of the Kung people's charge to me—"Tell our story to your people."

The Kung language is characterized by four clicks, sounds produced with an ingressive air stream when the tongue is drawn sharply away from the roof of the mouth at different points of articulation:

/	Dental click, as in */Xai/xai*. In spoken English this sound denotes a mild reproach, written "tsk, tsk."
≠	Alveolar click, as in *≠ Dau*.
!	Alveopalatal click, as in *!Kung*.
//	Lateral click, as in *//gebesi*. In spoken English this sound is used in some dialects to urge on a horse.

Other pronunciation features are:

~	Nasalization, as in *Zhũ/twasi*.
'	Glottal stop, as in *ts'i*.
"	Glottal flap, as in *k"ausi*.

Without these symbols, Kung words are pronounced phonetically. Following is a list of the Kung words used in this book, with their clicks and other pronunciation features shown in parentheses.

ama ama
Bau
Be
Bo
chi dole
chi num (chi n/um)
cho
choma
Chore
Chuko (Chu!ko)
Chumkwe (Chum!kwe)
chxi
daa (da'a)
Dau (≠ Dau)

Debe
deu (≠deu)
di
Dikau (Di//kau)
Dobe
dwa (≠dwa)
gaise noru noru (/gaise !noru !noru)
gam
Gana (//Gana)
Gao Na (≠Gao N!a)
Gasa (/Gasa)
Gau (/Gau)
gauwasi (//gauwasi)
gebesi (//gebesi)
geiha (!geiha)
geiha ama ama (!geiha ama ama)
go (≠go)
Goba
Goshe (!Goshe)
gwa (!gwa)
Gwi (/Gwi)
Hotun (Ho/tun)
Hwa Na (≠Hwa N!a)
hxabe (//hxabe)
hxaro
hxobo
Hxumi
Kaha (!Kaha)
Kamto (Kam/to)
Kangwa (!Kangwa)
Kanka (Kan/ka)
Kana (Kan//a)
Kashay
kau, *sing.* (k″au);
  kausi, *pl.* (k″ausi)
Kau Dwa (K″au /Dwa)
Kauha
kia (!kia)
Kinachau
Koka (//Koka)
Kore
Koshe (//Koshe)
Koto (Ko/to)
kow-ha-di-di
kow-he-di-i
kowhedili
Kumsa
Kung (!Kung)
kwara
kwashi (//kwashi)
na (n!a)
Naesi (N!aesi)
Nai (N!ai)
Nharo
Ninkau (/N!kau)
Nokaneng
nore (n!ore)
Nukha (N!ukha)
num (n/um)
num tchisi (n/um tchisi)
num chxi (n/um chxi)
num kausi (n/um k″ausi)
Tam
Tankau (/Tan!kau)
tara
Tikay (/Ti!kay)
Toma Zho (≠Toma Zho)
Tsaa (Tsa′a)
Tsama
Tsau
tsi (ts′i)
Tsumbe
Tuka (/Tuka)
twe (≠twe)
Wa Na (/Wa N!a)
Wi (/Wi)
xai (/″xai)
Xaixai (/Xai/xai)

Xam (!Xam)
xga ku tsiu (!xga ku tsiu)
Xoma (!Xoma)
ya ga da
yo
zhorosi
Zhutwa, *sing.* (Zhũ/twa);
Zhutwasi, *pl.* (Zhũ/twasi)

Glossary

ama ama: the real one; used to signify healers who are truly powerful.

blacks: a general term referring to non-San, Bantu-speaking African peoples, including the Hereros and Tswanas.

Chumkwe: a government-run San settlement in Namibia, occupied by close relatives of the Dobe area Kung San who have generally forsaken hunting and gathering.

Dobe: a permanent water-hole where one of the Kung camps is located for part of the year.

Dobe area: the area in the northwestern Kalahari where the Kung who are the subject of this book live; includes the water-holes of Dobe, Xai-xai, Kangwa, and Goshe.

drink num: the process or act of learning to heal; often refers to the first kia experience in which the person can also heal.

Drum dance: a form of healing dance which is less central to the dominant values of Kung hunting-gathering life and more female-oriented than the Giraffe dance.

Fanagalong: the *lingua franca* of the South African mine culture.

gaise noru noru: a root which apparently has psychoactive properties and helps activate num. Botanical identification: *Ferraria glutinosa* (Bak.) Rendle.

Gao Na: the great god.

gauwasi (plural): the spirits of Kung ancestors or of the dead.

gebesi: an area of the body from approximately the diaphragm to the hip bones, centered at the waist, sides, and stomach; also certain internal organs, apparently the spleen or liver. The condition of the gebesi is critical to the experience of kia.

geiha: someone who has "completely learned" to heal; also an experienced healer.

geiha ama ama: one of the few experienced healers with the most powerful num.

Ghanzi: an area dominated by large ranches of white Afrikaaners, where the San have mostly given up hunting and gathering and become squatters or poorly paid laborers.

Giraffe dance: the dominant healing dance in the Kung hunting-gathering camps of the Dobe area, which expresses most fully the values of that life-style; called here the "traditional" healing dance.

Goba: an unfamiliar black person; practically speaking, one who is not recognized as Tswana or Herero.

Goshe: a permanent water-hole which supports a Herero cattle-post and where several Kung camps are located for part of the year.

gwa: a root which apparently has psychoactive properties and is used in the Drum dance to help induce kia.

Herero: a black, Bantu-speaking group that is the Kung's most frequent neighbor in the Dobe area.

hxabe: literally "to unwind, unfold, or untie"; as used in the healing dance, "to unwind or unfold one's flesh," or "to feel oneself again," an experience felt by both the healer and the one being healed.

hxaro: the system of exchange by which material goods move throughout the Kung community.

Kangwa: a permanent water-hole which supports a Herero cattle-post, where several Kung camps are located for part of the year, and where the only trading-store in the Dobe area is located.

kaross: an animal-hide garment worn by women which serves as both a covering and a carrying device.

Kauha: the lesser god.

kia: an enhanced state of consciousness, with associated behaviors, which results from the activation of num and is a prerequisite for healing. The word is both a verb and noun.

kowhedili: an aspect of kia that occurs when healers expel the sickness from themselves, referring to both a state of consciousness in which there is great pain and a set of behaviors and sounds dramatically expressing that pain.

Kung: the name used in the anthropological literature to refer to a distinct ethnic and linguistic group of people living in southern Africa.

na: old, big.

Nokaneng: a permanent black settlement east of the Dobe area, separated from it by a long stretch of waterless land, where Kung live and work for the blacks.

nore: literally "our area" or "our place"; the area in which a particular camp is located and where it hunts and gathers. Its boundaries are informal and permeable because it is not defended against other camps.

num: energy that originates from the gods and is the most powerful force in the Kung universe of experience. It appears in different forms, its main action being as healing energy.

num kausi: an owner or master of num, a healer.

San: Kung-speaking people as well as other groups who speak a different but related language.

tara: another word for the women's experience of kia in the Drum dance; literally "to tremble or shimmy," which describes the characteristic behaviors accompanying the women's kia.

Trees dance: a kia dance which is more peripheral to Kung hunting-gathering life and more recent in Xaixai than the Giraffe dance and is more male-dominated.

Tswana: the black, Bantu-speaking group which is dominant in Botswana.

Xaixai: a permanent water-hole which supports a Herero cattle-post and where five Kung camps are located for part of the year.

Zhutwa (Zhutwasi, plural): the name used by Kung in referring to themselves, meaning "true or real people," "we people," or simply "people."

Bibliography

Balikci, A. 1967. Shamanistic behavior among the Netsilik Eskimos. In J. Middleton, ed., *Magic, Witchcraft and Curing.* Austin: University of Texas Press.

Barker, R. 1968. *Ecological Psychology.* Stanford: Stanford University Press.

Barnard, A. 1979. Nharo Bushmen medicine and medicine men. *Africa* 49:68–80.

Bateson, G. 1972. *Steps to an Ecology of Mind.* New York: Ballantine Books.

Benedict, R. 1970. Synergy: Patterns of the good culture. *American Anthropologist* 72: 320–333.

Bennis, W., K. D. Benne, and R. Chin, eds. 1976. *The Planning of Change: Readings in Applied Behavioral Sciences.* New York: Holt, Rinehart & Winston.

Berger, P., B. Berger, and H. Kellner. 1973. *The Homeless Mind: Modernization and Consciousness.* New York: Vintage Books.

Bertalanffy, L. V. 1968. *General Systems Theory.* New York: George Braziller.

Biesele, M. 1969–1971. Field notes on the !Kung. University of Texas, Austin.

______. 1975. *Folklore and Ritual of !Kung Hunter-Gatherers.* 2 vols. Ph.D. dissertation, Harvard University, Cambridge, Mass.

______. 1976a. Some aspects of !Kung folklore. In R. B. Lee and I. DeVore, eds., *Kalahari Hunter-Gatherers.* Cambridge: Harvard University Press.

______. 1976b. Song texts by the master of tricks: Kalahari San thumb piano music. *Botswana Notes & Records,* vol. 7. Gabarone, Botswana.

______. 1978. Religion and folklore. In P. V. Tobais, ed., *The Bushman.*Cape Town: Human & Rousseau.

Biesele, M., and R. B. Lee. 1974. Hunters, clients and squatters: The Kalahari San today. Paper prepared for Symposium on the Future of Traditional "Primitive" Societies, University of Cambridge.

Bourguignon, E., ed. 1973. *Religion, Altered-states-of-consciousness, and Social Change.* Columbus: Ohio State University Press.

______. 1976. The effectiveness of religious healing movements. *Transcultural Psychiatric Research Review* 13: 5–21.

______. 1979. *Psychological Anthropology: An Introduction to Human Nature and Cultural Differences.* New York: Holt, Rinehart & Winston.

Caplan, G. 1964. *Principles of Preventative Psychiatry.* New York: Basic Books.

Caplan, G., and M. Killilea, eds. 1976. *Support Systems and Mutual*

Help. New York: Grune & Stratton.
Case, J., and R. Taylor, eds. 1979. *Co-ops, Communes and Collectives: Experiments in Social Change in the 1960's and 1970's*. New York: Pantheon.
Cashdan, E. 1980. Egalitarianism among hunters and gatherers: Reports and comments. *American Anthropologist* 82: 116–120.
Churchmen, C. W. 1979. *The Systems Approach and Its Enemies*. New York: Basic Books.
Devereaux, G. 1956. Normal and abnormal: The key problem of psychiatric anthropology. In J. B. Casa Grande and T. Gladwin, eds., *Some Uses of Anthropology,* vol. 6. Washington, D.C.: Anthropological Society of Washington.
Draper, P. 1975. !Kung women: Contrasts in sexual egalitarianism in the foraging and sedentary contexts. In R. Reiter, ed., *Toward an Anthropology of Women*. New York: Monthly Review Press.
Draper, P., and E. Cashdan. 1974. The impact of sedentism on !Kung socialization. Paper prepared for Annual Meeting of American Anthropological Association, Mexico City.
Durkheim, E. 1915. *The Elementary Forms of Religious Life*. 1965 ed. New York: Free Press.
Eliade, M. 1959. *The Sacred and the Profane*. New York: Harper & Row.
______. 1960. *Myths, Dreams and Mysteries*. New York: Harper & Row.
______. 1967. *From Primitives to Zen*. New York: Harper & Row.
England, N. 1968. *Music among the Zu/wasi of South Western Africa and Botswana*. Ph.D. dissertation, Harvard University, Cambridge, Mass.
Fabrega, H. 1977. The scope of ethnomedical science. *Culture, Medicine and Psychiatry* 1: 201–228.
Frank, J. 1971. Therapeutic factors in psychotherapy. In J. D. Matarazzo, A. E. Bergin, J. D. Frank, P. J. Lang, I. M. Marks, and H. H. Strupp, eds., *Psychotherapy 1971: An Aldine Annual*. New York: Aldine.
______. 1973. *Persuasion and Healing*. Rev. ed. Baltimore: Johns Hopkins University Press.
______. 1979. The present status of outcome studies. *Journal of Consulting and Clinical Psychology* 47: 310–336.
Fuller, B. 1963. *Ideas and Integrities*. New York: Macmillan, Collier Books.
Goffman, E. 1961. *Asylums*. New York: Doubleday.
Goodstein, L. D., and I. Sandler. 1978. Using psychology to promote human welfare: A conceptual analysis of the role of community psychology. *American Psychologist* 33: 882–892.
Gray, W., F. J. Duhl, and N. D. Rizzo, eds. 1969. *General Systems Theory and Psychiatry*. Boston: Little, Brown.
Guenon, R. 1962. *Crisis of the Modern World*. London: Luzac.
Guenther, M. 1975. The trance dancer as an agent of social change among the farm Bushmen of the Ghanzi district. *Botswana Notes & Records,* vol. 6. Gaborone, Botswana.
______. 1976. From hunters to squatters: Social and cultural change

among the San of Ghanzi, Botswana. In R. B. Lee and I. DeVore, eds., *Kalahari Hunter-Gatherers.* Cambridge: Harvard University Press.

Harner, M. 1972. *The Jivaro.* New York: Doubleday.

Harwood, A. 1977. Puerto Rican spiritism. Part 2: An institution with preventative and therapeutic functions in community psychiatry. *Culture, Medicine and Psychiatry* 1: 135–153.

Hilgard, E. 1978. *Divided Consciousness.* New York: John Wiley.

Hitchcock, R. 1978. Patterns of sedentism among hunters and gatherers in Eastern Botswana. Paper prepared for International Conference on Hunter-Gatherers, Paris.

Hoch-Smith, J., and A. Spring, eds. 1978. *Women in Ritual and Symbolic Roles.* New York: Plenum.

Howell, N. 1976. The population of the Dobe area !Kung. In R. B. Lee and I. DeVore, eds., *Kalahari Hunter-Gatherers.* Cambridge: Harvard University Press.

James, W. 1958. *The Varieties of Religious Experience.* New York: Mentor Books.

Janzen, J. C . 1978. *The Quest for Therapy in Lower Zaire.* Berkeley: University of California Press.

Jung, C. J. 1961. *Memories, Dreams and Reflections.* New York: Random House.

______. 1972. *Two Essays on Analytic Psychology.* Princeton: Princeton University Press.

Katz, R. 1973. *Preludes to Growth: An Experiential Approach.* New York: Free Press.

______. 1976. Education for transcendence: !Kia-healing with the Kalahari !Kung. In R. B. Lee and I. DeVore, eds., *Kalahari Hunter-Gatherers.* Cambridge, Mass.: Harvard University Press.

______. 1976–1978. Field notes on Fijian healers and healing systems. Harvard University, Cambridge, Mass.

______. 1979. The painful ecstacy of healing. In D. Goleman and R. Davidson, eds., *Consciousness.* New York: Harper & Row.

______. 1981. Education as transformation: Becoming a healer among the !Kung and Fijians. *Harvard Educational Review* 51: 57–78.

______. In press. Accepting "boiling energy." *Ethos.*

______. In press. Utilizing traditional healing systems. *American Psychologist.*

Katz, R., and M. Biesele. 1980. Male and female approaches to healing among the !Kung. Paper delivered at 2nd International Conference on Hunting and Gathering Societies, Quebec.

Katz, R., M. Biesele, and M. Shostak. 1982. Healing music of the Kalahari San. Folkways Records, New York.

Katz, R., and E. Rolde. 1981. Community alternatives to psychotherapy. *Psychotherapy: Theory, Research, and Practice* 18: 365–374.

Kessler, M., and G. W. Albee. 1975. Primary prevention. In M. R.

Rosenzweig and L. W. Porter, eds., *Annual Review of Psychology,* vol. 26. Palo Alto: Annual Reviews.

Kiev. A. 1968. *Transcultural Psychiatry.* New York: Free Press.

Kleinman, A. 1979. *Patients and Healers in the Context of Culture.* Berkeley: University of California Press.

Kleinman, A., and L. Sung. 1979. Why do indigenous practitioners successfully heal? *Social Science & Medicine* 13b: 7–26.

Konner, M. J. 1976. Maternal care, infant behavior, and development among the !Kung. In R. B. Lee and I. DeVore, eds., *Kalahari Hunter-Gatherers.* Cambridge: Harvard University Press.

La Barre, W. 1970. *The Ghost Dance: The Origins of Religion.* New York: Doubleday.

Lame Deer, J. and R. Erdoes. 1972. *Lame Deer, Seeker of Visions.* New York: Simon & Schuster.

Landy, D., ed. 1977. *Culture, Disease and Healing.* New York: Macmillan.

Lee, P., ed. 1977. *Symposium on Consciousness.* New York: Penguin Press.

Lee, R. B. 1963–1974. Field notes on the !Kung. University of Toronto, Toronto.

______. 1968a. The sociology of !Kung Bushman trance performances. In R. Prince, ed., *Trance and Possession States.* Montreal: Bucke Memorial Society.

______. 1968b. What hunters do for a living, or, how to make out on scarce resources. In. R. B. Lee and I. DeVore, eds., *Man the Hunter.* Chicago: Aldine.

______. 1969. !Kung Bushmen subsistence: An input-output analysis. In A. P. Vayda, ed., *Environment and Cultural Behavior.* New York: Natural History Press.

______. 1972a. The intensification of social life among the !Kung Bushmen. In B. Spooner, ed., *Population Growth: Anthropological Implications.* Cambridge: M.I.T. Press.

______. 1972b. The !Kung Bushmen of Botswana. In M. Bicchierei, ed., *Hunters and Gatherers of Today.* New York: Holt, Rinehart & Winston.

______. 1972c. Work effort, group structure and land use in contemporary hunter-gatherers. In P. J. Ucko, R. Tringham, and G. W. Dimbleby, eds., *Man, Settlement and Urbanism.* Cambridge: Schenkman.

______. 1974. Male-female residence arrangements and political power in human hunter-gatherers. *Archives of Sexual Behavior* 3: 167–173.

______. 1975. The !Kungs' new culture. In *Science Year: 1976.* Chicago: World Book Encyclopedia.

______. 1976. !Kung spatial organization: An ecological and historical perspective. In R. B. Lee and I. DeVore, eds., *Kalahari Hunter-Gatherers.* Cambridge: Harvard University Press.

______. 1978. Issues in the study of hunter-gatherers, 1968–1978. Paper delivered at Ist International Conference on Hunting and Gathering Societies, Paris.

______. 1979. *The !Kung San: Men, Women and Work in a Foraging Soci-*

ety. Cambridge: Cambridge Univerity Press.
Lee, R. B. and I. DeVore, eds. 1968. *Man the Hunter.* Chicago: Aldine.
______. 1976. *Kalahari Hunter-Gatherers: Studies of the !Kung San and Their Neighbors.* Cambridge: Harvard University Press.
Lehman, S., S. Mitchell, and B. Cohen. 1978. Environmental adaptation of the mental patient. *American Journal of Community Psychology* 6: 115–124.
Lessa, W., and E. Vogt, eds. 1979. *Reader in Comparative Religion.* 4th ed. New York: Harper & Row.
LeVine, R. 1973. *Culture, Behavior and Personality.* Chicago: Aldine.
Levi-Strauss, C. 1963. *Structural Anthropology.* New York: Basic Books.
Lewin, K. 1935. *A Dynamic Theory of Personality.* New York: McGraw-Hill.
Lewis-Williams, J. B. 1980. The economic and social determinants of southern San rock art. Paper delivered at 2nd International Conference of Hunting and Gathering Societies, Quebec.
Light, D. 1980. *Becoming Psychiatrists.* New York: W. W. Norton.
Marshall, J. 1965. *N/um Tchai: The Ceremonial Dance of the !Kung Bushmen.* Documentary film distributed by Documentary Educational Resources, 5 Bridge St., Watertown, Mass. 02l72.
Marshall, L. 1961. Sharing, talking and giving: Relief of social tensions among the !Kung Bushman. *Africa* 31: 231–249.
______. 1962. !Kung Bushman religious beliefs. *Africa* 32: 221–252.
______. 1965. The !Kung Bushman of the Kalahari Desert. In J. L. Gibbs, ed., *Peoples of Africa.* New York: Holt, Rinehart & Winston.
______. 1969. The medicine dance of the !Kung Bushmen. *Africa* 39: 347–381.
______. 1976. *The !Kung of Nyae Nyae.* Cambridge: Harvard University Press.
Maslow, A. 1971. *The Farther Reaches of Human Nature.* New York: Viking Press.
Mintz, J. 1972. What is "success" in psychotherapy? *Journal of Abnormal Psychology* 80: 11–19.
Mohatt, G. 1975. Perspectives on non-Western healing. Qualifying paper, Harvard University, Graduate School of Education, Cambridge, Mass.
Moos, R. 1973. Conceptualizations of human environments. *American Psychologist* 28: 652–665.
Murphy, J. 1976. Psychiatric labeling in cross-cultural perspective. *Science* 191: 1019–1028.
Neihardt, J. 1972. *Black Elk Speaks.* New York: Pocket Books.
Ornstein, R., ed. 1973. *The Nature of Human Consciousness.* San Francisco: W. H. Freeman.
Rappaport, J. 1977. *Community Psychology.* New York: Holt, Rinehart & Winston.
Rappaport, R. 1978. Adaptation and the structure of ritual. In N. Blurton-Jones and V. Reynolds, eds., *Human Behavior and Adaption,* vol. 18.

New York: Halsted Press.
Richardson, H. W. and D. R. Cutler, eds. 1969. *Transcendence.* Boston: Beacon Press.
Rogers, C. 1979. *Carl Rogers on Personal Power.* New York: Delacorte.
Scheff, T. J. 1979. *Catharsis in Healing, Ritual and Drama.* Berkeley: University of California Press.
Shostak, M. 1981. *Nisa: The Life and Words of a !Kung Woman.* Cambridge: Harvard University Press.
Siskind, J. 1973. *To Hunt in the Morning.* New York: Oxford University Press.
Smith, H. 1969. The reach and the grasp: Transcendence today. In H. W. Richardson and D. R. Cutler, eds., *Transcendence.* Boston: Beacon Press.
Smith, M. L., and G. Glass. 1977. Meta-analysis of psychotherapy outcome studies. *American Psychologist* 47: 310–316.
Tart, C., ed. 1969. *Altered States of Consciousness.* New York: John Wiley.
______. 1975. *States of Consciousness.* New York: Dutton.
Thomas, E. M. 1958. *The Harmless People.* New York: Random House, Vintage Books.
Thomas, K. 1971. *Religion and the Decline of Magic.* New York: Charles Scribner's Sons.
Triandis, H. C., and J. W. Berry, eds. 1980. *Handbook of Cross-Cultural Psychology. Vol. II: Methodology.* Rockleigh, N. J.: Allyn and Bacon.
Triandis, H. C., and J. G. Draguns, eds. 1980. *Handbook of Cross-Cultural Psychology. Vol. VI: Psychopathology.* Rockleigh, N. J.: Allyn and Bacon.
Truswell, A. S., and J. D. L. Hansen. 1976. Medical research among the !Kung. In R. B. Lee and I. DeVore, eds., *Kalahari Hunter-Gatherers.* Cambridge: Harvard University Press.
Turner, V. 1967. *The Forest of Symbols.* Ithaca: Cornell University Press.
______. 1969. *The Ritual Process.* Chicago: Aldine.
Van Gennep, A. 1960. *The Rites of Passage.* Chicago: University of Chicago Press.
Vinnicombe, P. 1975. *The People of the Eland.* Pietermaritzburg: Natal University Press.
Waxler, N. 1977. Is mental illness cured in traditional societies? A theoretical analysis. *Culture, Medicine and Psychiatry,* 233–253.
______. 1979. Culture and mental illness: A social labeling perspective. *The Journal of Nervous and Mental Disease* 159: 379–395.
Weatherhead, L. 1952. *Psychology, Religion and Healing.* Nashville: Abington Press.
Weisnner, P. 1977. Hxaro: A regional system of reciprocity for reducing risk among the !Kung San. Ph.D. dissertation, University of Michigan, Ann Arbor.
Whiting, B. 1950. Paiute sorcery. *Viking Fund Publication in Anthro-*

pology, no. 15. New York: Wenner-Gren Foundation.

Woodburn, J. 1980. Hunters and gatherers today and reconstruction of the past. In E. Gellner, ed., *Soviet and Western Anthropology.* London: Duckworth.

Zaretsky, I., and M. P. Leone, eds. 1974. *Religious Movements in Contemporary America.* Princeton: Princeton University Press.

Index